GENDER, DISCOURSE AND THE SELF IN LITERATURE

# Gender, Discourse and the Self in Literature
ISSUES IN MAINLAND CHINA, TAIWAN AND HONG KONG

Edited by

Kwok-kan Tam

and

Terry Siu-han Yip

**The Chinese University Press**

*Gender, Discourse and the Self in Literature:*
*Issues in Mainland China, Taiwan and Hong Kong*
 Edited by Kwok-kan Tam and Terry Siu-han Yip

© **The Chinese University of Hong Kong,** 2010

ISBN: 978–962–996–399–6

THE CHINESE UNIVERSITY PRESS
The Chinese University of Hong Kong
SHA TIN, N.T., HONG KONG
Fax: +852 2603 6692
    +852 2603 7355
E-mail: cup@cuhk.edu.hk
Web-site: www.chineseupress.com

Printed in Hong Kong

# Contents

# Preface

Being transdisciplinary in methodology, gender studies is a growing field that addresses metalingual and metatextual issues of the self, culture and society. With the cultural map of the world redrawn by trends of postcoloniality and globalization, gender studies in the twenty-first century has become a field of critical inquiry exploring the self in all spheres of transnational culture and politics. Closely connected with issues of identity and representation, gender studies has also become one of the focuses of comparative studies that involve the re-examination of theory in transcultural contexts.

This project on gender issues in literary writings from mainland China, Taiwan and Hong Kong aims at re-examining literature and culture in three Chinese communities, with their distinct course of socio-cultural development, from the perspective of global cultural formations. It is believed that the uniqueness of Chinese literature and culture can be seen in a better light when juxtaposed against the global cultural transformations, such as feminism and gender discourse.

Feminism in mainland China has undergone three stages of development that are all closely related to political and cultural change of the time. The initial stage was the May Fourth era, in which women emerged as individual selves freed from the collective definition of their role selves. The next stage was the socialist era, in which the female self was reconstructed as part of the socialist collective. The third stage is the post-socialist era in which the self is again freed from social(ist) confinement. In each of these periods, there is a dominant discourse that defines women: the individualist, the socialist and the feminist.

In the case of Taiwan and Hong Kong, women's development and hence gender issues have taken very different paths, for they have developed outside the socialist tradition and have been exposed to Western cultural definitions of the self and feminist discourses since the 1960s. As the essays in this collection demonstrate, revealing the hidden assumptions about gender entails a critical examination of the gender discourses, and therefore is deconstructionist in nature.

In the preparation of this book, we are indebted to many individuals and institutions. Gerald Cheung, Yomei Shaw and Katrine Wong provided assistance in translation and proofreading. Liu Yan, Xie Qun and Liao Weichun helped in organizing exchange activities with mainland Chinese institutions. Zhang Jiong, Wu Sijing, Li Xiaojiang, Lin Shuming, Lin Danya, Tan Xiang and Huang Lin invited us to all the gender studies conferences that they organized. Our participation in all these conferences informed us of the pressing issues that women face in mainland China. The Hong Kong Arts Development Council provided us with funds to invite eminent writers and scholars to meet in Hong Kong and discuss gender issues in literature. Much of the idea for this book came from that meeting. Hong Kong Baptist University and its Department of English Language and Literature have all along been supportive of our project. To all of them, we would like to express our deepest gratitude.

Special thanks are given to Flo Lai-on Chan, editor of The Chinese University Press, for her careful reading of the manuscript. Without her assistance, many of the inconsistencies might have passed unnoticed.

Kwok-kan Tam
Terry Siu-han Yip
May 2009

# Introduction

*Feminism and Gender Discourse in Mainland China, Taiwan and Hong Kong*

KWOK-KAN TAM

"GENDER," AS THE WORLD HEALTH Organization defines it, "is used to describe those characteristics of women and men, which are socially constructed, while sex refers to those which are biologically determined. People are born female or male but learn to be girls and boys who grow into women and men. This learned behaviour makes up gender identity and determines gender roles" (WHO, 2002, "Annex," p. 1). While it seems simple and common sense to say that gender is a cultural construct and sex is biological make-up, much complex theorization is involved when consideration is given to the fact that the knowledge about sex is also based on a cultural construct, and may be biased. If both knowledge of sex and gender are culturally constructed, then what people learn about their sex is subject to the discursive function of gender-related knowledge. Since it is society that produces knowledge about gender, learning about gender can be regarded as learning the culturally constructed knowledge about gender, and learning about one's gender is learning to define oneself according to a community's rules and expectations of gender behaviour. In the Foucauldian sense, gendering oneself is disciplining oneself. It is in the process of socialization that gender identity is acquired. This notion of gender identity is in line with recent philosophical enquiry, particularly with that proposed by Judith Butler, who argues that gender identity is a matter of performativity and is formed as a result of socially or culturally prescribed rules of "performance" imposed upon an individual.

Although gender identity is acquired, it is not entirely socially constructed, as it has to be an effect of ego development in its relation to the love-object. In Freud's argument, gender identity does not come with birth, but is acquired upon the emergence of the ego. In such a notion, gender identity is formed as a result of the ego's development, which is based on its interaction with the so-called "love-object." In

Freud's theory, a boy would have his mother as the love-object and therefore will become masculine, while a girl will have to change her love-object from the mother to the father to become feminine. A key concept in Freud's theory is that human beings are driven by their sexual instinct and therefore the inclination towards the love-object is natural and it comes with birth. This theory assumes that an infant will have difficulty in developing a gender identity in the lack of a love-object, or when a love-object ceases to be so or even becomes a hate-object. While Freudian theory maintains that the ego plays a crucial role in the formation of a person's gender identity, feminist sociologists argue that it is socialization that plays a significant role in the formation of gender identity.

Over the past half century, there have been many debates on how gender identity is formed and whether it is formed at the Oedipal or pre-Oedipal stage, but there does not seem to be any general agreement among the psychoanalysts and feminist sociologists. In the Freudian view, gender identity is formed at the Oedipal stage. Post-Freudian psychoanalysts as well as some feminists, such as Nancy Chodorow, however, provide a new theory by arguing that gender identity is formed at the pre-Oedipal stage, that is, before the emergence of the ego. Such a view of gender formation is based on the belief that gender is learned by role-imitation: a girl would imitate the mother and becomes a woman, while a boy would imitate the father and becomes a man. This is true in the case of a person who has already formed an ego, but it is difficult to argue that a person will role-imitate a certain gender model before his/her ego is formed.

Although the issues involved in the debates over the formation of gender are crucial to an understanding of identity, not many of them have been reflected in Chinese scholarship or cultural critique. There are many explanations for the lack of interest in such theoretical debates in China. For one, China has not been engaged in the same debate on the tradition of psychoanalysis. Not many Chinese scholars are well-informed about such arguments in the Western tradition. Furthermore, gender is not simply an identity issue, but also a social issue of representation that has implications for contemporary Chinese politics. Rapid political developments in China since the 1980s, however, have forced many scholars to address gender issues with more theoretical reflections on social problems. This explains why it has become a much more pressing issue in mainland China, Taiwan and Hong Kong today.

## THE TRADITIONAL CHINESE ROLE-GENDERED SELF

Concepts like "men/women," "male/female" and "masculinity/ femininity" can be found in traditional Chinese discourses. In the Chinese language, the word "*xing*" covers both sex and gender. It may mean biological nature, sex, gender, or character. Sex (*xing*) is taken by the Chinese as one of the categories to understand human relationships, while gender (*xiongxing/cixing*) is a marker of sexual characteristics. In both Daoist and Confucian discourses, sex is not simply a biological term, but also a philosophical concept that originates from a binary relation in the dialectic of "*yin/yang*," which includes cosmic principles relating to the "moon/sun," "negative/positive," "darkness/brightness" and "female/male." Hence, the traditional Chinese worldview is an interactive one, which believes that harmony can be achieved in the balance of *yin* and *yang*. The male/female is more than an opposition; it also denotes relations of interdependence. In this relation, the male/ female is a manifestation of the *yang* and *yin* principles. In such a binary opposition, the male is often associated with heaven (*qian*) and the sun, the female with the earth (*kun*) and the moon. Seen as part of the natural order, the male/female is understood as forming a binary relation, in which the male is different from and superior to the female, though they are interdependent. In such a cosmic view, the differences between the male and the female are accepted as part of the natural order.

Extended from the traditional Chinese *yin/yang* natural order or cosmic view is a hierarchy, in which the male self has a position dominating the female. Hence, the cosmic hierarchy is extended to the human world and forms a social hierarchy, in which the self is seen as a process of realizing the different roles a person has at different stages of life. When such female/male differences are extended to social categories, they often become inequalities resulting from the subjugation of the female to the male. Female subjugation is thus taken as "women's fate," meaning the natural course which a person's life follows. Furthermore, the traditional Chinese notion of the self is a body-mind process of socialization, in which little heed is given to psychoanalytic, or metaphysical, consideration. The Western model of identity formation, with its emphasis on the ego as described by Erik H. Erikson, does not seem to throw any light on the issue of Chinese identity in this context.

The traditional Chinese concept of self speaks of a person's relation, not to himself/herself, but to others with himself/herself as an object and not as a subject. Thus selfhood is emphasized, but not the constitution of the self in relation to psychology and social formation. Numerous examples can be found in Chinese history and literature to show the effect of the Confucian discourse on the construction of the Chinese self. Briefly summarized, the traditional Chinese self is a relational role-self, an object-self, as well as a no-agent self constructed merely as a product of Confucian discourse which is psychologically and politically repressive. In traditional Chinese thinking, a person is defined according to his/her familial and social roles, which are specifically prescribed according to the division of duties and obligations. In such a context, sex is taken into consideration, but not gender.

## THE MODERN CHINESE CONCEPT OF SELF AND ITS PROBLEMATIZATIONS

As a result of the emphasis on the social and familial roles that define a person's identity, the psychoanalytic concept of gender identity can hardly be found in traditional Chinese discourse. In such a tradition, a person is often seen as a product of social formation, in which identity is the realization of roles. Identity is not considered as a psychoanalytic issue, but as a moral one, which has more to do with the "hows" and "shoulds" than with the "whys" of identity formation. As illustrated in the Chinese classic *Great Learning (Daxue)*, a person has to realize himself/herself by fulfilling various roles in the service of the family, state and the world. A person's identity is seen in the Chinese tradition mainly as a matter of the roles he/she fulfils in life, and thus refers to role-identity rather than self or personal identity. Even up to recent times when the Chinese speak of identity, they often take it as referring to a person's social responsibilities, because responsibilities come with roles. In this sense, gender identity is viewed as inseparable from gender roles: a person's gender identity is derived from that person's gender roles. A person's identity is thus not, according to the traditional Confucian discourse, a personal or individual matter; it is a process of socializing a person and extending the person into a social realm. Gender in this context can often be reduced to or understood as male and female social roles, and hence does not serve as a marker of personal character traits. When the externalization of a person becomes socially accepted, gender will be treated mainly as a social category, and people will no longer consider it as a psychoanalytic issue. A person is merely a social subject when his/her life is regarded simply as the realization of roles imposed from the outside. As a product of the Chinese discourse of self, a woman in traditional China held a much lower status than a man did and was expected to fulfill the subordinate role in support of man's realization of his self. A woman's self is doubly denied and negated, for her role is realized through her support of other people's roles, especially those of men.

This situation remained largely unquestioned until the May Fourth era when awakened intellectuals struggled to live life as an individual, with the gradual disintegration of the Confucian self based on authority and subordination and defined by its relation to others. Lu Xun, for example, was among the first few intellectuals to introduce the revolutionary spirit of European romanticism and individualism as an antidote to the collapsing Confucian moral order. In his seminal essays "On the Power of Mara Poetry" (Moluo shili shuo) and "On Cultural Extremes" (Wenhua pianzi lun), he introduced to the Chinese the sense of the individual as an existential self. Hu Shi also regarded the Confucian concept of self as the basis for traditional Chinese institutions of law, religion and morality which tended to suppress the formation of the individual self.

The self as a free agent and subject, independent of a passive object-relation to others was thus advocated by such Chinese intellectuals as Lu Xun and Hu Shi. A new morality combining iconoclasm with individualism came into being, and a new generation was born in China with a heightened sense of self defined by individualism. The leading May Fourth writers, such as Lu Xun, Guo Moruo, Tian Han and Mao Dun, often depicted their young protagonists in conscious defiance of tradition and all kinds of socio-moral bondage that posed as obstacles in their journey to individual freedom.

To the new generation of Chinese, the self is represented as the "experiencing I," the subject of knowledge and action. Captured in these writers' works is the spirit of the time when China's youths were groping for the means to transform themselves from their old role-selves to take up new identities characterized by free expressions of the self.

Subjectivity, problematized in modernity by Jürgen Habermas and understood as the psychological and emotional state of the self, has become a prominent feature of twentieth-century Chinese literature (Chou, 1992; Larson, 1993; Lee, 1990). The emergence of this self echoes what Anthony Giddens observed in his book *Modernity and Self-Identity* and what Stephen Frosh stated in *Identity Crisis: Modernity, Psychoanalysis and the Self*. The self is a complex matter of identity and is seen as a reflexive project: "We are not what we are, but what we make of ourselves" (Giddens, 1991, p. 76). Identity is seen not as "object identity" as discussed by the philosopher David Hume, and the self under modern conditions is an amorphous self, which is "always in danger of being undermined, of withering away or exploding into nothingness" (Frosh, 1991, p. 187). Self-identity "is not something that is just given as a result of the continuities of the individual's action system, but something that has to be routinely created and sustained in the reflexive activities of the individual" (Giddens, 1991, p. 76), which, as a coherent phenomenon, presumes a narrative.

Lu Xun's short story "The True Story of Ah Q" (A Q zhengzhuan) stands for an early modern Chinese attempt at problematizing the quest for self-identity. In Lu Xun's story, the anti-hero Ah Q is represented as a literary figure symbolic of the Chinese national character at the end of the Qing dynasty, a figure who is caught between and lost in the conflicting values in the dichotomy of tradition vs. modernity, revolution vs. anti-revolution, urban values vs. rural morality, and the role-self vs. the individual self.

In another story, "New Year's Sacrifice" (Zhufu), Lu Xun confines his discussion of the quest for an identity of the self to a problematization of gender roles in the definition of women's self. The problematization focuses on the characterization of a traditional Chinese woman, Xianglin's Wife, who does not have a life of her own. Instead, she is "passed" from one husband to another as a commodity. This echoes Luce Irigaray's idea about women becoming men's products of exchange. Xianglin's Wife is simply not treated by anybody, including herself, as a human subject, but as an object that can be handed over from one man to another. The problem is that no one, including Xianglin's Wife herself, sees this as a problem. What bothers Xianglin's Wife is her identity after death, when the ghosts of her dead husbands may come back to claim her.

The Chinese discussion on female identity and perhaps gender witnessed a turn after the publication of this story in the early 1920s. It aroused much attention among young intellectuals and caused a debate over the liberation of women's self in China.

## SOCIAL(IST) DISCOURSE IN THE CONSTRUCTION OF THE NEW FEMALE

Noticing an urgent need to "liberate" women, editors of many influential journals in the 1920s devoted themselves to the promotion of a new consciousness among Chinese women. Feminist journals such as *Women's Bell* (*Nüxing zhong*), *Women's Magazine* (*Funü zazhi*), *Women's Review* (*Funü pinglun*) and *Womens' Life* (*Funü shenghuo*), published articles attacking the evils of footbinding and inequality between the sexes. In addition, these feminist journals also published translations of feminist literature, particularly the plays of Henrik Ibsen and Bernard Shaw. In the midst of this feminist debate, Nora became a model of the new woman for the Chinese. The qualities of individualism embodied in her character represented to the newly-awakened Chinese youths a new morality based on the concept of an individual self.

While Lu Xun considers economic independence as the first step to women's liberation, Mao Dun vaguely anticipates revolution as a final resolution for all other problems. In his novel on woman, *Rainbow* (*Hong*, 1929), Mao Dun portrays the psychological and spiritual growth of a young girl, Mei, under the influence of Ibsen's *A Doll's House*, and depicts how, after leaving home, she comes to understand that personal freedom and liberation can only be achieved through participation in social revolution. Through the portrayal of such a revolutionary figure and her search for identity, Mao Dun constructs Mei as a new woman defying her own sex in favour of a genderless self, which can be interpreted ideologically as a conscious and political act in subsuming gender considerations under the national cause of revolution.

It is interesting to note that both the traditional Confucian discourse and the revolutionary discourse of the 1930s have discouraged the construction of a self-identity. Not only is the project of constructing a new female self a failure in modern China, that of the male self has also encountered numerous problems. Ibsenism has exerted its impact mainly in freeing the Chinese self from the Confucian discourse, but not from the ideological fetters of the communitarianist-oriented Chinese culture. The socialist construction of the self as a product of class is simply a substitution of the family with class. In such a construction, the self is denied as an individual. In Han Shaogong's story "Homecoming" (Guiqu lai, 1986), for example, there is the description of a man who has been mistaken as another person and gradually loses his own sense of self by taking on a new identity imposed by other people. The story is set in a contemporary Chinese village, which retains much Chinese traditional culture even while it has become a socialist community. Setting the self against such a combination of tradition with socialism has two implications in the portrayal of the contemporary Chinese self. First, socialism has much in common with the Chinese tradition in terms of denial of the individual in favour of collectivism. Second, the socialist liberation of self is just another framing of the self in socialist collectivist terms, and signifies another form of denial of the individual.

## CHINESE FEMINISM: NEW VOCABULARY AND NEW AGENDA

The socialist construction of the female subject as a collective self in mainland China has its origin in the 1930s, when women were represented as subjects of a class structure, particularly in the fictional works of Mao Dun and other writers of the Literary Studies Association who saw the definition of femininity as a political issue in the women's movement. In all major histories of modern Chinese literature published on the mainland since 1949, social construction has become the dominant representation of women, and hence, for a long time, works of the 1930s have been regarded by historians as the peak of modern Chinese literature as well as the origin of the socialist orientation. During the Cultural Revolution of 1967–1976, writers like Hao Ran took the works of Mao Dun and other social experimentalists as models of socialist portrayal. The dominant image of women in mainland China during the Cultural Revolution was still that of Nora, who became a revolutionary icon for all women, including Jiang Qing, who openly acknowledged her indebtedness to Nora (Tam, 1987, pp. 197–200).

Conceived as products of class structure, women in the socialist era were subjected to a collectivist delineation of womanhood. As Elisabeth Croll has pointed out, the Chinese socialist construction of women since the 1930s was based on a socialist interpretation of feminism as a movement that fought for women's rights, rather than as a critical enquiry seeking to redefine womanhood (Croll, 1980, pp. 3–11). Hence, there are two terms in modern Chinese politics that play a crucial role in defining women: *"funü yundong"* (women's movement) and *"nüquan zhuyi"* (women's-rights-ism). Both of these terms situate Chinese women in the arena of national politics. Thus Elisabeth Croll has the following observation about the different meanings of "feminism" in modern China:

> Feminism is not an easy term to define. In China its meaning has been constantly reinterpreted. For the first two decades it was used to denote the exclusive advocacy of women's rights, later it referred to the women's

movement which worked to forward the interests of its members within the context of the wider revolutionary movement to alter the basic structures of society. In the last two decades the term feminism has become much more a term of abuse referring to those who exclusively pursue women's interests without regard for the forms which political and economic systems take. (Croll, 1980, p. 3)

The term "*nüxing zhuyi*" (an ism of female-ness, or feminism) was never used in any Chinese discussion of women before the 1990s. References to related issues can only be found in the term "*nüquan zhuyi*" (women's-rights/power-ism), which is apparently a concept adapted from English. The understanding of feminism as *nüquan zhuyi* not only marks the Chinese social reality in which women have to fight for their rights and power, but also denotes the Chinese understanding that women's issues are no more than a matter of rights and power. Such an understanding of women's issues also reveals much of the gender politics in China today. The term "*nüquan zhuyi*" may mean an antagonism to male power and a strong desire to dominate over men. On the other hand, it may show a hidden fear among men for loss of power to women.

Most of the literary works published by women in the 1980s dealt with the added pressure Chinese women had to face when they battled to become equal with men, while they continued to be deprived of their right to work and were confined to household work. The voice for equity can be found in such celebrated works as Zhang Xinxin's "On the Same Horizon" (Zai tongyi dipingxian shang) and Zhang Jie's "The Ark" (Fangzhou). However, the critic may also discover that in many female writings there is a strong desire for a new identity for women. Hidden under the social theme of equity for women is a new consciousness that women need to reinvent and redefine themselves in mainland China today. As Terry Yip remarks in "Women's Self-Identity and Gender Relations in Twentieth-Century Chinese Fiction" (Chapter 1), "women's hope of redefining their gender roles reveals the increasing need for voice and identity in society" (p. 14). From fighting for equal social rights to redefining female identity, the literary construction of new women has gone through a sophisticated process of theoretical rethinking. Such a process also shows that feminism is not simply a matter of social struggle in modern China. It is a new consciousness that calls for women's self-reflection on their identity. In "Women as Human vs. Women as Women: Female Consciousness in Modern Chinese Women's Literature" (Chapter 5), Qiao Yigang shares a similar view that "[f]emale consciousness in the modern sense still embodies the idea of women being a natural/biological formation, but the associations with women as social beings have actually changed. The most important of these changes lies in the recognition of women as individuals" (p. 86).

With the understanding of feminism as *nüquan zhuyi*, many Chinese critics for a long time have regarded *nüquan zhuyi* as a threat and have been worried about the rise of a new female consciousness that would challenge the establishment. The Fourth World Conference on Women held in Beijing in 1995 gave the new generation of Chinese feminists an opportunity to present their views, not only to feminists from overseas, but also to the Chinese people, male and female alike, on what they thought feminism was and what feminism could do for women and for the nation. Numerous books that reassess traditional Chinese female writings and re-evaluate the representation of women in mainland China were published around this time. As Lin Shuming and He Songyu have concluded in "Feminist Literary Criticism in China since the Mid-1990s" (Chapter 3), "the year 1995 can be regarded as the beginning of the second wave [of Chinese feminism]" (p. 35), when many female Chinese scholars began to reflect on issues connected with women from feminist perspectives, showing their eagerness to engage in dialogue with feminists from other parts of the world.

The mid-1990s saw the emergence in mainland China of a new group of Chinese female critics who openly called themselves feminists. Besides Li Xiaojiang, the incessant lonely fighter for a voice for women in mainland China, there were other scholars advocating a reconsideration of women's lives, as well as of their writings. Particularly vocal were scholars from academic institutions such as the Academies of Social Sciences in various provinces, where women's studies centres were set up with plans for research and publications. Since 1996 annual conferences on women's literature have been held in cities such as Chengde, Shanghai, Xiamen, Guiyang and Nanjing. As Lin and He remark in their chapter, such efforts proved to have fruitful results:

> By the end of the twentieth century, there were already great achievements in feminist literary criticism in China, which brought modern Chinese literary criticism to new heights. Influenced by feminist ideas, more and more critical studies on sex, sexual problems and gender began to emerge on the scene of contemporary Chinese cultural studies. Representative works include *Tang Goddesses and Venus* (*Gao Tang shennü yu Weinashi*) (Ye Shuxian, 1997), *Female Literature of the Song Dynasty* (*Songdai*

*nüxing wenxue*) (Su Zhecong, 1997), *Beijing Opera, Stilts and Gender in China* (*Jingju, qiao he Zhongguo de xingbie guanxi*) (Huang Yufu, 1998), *Dunhuang Sex Culture* (*Dunhuang xing wenhua*) (Shi Chengli et al., 1999), and *A History of Female Ci Poetry* (*Nüxing ci shi*) (Deng Hongmei, 2000). In the last decade of the twentieth century, there was further diversification of Chinese feminist criticism into gender studies and critiques of Chinese cultural traditions. (Chapter 3, p. 36)

One unique feature of this second wave of feminism in mainland China is the quest for a genuine Chinese feminist voice, quite distinct from its European or American counterparts. Several gender studies centres have been set up in China since 2001, including the one presided over by Li Xiaojiang at Dalian University and another headed by Huang Lin (penname of Liu Qunwei) at Beijing's Capital Normal University, marking the official recognition of gender research as an academic discipline in mainland China. Both centres have worked out an impressive publication agenda. In the mid-1980s to early 1990s, Li published six volumes of essays that aimed at promoting a new consciousness among women, "putting the spotlight on 'culture,' to some degree to reverse Maoist theoretical preoccupations" (Barlow, 2004, p. 269). In Li's programme, the focus was placed on the re-education of women, which critics sometimes characterized as "Enlightenment" (Barlow, 2004, p. 268). At Dalian University, Li Xiaojiang has successfully made gender studies a required subject for all undergraduate students in her university. Her gender studies centre also holds international conferences on a regular basis to explore collaboration among feminists in Asia. The annual workshops that the centre organizes form part of its education programme to promote gender research in mainland China. Equally exciting projects were carried out at Capital Normal University under the leadership of Huang Lin who edits two journals, *Feminism in China* (*Zhongguo nüxing zhuyi*) and *Female Culture in China* (*Zhongguo nüxing wenhua*) and a book series, *Chinese Feminist Studies* (*Zhongguo nüxing zhuyi xueshu luncong*). She also organizes monthly seminars on gender studies and research. These two centres promote collaborative research projects and exchanges that aim at exploring the latest theoretical frameworks for gender studies. With the formation of gender research centres at universities and the Academies of Social Sciences, and the organization of academic conferences, a network and programmes of gender studies have put down roots in mainland China.

The scene of gender studies and criticism in mainland China began to change with the emergence of a new generation of feminist critics in the mid-1990s. Gender studies programmes have mushroomed in academic institutions, and institutions offering gender studies include Peking University, the Central Party School, Nankai University, Zhejiang Normal University, Capital Normal University, Xiamen University, Fujian Normal University and Henan University. Together with the research centres, these academic programmes offer a research agenda that aims at promoting gender studies as an academic discipline in mainland China, advocating feminist views, and developing meaningful dialogues with male critics and writers. Feminism is not just the business of female writers; it is also the concern of critics. These new feminist critics have become more and more active since the Fourth World Conference on Women was held in Beijing. Furthermore, with the rise of cultural studies in mainland China, some prominent feminist critics have begun to emerge, demanding to have their voices heard in different fields, such as literature, film studies, sociological studies and education studies. Among these new feminist critics are Chen Huifen, Cui Weiping, Dai Jinhua, Huang Lin, Jin Yanyu, Lin Danya, Liu Huiying, Liu Siqian and Sheng Ying, all of whom are either professors working at universities or researchers at the Chinese Academies of Social Sciences. Their views and research interests are revealed in the themes selected for the annual conferences they have organized since 1996: "female/gender identity," "female writings," "feminist films," "critique of patriarchal discourse," "sexual discrimination," "gender differences," "representation of women," "gender education," "feminism in other parts of the world," and "comparative studies and Western concepts of gender." A survey of the articles and essays published in the journal *Feminism in China* (*Zhongguo nüxing zhuyi*) further shows that there is a growing interest in gender-related issues in mainland China and that there exists a forum for feminist critics to deliberate over gender and feminist issues.

## IN SEARCH OF FEMININITY: MAINLAND CHINA, TAIWAN AND HONG KONG

The burgeoning interest in gender studies may serve as an index to show the social changes that are taking place in mainland China. A look at the strategies adopted by Chinese feminist critics reveals much about the theoretical perspectives they have adopted in dealing with gender issues and in responding to the representation of women in mainland China. As Kwok-kan Tam observes in "Gender Construction, Stereotyping and

Cross-Gender Writing" (Chapter 2), there is a tendency among Chinese feminist critics to limit their discussion of gender identity to social construction at the expense of its psychoanalytic dimension: "Added to the complexity of these issues is the theoretical dimension: Is it possible to construct a theory of Chinese feminism which does not have any reference to the specific psychological workings of gender identity in the Chinese context? The answer, perhaps, can only be provided by Chinese critics who claim to be feminists" (p. 30). This may be seen as a theoretical pitfall in the Chinese approach to feminism.

In reviewing relevant works in both Chinese and Western literature, Jessica Li, in her essay "Food, Body and Female Subjectivity: Reading between Western and Chinese Perspectives" (Chapter 4), puts forth the view that there is a discourse behind food and body which defines the female according to male-dominated and commercial values:

> [I]n the gender-based division of labour, women are expected to perform domestic duties, such as food preparation and washing the dishes, that limit their space for personal development. Women are also subjected to commercially idealized images of the female body, thus being forced to control their appetites and exhaust their energies. All such restrictions and images may hinder women from achieving power and developing a positive self-identity. (p. 53)

Using an anthropological perspective, Li points out that body and food are determinants in the social and cultural construction of female identity and argues for a materialistic basis in the formation of female subjectivity. This materialistic foundation is inseparable from the cultural space of food and body to which women are subjected. The concept of cultural space and its function in the formation of women's identity are seldom discussed in mainland Chinese criticism. Hence, Li's work can be seen as an attempt to deconstruct the patriarchal discourse behind ideas that shape social values.

Looking at the various experimentations with the characterization of women in modern Chinese literature, Qiao Yigang argues in "Women as Human vs. Women as Women: Female Consciousness in Modern Chinese Women's Literature" (Chapter 5) that "Chinese women's literature over the past hundred years is often characterized by the optimistic desire for the social liberation of women. Among the cultural issues, gender ranks as the most crucial in different historical contexts and it manifests itself in various ways, some more explicit than others. The most characteristic of the age's concerns is women's redefinition of themselves as human beings first, and women second" (p. 78). Qiao sees the need to probe the question of what women are. This is not a question about the biological makeup of women, but about the ways in which women define themselves. As she puts it, femininity is a question of self-awareness.

In her essay "Liberation of Femininity? Women's Poetry in Post-Mao China" (Chapter 6), Lisa Wong discusses the concept of women's space in relation to the quest for liberation in contemporary Chinese politics of gender:

> Writing back against the national collective self, women poets in post-Mao China seek liberation in a private space into which women can retreat from the external world and divest themselves of a public role. This withdrawal into a room of one's own is a manifestation of autonomy and independence. The room becomes a base from which the female self sets off for her journey of discovery and to which she can return at will. (pp. 99–100)

Wong concludes that "far from being liberated from the fetters of patriarchal culture and moral convention, women poets are still exploring new roles and consciousness under constriction" (p. 105). It may, however, be argued that while the project of constructing a liberated femininity may never be completed so long as there is patriarchy, Chinese women poets, as well as feminists, can still be considered as partially liberated, at least in mind, when they are aware of the fact that they are not yet liberated. In exploring the concept of women's space, Wong points out that there is a discourse that defines women in terms of space, though it is a changing discourse.

The lack of space reveals so much about the oppressive social reality experienced by women. As Suying Yang comments in the essay "Gender Construction in the Novels of Zhang Kangkang and Liang Xiaosheng" (Chapter 7):

> At the public level, women were, like men, members of society. They were financially independent and enjoyed equal opportunities for education and jobs of various kinds. Their ability and competence were recognized in society. However, at the private level, they felt gender inequality. Unfortunately, they tended to ignore this feeling of gender inequality at the private level because of their greater concern with society and the social system. (p. 113)

Yang believes that social oppression imposed upon Chinese women stems from linguistic structures which place men in a superior position to women. Yang offers the following view in her analysis of language as social practice that causes the inequality between men and women:

> [M]any linguists have studied how females and males use language in different language situations. They have found some general patterns. For example, females usually speak with a softer tone. They tend to make requests in a consultative manner, even when they speak from a more authoritative position (such as a doctor speaking to a patient). While women often resort to hedges and explanations to make their requests more acceptable, male language displays very different characteristics. Men are usually more direct in making requests and they usually do not make an effort to soften the tone of their requests. (p. 115)

Yang points out the close relation between women's space and language, stating that women lack social space because they lack a language that can put them in a superior position to men.

In a similar vein, Sheng Ying explores women's space as a social discourse that is constituted of different "myths" created by men. In "Feminist Critique: The Patriarchal Discourse of Chinese Male Writers" (Chapter 8), she suggests that women can be liberated only when they are freed from these myths, or discourses. In deconstructing these myths, Sheng points out that Chinese male writers like to fantasize women because they feel unfulfilled in their lives:

> Some Chinese male writers do not seem to be aware that when they write about women in such ways, they are actually treating women as an instrument for men to satisfy their desire for domination and power. Some male writers not only refrain from questioning the traditional patriarchy, they even pick up the debris of pornography and perversion from the ancient warehouse of sexual culture, and use it openly to propagate phallic imagery, in a vain attempt to keep women as the material object of men's desires. (pp. 140–141)

It is interesting to note Sheng's view on the writings of male authors who, in fantasizing women, attempt to compensate for their "severely repressed" egos (p. 125).

In her essay "Three Chinese Women Writers and the City in the 1990s" (Chapter 9), Jin Yanyu proposes to situate the study of contemporary Chinese women's writings in an urban space, which serves the function of defining women's identity in the changing social landscape. The city is no longer a backdrop or simply a social setting for women's writings, but provides the space for a new social imaginary, which, as Jin says, "is a double-edged sword, with dual functions of construction and demolition. The city can make women's lives more dynamic, more colourful, and more poetic; it can also throw women into dark terrors when the female body becomes a commodity" (p. 147). By comparing the works of three women writers, Wang Anyi, Shi Shuqing and Zhu Tianxin, Jin contrasts the differences and points out the similarities in these writers' discourses, showing how women are portrayed, or constructed, in mainland China, Hong Kong and Taiwan. This is also a comparison of the urban space women have in Shanghai, Hong Kong and Taipei. As Jin says, these three writers deliberately place their women characters in urban space to explore female subjectivity:

> It is not a coincidence that all three female writers seek to write about woman and city in the form of a trilogy, which is a powerful tool for telling history from an evolutionary and linear, muscular way. The three female writers' trilogies, however, all seek to go back from the third part to the first part so as to find faults in the seemingly truthful perceptions of the beginnings. They rewrite the history of city and woman through questioning their origin. Only by so doing can they eventually go beyond the limit of the trilogy and find possibilities of rewriting female subjectivity. (p. 156)

By comparing the three female writers and their writing strategies, Jin shows how women are constructed in the gaze of others as well as in the urban space in three cities which typify the diversities in contemporary Chinese culture and politics.

From a sociological point of view, Guo Shumei addresses how women's writings have developed in mainland China with the material growth in social life. In "New Modes of Women's Writing in the Age of Materialism" (Chapter 10), she suggests that Chinese women's writings, particularly those that deal with private feelings and the private parts of a woman's body, should be read as resistance against the Chinese socialist tradition which upholds that literature must deal with grand social themes. As she points out, "Now, in the age of materialism, the picture is totally different. Anyone can take part in literary creation. It is easy to publish a book. Anyone can write, as long as he or she is recognized by publishers. Publishing an article is even easier, as a large number of newspapers and magazines need contributions. Therefore, more women start to write and they write anything they wish. The field has become free, liberal and open" (p. 162). The market economy has brought about the commercialization of literature and the publishing industry and, in a direct way, has led to the flourishing of women's writing: "Women writers would not have emerged in such great numbers and there would not have been such colourful stories from all walks of life told in so many different tones, had there not been the market demand, the active participation of women in writing, or the pluralistic values, psychologies and styles that now exist" (p. 163). Guo further points out that many women's writings tend to be plotless, with the focus placed not on story and events, but on feelings and memory, which are achronological and non-linear. Such a style reveals that the writer views real life as plotless and non-linear.

While women's writings in mainland China tend to exhibit a strong sense of resistance, struggling to redefine femininity beyond prescribed Chinese social conventions, those in Taiwan tend to engage intensely in a politics of rewriting that aims at "empowering a female poetics to counter the male-dominated historiography of Taiwan literature and, by implication, to construct a literary female subjectivity" (Chapter 11, p. 171). As Mei-hwa Sung argues in "Writing Women's Literary History: Gender Discourse and Women's Literature in Taiwan" (Chapter 11), women's writings in Taiwan, as demonstrated in poetry, tend to be tied in with political enquiries: "The overwhelming majority of women poets have dealt with love (romantic and maternal) in their poems, and very often their poems tend to be philosophical treatises on the female self and its emancipation. A small number of them, on the other hand, have moved beyond the private/domestic realm to write about public issues such as national identity and women's place in the national/post-capitalist context" (p. 173). In her study of Taiwan women's poetry, Sung shows that "writing women's literary history is a political act as well as a poetic one" (p. 188). She points out that the effort to anthologize women poets is both politics and poetics in establishing a tradition of women's writings. As she puts it at the end of her essay, anthologizing women's poetry is to inscribe order on the voices of the other.

In a review of recent documentaries, Kuei-fen Chiu shows how a different strategy has been employed in the representation of women as minority in Taiwan. Chiu argues that giving the subaltern a voice is resistance. However, the issue of voice and self-representation is so complex in Taiwan that "the ideological ambiguity of the subaltern's speech performance" has to be examined critically (Chapter 12, p. 206). In her essay "The Subaltern Woman's Voice and the (Film-)making of Modern Taiwan" (Chapter 12), Chiu poses the question of how modernity can be envisioned, whether it is in Taiwan or in mainland China, since a wide gap exists between the literary wor(l)d and the illiterate masses: "The gap between the literary word and the illiterate people was not easy to overcome, for the representation endeavour by the literary word could do no more than performing representation as 'speaking for,' often at the sacrifice of 're-presentation'" (p. 211). It is the word that constitutes a different world of the literary. Chiu believes that, thanks to documentary filming, the "grass-roots vision" can be represented in "shaping the history of Taiwan under transformation" (p. 211).

Gender representation is a matter of politics, but it is seldom represented as such in Hong Kong writings. Instead, it is tied in with Hong Kong people's quest for an identity which is very often problematized as transcultural or transnational. Because of its location between East and West, and between mainland China and other parts of the world, Hong Kong has a unique identity that is not purely Eastern or Chinese, not purely Western or British. What is interesting in this quest is a strong emphasis on the fluidity of identity. In recent Hong Kong writings, as exemplified in Dong Qizhang's novel *Dual Body* (*Shuangsheng*), (dis) location of the self is always central to any identity quest. Gender fluidity also denotes the lack of a fixed identity. As Kwok-kan Tam argues in the essay "Desire, Fear and Gender in Dong Qizhang's Novel *Dual Body*" (Chapter 13), representation of the self in terms of gender is politics:

> The lack of an identity that can be categorized and can fit into people's stereotypes implies Hong Kong people's lack of a cultural identity that can be categorized as Western or Chinese. In another sense too, the novel can be read as a symbol of Hong Kong people's lack of a definable identity. Hong Kong people are bilingual, bicultural, and now also bi-sexual and bi-gendered. This bi-sexual and bi-gendered identity and the trouble of misrecognition that it brings is perhaps the unique gender politics that Hong Kong has. (p. 224)

The novel *Dual Body* can thus be read as a political satire on Hong Kong people's confusion about themselves in terms of their national and cultural identity in the 1990s, when they found themselves caught in a dilemma of imaginaries between their old selves of being Chinese in a British colony and their new selves of being neither Chinese nor British.

In his essay "Men Aren't Men: Feminization of the Masculine Subject in the Works of Some Hong Kong Male Writers" (Chapter 14), Kwai-Cheung Lo relates gender identity to political identity in Hong Kong. He begins by asserting that "[t]he historical construction of the Chinese male in Hong Kong may shed light on this issue. Masculinity in

Hong Kong is not only related to the reconstruction of Chineseness (or Chinese cultural identity in particular), but is also related to the fact that the colonial modernity of the port city over the last several decades has been displacing traditional concepts of what a Chinese male is supposed to be" (p. 226). Lo argues that the feminization of men in Hong Kong is related to social change in which more and more men are turned into "househusbands." In literary representation, however, he sees the feminization of men as an attempt "to de-legitimize the discovery of one's inner self and to lay bare just such a process of a man's becoming a woman" (p. 236). The novel *Dual Body*, as Lo reads it, "reject[s] the differentiation of sexual identities as a fixed and stable set of symbolic inclusions and exclusions" (p. 237). In his conclusion, Lo states:

> The process of becoming-female either in a literal or metaphorical sense in these texts is linked with contemplation of the masculine subject itself and the issue of Chinese identification. Hong Kong men appropriate the notion of femininity to reconstruct not only the male identity but also their national identity. But when the new meaning of masculinity or nationality is built around the idea of a becoming-woman, it also suggests that there is no longer any positive consistency in a Chinese male subjectivity, which could only lie in the imaginary "woman" or in something that does not exist. (p. 240)

In *The Lenses of Gender*, Sandra Bem points out that "hidden assumptions about sex and gender remain embedded in cultural discourses, social institutions, and individual psyches that invisibly and systematically reproduce male power in generation after generation" (Bem, 1993, p. 2). She calls these assumptions "the lenses of gender," and she points out that "[n]ot only do these lenses shape how people perceive, conceive, and discuss social reality, but they also shape the more material things—like unequal pay and inadequate day care—that constitute social reality itself" (Bem, 1993, p. 2). The study of gender, in this collection of essays, necessitates a discovery of the hidden lenses embedded in the culture of the three Chinese communities, namely, mainland China, Taiwan and Hong Kong. It is apparent from these essays that the study of gender is inseparable from the study of society, politics and discourse. While gender can be viewed as a lens that provides perspectives for a critical understanding of the world, it can also construct a discourse that disciplines people's behaviour and shapes their thinking of themselves and other people's selves. This collection can be seen as the product of a concerted effort to render the Chinese gender lenses "visible rather than invisible, to enable us to look *at* culture's gender lenses rather than *through* them" (Bem, 1993, p. 2).

## REFERENCES

Ames, Roger T. (1993). "The Meaning of the Body in Classical Chinese Philosophy." In Thomas P. Kasulis et al., eds., *Self as Body in Asian Theory and Practice*, pp. 157–177. Albany: State University of New York Press.

Barlow, Tani E. (2004). *The Question of Women in Chinese Feminism*. Durham, NC: Duke University Press.

Bem, Sandra Lipsitz (1993). *The Lenses of Gender: Transforming the Debate on Sexual Inequality*. New Haven, CT: Yale University Press.

Chou, Ying-hsiung (1992). "Zhongguo xiandangdai zhiwo yishi chutan" [A preliminary study of subjectivity in modern and contemporary China]. In Chen Bingliang (Chan Ping-leung), ed., *Zhongguo xiandangdai wenxue tanyan* [Studies in modern and contemporary Chinese literature], pp. 16–25. Hong Kong: Joint Publishing.

Croll, Elisabeth (1980). *Feminism and Socialism in China*. New York: Schocken Books.

Erikson, Erik H. (1959). *Identity and the Life Cycle: Selected Papers*. New York: International University Press.

Frosh, Stephen (1991). *Identity Crisis: Modernity, Psychoanalysis and the Self*. London: Macmillan.

Gardiner, Judith Kegan (1981). "On Female Identity and Writing by Women." *Critical Inquiry*, Vol. 7, No. 4 (Winter), 347–361.

Giddens, Anthony (1991). *Modernity and Self-Identity: Self and Society in the Late Modern Age*. Cambridge: Polity Press.

Hu Shi (1918). "Yibusheng zhuyi" [Ibsenism]. *Xin qingnian* [New youth], Vol. 4, No. 6 (June), 489–507.

Ibsen, Henrik (1980). *A Doll's House* (1879). In Michael Meyer, trans., *Ibsen Plays: Two*, pp. 23–104. London: Methuen.

Irigaray, Luce (1985). *This Sex Which is Not One*. Trans. Catherine Porter and Carolyn Burke. Ithaca, NY: Cornell University Press.

Larson, Wendy (1993). "Female Subjectivity and Gender Relations: The Early Stories of Lu Yin and Bing Xin." In Liu Kang and Xiaobing Tang, eds., *Politics, Ideology, and Literary Discourse in Modern China*, pp. 124–143. Durham, NC: Duke University Press.

Lee, Leo Oufan (1990). "In Search of Modernity: Some Reflections on a New Mode of Consciousness in Twentieth-century Chinese History and Literature." In Paul A. Cohen and Merle Goldman, eds., *Ideas across Cultures: Essays on Chinese Thought in Honor of Benjamin I. Schwartz*, pp. 109–136. Cambridge, MA: Harvard East Asian Monographs.

Lu Xun (1973). "Shangshi" [Regret for the past]. In Lu Xun, *Panghuang* [Hesitation], pp. 114–137. Beijing: Renmin wenxue chubanshe.

Lu Xun (1981). "Moluo shili shuo." In *Lu Xun quanji* [Complete works of Lu Xun], Vol. 1, pp. 63–115. Beijing: Renmin wenxue chubanshe.

Lu Xun (1981). "Wenhua pianzi lun." In *Lu Xun quanji* [Complete works of Lu Xun], Vol. 1, pp. 44–62. Beijing: Renmin wenxue chubanshe.

Mao Dun (1928). "Chuangzao" [Creation]. In *Mao Dun duanpian xiaoshuo xuan* [Short stories by Mao Dun], Vol. 1, pp. 17–34. Hong Kong: Yixin shudian.

Mao Dun (1935). *Hong* [Rainbow]. Hong Kong: Lingnan chubanshe.

Tam, Kwok-kan (1987). "The Shanghai Performance of *A Doll's House* and the Mystery of Jiang Qing's Role in the Stage Production and in the Revolution: A Research Note and Review." *Journal of Oriental Studies*, Vol. 25, No. 2, 197–201.

Tam, Kwok-kan, and Terry Siu-han Yip (1998). "The Self in Transition: Moral Dilemma in Modern Chinese Drama." In Roger T. Ames et al., eds., *Self as Image in Asian Theory and Practice*, pp. 200–216. Albany: State University of New York Press.

Tu, Wei-ming (1985). "Selfhood and Otherness in Confucian Thought." In Anthony J. Marsella et al., eds., *Culture and Self: Asian and Western Perspectives*, pp. 231–251. New York: Tavistock Publications.

World Health Organization (2002). "Integrating Gender Perspectives into the Work of WHO." <http://whqlibdoc.who.int/hq/2002/a78322.pdf>.

## GLOSSARY

cixing 雌性

*Daxue* 《大學》

Dung Kai Cheung (Dong Qizhang) 董啟章

"Fangzhou" 〈方舟〉

*Funü pinglun* 《婦女評論》

funü yundong 婦女運動

*Funü shenghuo* 《婦女生活》

*Funü zazhi* 《婦女雜誌》

"Guiqu lai" 〈歸去來〉

Guo Moruo 郭沫若

Han Shaogong 韓少功

Hao Ran 浩然

*Hong* 《虹》

Hu Shi 胡適

Jiang Qing 江青

kun 坤

Liang Xiaosheng 梁曉聲

Lu Xun 魯迅

Mao Dun 茅盾

Mei 梅

nüquan zhuyi 女權主義

*Nüxing zhong*《女性鐘》

nüxing zhuyi 女性主義

qian 乾

Tian Han 田漢

xing 性

xiongxing 雄性

yang 陽

yin 陰

"Zai tongyi dipingxian shang"〈在同一地平線上〉

Zhang Jie 張潔

Zhang Kangkang 張抗抗

Zhang Xinxin 張辛欣

"Zhufu"〈祝福〉

Women's Self-Identity and Gender Relations in
Twentieth-Century Chinese Fiction

TERRY SIU-HAN YIP

SELF AND IDENTITY ARE TWO interlocking concepts that have caught the
enduring interest of many writers and scholars. What one identifies
oneself with, and how one does it, are questions that have been explored
by philosophers, psychologists, anthropologists and sociologists since
the nineteenth century. With the advent of the women's movement and
feminist discourse in the twentieth century, discussions on self and iden
tity have often been linked with discussions on the "engendered power
imbalance" between men and women, as Kate Millett calls it. In literature, for example, the relationship between sex and power is often
explored through tangled relationships and myriad forms of struggle
between men and women. Writers often present those social, ideological
and/or historical circumstances that tend to hamper women's quest for
an autonomous self or highlight the aspirations and frustrations of those
women who search for a specific type of identity in tradition-ridden
societies. Henrik Ibsen, for example, is among the few early writers in
Europe to explore the modern notion of the individual self, especially
the female self, in his plays. Placing his female characters in struggles
against confinement in domestic settings, Ibsen studies the transformation of the female and points out how the imbalance in gender relations
has led to repression of the self.

His play *A Doll's House* (1879) is a classic example, elucidating the
general conditions of women in Norway in the late nineteenth century,
when women's differential social positions, or domestic roles to be more
accurate, made them subordinate to men. Most women at the time were
expected to seek no other goals in life than to fulfil their stereotypical
gender roles as daughters, wives and mothers. In *A Doll's House* Ibsen
scrutinizes those social, moral and ideological assumptions regarding
gender roles that were in full operation and highlights the female
protagonist's moral crisis in life and her subsequent self-awakening. The
play focuses on Nora's transformation from a dependent daughter,

dutiful wife and caring mother, who at the beginning diligently performs her assigned gender roles, to an awakened woman and an assertive individual eager to find her own voice and to establish her own space. Her decision to leave her husband and her family at the end shows a woman's determination to embark on a life of her "own," searching for a coherent identity. It further shows the distribution of power in society where men often assume dominating positions, play domineering roles in gender relationships and exercise absolute power over women.

Situating his female protagonist in a society resistant to socio-moral changes, Ibsen challenges the general social assumptions that the family or home is the natural shelter or resting place for individuals. For Ibsen, family is often one of the many social institutions that imprison the free spirit of the individual. It can be a battlefield where men and women fight for power and supremacy. Nora comes to realize that she is just a plaything, a commodity that has been passed from one man (her father) to another (her husband). She has no place or position in her own family other than a subordinate or a supporting one. As she tells her husband Torvald before her departure, "You [Torvald] arranged everything to suit your own tastes, and so I came to have the same tastes as yours.... But our home has been nothing but a play-room. I've been your doll-wife here, just as at home I was Papa's doll-child" (Ibsen, 1986, pp. 225–226). Nora comes to realize that she has never been treated as equal by her husband and her identity has been defined primarily by her social roles and by her relationships with men as daughter, wife or mother. Through Nora's interactions with other male characters in the play, Ibsen shows the imbalance of power between the sexes as well as the patriarchal prejudices and values that tend to oppress the female sex. Ibsen foregrounds the pressing need for women to take note of their situation and act to change the status quo. Nora's departure thus marks her first step toward self-actualization; it further signifies an "awakened" woman's conscious attempt to define her own self based on the romantic notion of individualism on the one hand and her determination to live not for men but, more importantly, for the realization of her self on the other.

## THE SELFLESS WOMAN IN THE 1920S

When Ibsen's *A Doll's House* was translated and made available to Chinese readers in 1918, Nora's defiance against prevailing socio-moral norms and patriarchal injustices caught the attention of thousands of young intellectuals who regarded Nora as a role model for Chinese women at the time. Ibsen's play also prompted many Chinese writers, male and female, to re-examine notions of self and identity as well as gender relations in twentieth-century China. Lu Xun, for example, was among the early male writers to examine the notion of self with reference to the causes of women's predicaments in modern China and advocated radical reforms of the self. In his oft-studied short story "New Year's Sacrifice" (Zhufu) published in 1924, for example, he traces the emotional and moral crises faced by an uneducated woman whose self is never developed nor recognized and whose identity is unidentifiable except at the social level, where she is known primarily as the wife of Xianglin.

Told from the perspective of an educated outsider-narrator, the story reveals the ghost-like existence of Xianglin's Wife, who is treated as a commodity not only by men but also by other women. Notions like self, identity, or womanhood are unknown to women in this Chinese tale. The female protagonist was forced into an arranged marriage with Xianglin, who soon died of typhoid. Though uneducated, Xianglin's Wife tries to lead a self-sufficient life working as a domestic helper in Lu province after her husband's death. Her attempt to preserve her integrity, however, comes to an abrupt end when her mother-in-law hunts her down and forces her into a second marriage. Her frustration and helplessness are epitomized by her attempted suicide on the wedding day of her second marriage. Xianglin's Wife comes to realize that she is never her own mistress and that she has no control over her own life because even suicide is not permitted. With the "accidental" death in the wilderness of her child from her second marriage, Xianglin's Wife undergoes another round of ordeals.

Labelled as a woman of bad luck by the villagers, Xianglin's Wife becomes an outcast socially, emotionally and physically in the village. Her obsessive telling of her predicaments to others and her eagerness to buy a threshold at the Temple of the Tutelary God reveal not only her pathetic situation as a self-less woman but also her hellish existence. Desperately, she tries to end her alienation and reintegrate into the community that holds prejudices against her by doubling her efforts to please others and by making sacrifices. Amah Liu's advice to Xianglin's Wife shows the absurdity of Xianglin's Wife's situation in particular and of Chinese society in general: "Better guard against that in good time, I say. Go to the Temple of the Tutelary God and buy a threshold to be trampled on instead of you by thousands of people. If you atone for your sins in this life you'll escape torment after death" (Lu Xun, 1989, p. 198). Instead of seeing herself as a victim of Confucian ideology, feudal practices and patriarchal mentality that subvert a woman's self, Xianglin's Wife regards herself as a sinner who has to atone for her sins and wrong deeds.

It is apparent from the way the story is told that Lu Xun considers ignorance as a sin, for it prevents society and its people from changing. Part of Xianglin's Wife's sufferings stems from people's indifference. The general public, including the educated narrator-observer, seem to be sympathetic, but they would not do anything to change the conditions for women like Xianglin's Wife. Nor would anyone interfere with her mother-in-law's decision to "sell" her to another man for money. However, Lu Xun also shows that Xianglin's Wife herself is partially responsible for her own predicament because she has allowed her life to be run by others. No one can save Xianglin's Wife from her ordeals, for she has accepted her plight as her fate.

As in the case of Shen Congwen's short story "Xiaoxiao" (1929), the protagonist Xiaoxiao has no sense of her self. As a result, she is unaware of her own exploitation by men. At the age of twelve, Xiaoxiao was sold as a child-bride. Her marriage to a three-year-old child did not bother her much as long as food was provided and her survival secured. For young Xiaoxiao, subsistence seems more important, immediate and real than human pride or dignity. Happiness for someone like her simply means food and shelter. That explains why she took her marriage as a mere move from one home to another. When she is sexually exploited by a villager and becomes pregnant, she is left to deal with her situation alone. Shen reveals woman's subordination and exploitation in rural China, where Xiaoxiao is at the mercy of men and patriarchy. She has neither power nor any say over her own body, life and "fate." Patriarchal prejudices against women, the imbalance in power between the sexes, or the rights of women are issues beyond her comprehension or concern due to her ignorance and lack of self. Through the tale, Shen shows that male supremacy was seldom challenged and female resistance remained minimal in tradition-ridden China. Women like Xianglin's Wife and Xiaoxiao were defenceless and vulnerable under the patriarchal order in which their female bodies were treated as sites of male domination.

Furthermore, it must be noted that Chinese women often suffer not simply because they are victimized by men. In "New Year's Sacrifice," Xianglin's Wife is manipulated and exploited by her mother-in-law as well. Xianglin's mother is presented not just as a monstrous woman who "feeds" on other women for mere survival: she is portrayed as both a victim and a victimizer in one, for she has been "colonized" by patriarchy and sided with men in her oppression of other women. Like Manlu in Eileen Chang's *Eighteen Springs* (*Bansheng yuan*), Xianglin's mother has submitted herself to patriarchy and has acted in an extremely selfish way in victimizing other helpless women, including her own family members. She shows no sympathy to Xianglin's Wife, for she treats the latter not as a human being but as a mere commodity for sale or exchange. In a comparable way, Manlu has also sacrificed her younger sister, Manzhen, in her desperate attempt to "keep" her man, Zhu Hongcai. Not only has she betrayed her younger sister and abused the trust the latter has in her, Manlu has also debased herself to the level of animal existence when her humanity is forsaken. Serving as an accomplice of her wicked husband Zhu, Manlu uses tricks to trap her younger sister and offers her as a "gift" to please her husband and to gratify Zhu's greed and excessive sexual appetite. Manlu's selfishness and ignorance typify many Chinese women who failed to develop a distinct self. Though Manlu has already become a victim of men due to economic and family circumstances, she has not properly registered the injustice and inequality she experienced. Instead, she chooses to side with men like Zhu in their violation of women's physical beings. As Eileen Chang succinctly states in her tale, there can never be a bright future for women if they fail to understand their situation and act upon it. There will be no future for women like Manzhen, though awakened and educated, if they do not receive support from their own womenfolk. It is apparent from the story that women have not only forsaken their lives, together with their happiness and future, for their family, but they have also forfeited their selves, together with their pride and dignity, when they rely on men for happiness, fulfilment and/or livelihood.

In the case of Xianglin's Wife, she neither understands the causes of her predicament nor realizes the injustices done to her and the prejudices held against her. Presented as a victim of the patriarchal system that has "trampled" on women for centuries, Xianglin's Wife is trapped in her position as a woman and in her gender relations. There seems to be no escape from such "torments" for women like Xianglin's Wife when their predicaments are closely linked to their ignorance and lack of self-awareness, as well as lack of support from their female family members. Without addressing the notion of self, especially the female self, and without attending to women's ignorance, it seemed that

Chinese women would continue to find themselves caught in such pathetic and hopeless situations that are beyond redemption, according to Lu Xun. Unlike Nora, who strives to preserve her integrity, develop her coherent identity and establish her autonomous self, Xianglin's Wife is eventually smothered to death in a feudal society owing not only to prevailing patriarchal practices, but also to her own acceptance of her "fate" and ignorance.

## AWAKENING TO THE FEMALE SELF

The promise held out by Ibsen's Nora in the 1910s and the predicament of women like Xianglin's Wife and Xiaoxiao in the 1920s have prompted many female intellectuals to reflect upon their lives and actively re-examine the notion of self and identity in China. Moral and emotional crises often arose when women's self-searching voyages were checked or swept off course by the strong social, moral or ideological currents of the time. A look at some exemplary works in Chinese women's literature since the 1920s will show how Chinese women writers have, under the influence of the Western notion of individualism, struggled to abandon their old role-selves defined basically by Confucianism in search of new selves characterized by romantic individualism and a heightened sense of identity. Women's search for a distinct female identity has become a recurrent motif in Chinese women's writings, which are considered by many as "an extension of their feminine role, an activity that [does] not detract from their womanhood," but in some sense augments it (Showalter, 1977, p. 85). Women's quest for selfhood also became a prominent theme of the time when writers often took a subjective stance in their depiction of domineering men and assertive women, and explored such notions as gender and sexuality, selfhood and motherhood, self-actuality and domesticity, as well as career and marriage, in their narratives.

While Chinese male writers have devoted much effort to depicting women's sufferings and exploitation in male-dominated Chinese society in the 1910s and 1920s, women writers focused on the problematization of gender roles in the construction of the female self in the 1920s. They openly resisted those reactionary external forces that tended to hamper their personal growth and self-expansion and consciously registered the engendered power imbalances between men and women in their writings. Taking an autobiographical or semi-autobiographical approach to their treatments of the female self, including female subjectivity, they scrutinized tensions in gender relations with the hope of making better sense of their selves and identifying the causes of their frustrations. With concerted effort, Chinese women writers presented an array of enlightened women in twentieth-century Chinese literature— women characters who distinguish themselves by their efforts to define their selves and by their open expressions of their sexual awakening. A new type of women characters emerged in modern Chinese literature as their "creators" attempted to address issues pertaining to the liberation of the self, including the sexual self. Central to their advocacy is the importance of self-consciousness, action and self-realization. Often presented as lonely young women caught in a state of love-sickness or entangled in a web of relationships, these "new" women struggle to establish their space and to find their own voice. Lu Yin's early short stories such as "The Sorrows of a Certain Youth" (Huoren de bei'ai) and "Where Would My Destiny Be?" (Hechu shi guicheng?), published in 1922 and 1927 respectively, are prime examples elucidating modern Chinese women's desire to be their own mistresses. Their yearning for romantic love and their eagerness to express their selves, especially their psychological and sexual selves, found resonance in many women of the time. Typical of these tales is the writers' focus on their female characters' confused selves. Inner struggles and profound emotional disturbances arose when women's aspirations were met with family intervention or socio-moral disapproval. Their awareness of their social role-selves with family obligations continues to weigh many women down today in their attempts to transcend their current state of being.

In "The Sorrows of a Certain Youth," for instance, the newly awakened woman, Yaxia, feels frustrated because of her failure in defining her self and in establishing a meaningful love relationship with the opposite sex, and in her inability to cast off her old morality with its socio-familial obligations. Although Yaxia openly rejects those traditional gender roles ascribed to her as a woman, she fails to acknowledge properly her emotional and sexual self. Her conscious effort to repress her strong amorous feelings for her lover can thus be regarded as a manifestation of her timidity and fear—timidity about asserting her newly acquired individual self and fear of confronting the world of tradition and convention. Yaxia's emotional and moral crises are typical of many Chinese women at the crossroads—women who found themselves completely lost as they embarked on a journey of self-discovery, looking earnestly for fulfilment. This sense of frustration and alienation is common in many of Lu Yin's writings that deal with women's struggle for self-definition. Their confusion and sense of loss are highlighted, for such a quest proves to be a difficult and painful one. In "Where Would My Destiny Be?" for example, Shanü feels desperate in her attempt to free herself from her household chores and domestic shackles. Her enthusiasm for developing her career gradually fades away as she fails to disentangle herself from her social roles and gendered relations. She comes to realize that she is fighting a losing battle alone, with no support from either her family or society.

Published in 1929, Chen Ying's short story "The Charming One" (Wujun) accentuates the desperation of a young woman in her defiance of her social role self defined by her socio-familial obligations. Wujun's radical act of leaving her oppressive parental home in search of romantic love shows her assertive step toward fulfilment in life. She is determined to live an independent life with her lover despite family disapproval. Unlike Yaxia, Wujun is ready to brave the world's criticism and indictment when she decides to elope with her lover. However, her lover is presented as a coward, a weakling who is not prepared to confront social institutions for love's sake. His last-minute change of mind and withdrawal from their planned elopement leave Wujun with no other alternative but death. Having chosen the road of no return, Wujun would rather die than live a ghost-like life of submission, emotional deprivation and spiritual imprisonment. Wujun is presented as a Nora figure who asserts her self and openly defies all forces that tend to subvert her female self and jeopardize her moral integrity. For her, there is no compromise in her quest for selfhood. Once she embarks on this journey to independence, it is impossible for her to turn back or be side-tracked. She is ready to pay a high price for her romantic ideal and to sacrifice her life for her cause.

A similarly heightened sense of self is delineated in Ding Ling's narratives about Chinese women's problematic self. Unlike Lu Yin's Yaxia, who represses her love, Ding Ling's Miss Sophie in "Miss Sophie's Diary" (Shafei nüshi de riji) voices her burning desire for her lover and expresses in frank language her sexual frustrations. Ding Ling's tale centres on Miss Sophie's emotional anxiety and highlights her frustrations and moral dilemma. Presented as an enlightened Chinese woman with a developed sense of consciousness, Miss Sophie consciously pursues the liberation of the self, especially the female self. She sees her freedom in love and choice of marriage partner as manifestations of her independence and the actualization of her self. Miss Sophie is often regarded as Ding Ling's leading woman character and is recognized for her boldness in acknowledging her sexuality and in expressing her quest for romantic individualism. A look at Chinese writings in the 1920s and 1930s shows the emergence of a generation of Chinese women who gradually left behind them their traditional social roles of domesticity and social marginality as they assumed increasingly active positions in society as career women, goal-seekers and advocates of women's rights.

## NATIONALIZING THE FEMALE SELF

It is interesting to note that these modern Chinese women started their emancipation campaign as bold fighters against Confucian morality that tended to treat women as men's subordinates and against patriarchal practices that subvert women's self-development. As seen in the writings by Chinese women in the first few decades of the twentieth century, women's self has been dealt with at the personal and social levels and has been closely linked to women's battle for freedom in love and marriage. Established socio-moral norms were challenged, women's emotional and spiritual awakening was emphasized and notions of self and sexuality were explored. It is this romantic zeal for independence that distinguishes women's writings of the time. However, this quest for independence on the part of Chinese women took a drastic turn in the late 1930s when China, as a young nation state, was under political threat from foreign powers such as Japan. Discussions about the emancipation of the self were often linked to debates over the liberation of the country from foreign invasion and occupation.

It was in such a climate of social and political upheaval in the country that Chinese women's writings witnessed an ideological shift from an advocacy of individual freedom to a celebration of national solidarity. The distinct female/feminine discourse that characterized the writings of the 1920s was replaced by a socialist/national discourse. Xie Bingying's famous autobiographical novel *Autobiography of a Girl Soldier* (*Nübing zizhuan*) marks the beginning of such a discoursal and ideological change in the narration of the female self. She makes it clear that personal independence and freedom would not be possible if the nation is politically under threat. Instead of focusing on the young female narrator's dream of romantic love and quest for personal happiness, Xie highlights her determination to serve her country in the battle against Japanese invasion. The engendered power imbalance highlighted by earlier writers was replaced by deliberation over unbalanced power relations between nations. Notions of self and identity were from then on discussed from a nationalistic perspective. Dramatized by the narrator in Xie's story, Chinese women came to assume a new masculine identity and took on a new militant look as they fought side by side with men for national solidarity and the betterment of the country. Xie's protagonist takes the defence of her country as her mission and responsibility. Without a second thought, the young girl soldier "unsexes" herself and assumes a masculine identity in her anti-Japanese campaign. Proud of her "defemininized" self, she sheds all her gendered social roles as a woman and abandons all traits of femininity as she enthusiastically joins the army as a girl soldier. Adopting a socialist discourse in her delineation of the young woman's transformation of her personal battle for selfhood into one that concerns national defence and national solidarity, Xie Bingying traces the girl soldier's transformation from a romantic dreamer to a romantic revolutionary. Her girl soldier became a new "role model" for Chinese women, redefining not only the female self but also the female mentality for decades to come.

A look at the array of women characters discussed above shows that Chinese women have gone a long way in their efforts to construct for themselves new identities in the twentieth century. From the ordeals and injustices experienced by Xianglin's Wife through the soul-searching and self-questioning crises undergone by Yaxia and Wujun to the outcries of Miss Sophie and the militant stance of Xie Bingying's girl soldier, Chinese women have tried various means to define their selves or to seek their way out of their emotional imprisonment or socio-moral confinement. Many thought that they had found an answer to their quest for self and that their new identity was secured when they sought alliance with the militant girl soldier. Such a conviction was publicly advocated by Jiang Qing, who gave Ibsen's Nora an abrasive character and a militant look on the stage in Shanghai in 1935. Both Jiang Qing and Xie Bingying thought that they had successfully taken Chinese women out of their spiritual labyrinth by advocating a pseudo-feminist mentality, a mentality which has affected many women since the 1930s. It was only decades later that Chinese women came to realize the absurdity of assuming a pseudo-male identity or putting on a masculine appearance, as this constitutes the denial of one's identity and the negation of the female self. As Randy Kaplan rightly puts it, many Chinese women have been deeply involved in competition with men in "socio-political spheres in which the rules and goals for achievement are defined by males" so that women's "potential energies for internal, psycho-sexual conflict are utterly short-circuited" (Kaplan, 1988, p. 87).

The socialist attempt to define the female self with a militant orientation came under scrutiny and challenge in the 1970s when contemporary women writers re-examined notions of self and sexuality, as well as female subjectivity. The masculine identity that many Chinese women have assumed since the mid-1930s was questioned and gender relations under the socialist system were scrutinized. Writers such as Zong Pu, Zhang Jie, Zhang Kangkang, Wang Anyi and Zhang Xinxin began to reassess in their fiction the meaning of "equality," the power relations between the sexes and the price women have paid for their liberation. Female subjectivity and sexuality come under the limelight in their stories that attempt to find out what constitutes true equality for women and what causes perpetual frustrations in women. Very often women's moral choice forms the backbone of their narratives in which metropolitan women find themselves caught in moral dilemmas that demand they take an inward look at their aspirations and selves in relation to their sexual other. For those women who resist compromise and choose to further develop their careers and preserve their individual selves, women are forced to admit the stark fact that women are still marginalized in society and that their female selves, including their bodies, are still subordinated to men. Divorce or separation from their husbands seems inevitable when these women fail to maintain a balance between their personal aspirations and family obligations.

## THE POST-SOCIALIST LOST SELF

In "The Ark" (Fangzhou), for instance, Zhang Jie details the causes of women's subjugation in contemporary China, where they remain marginalized, although they have successfully integrated into a men's world at the political and economic levels. Perplexity and a sense of loss arise when educated women fail to construct a distinct female self or develop meaningful relationships with the opposite sex. The title reveals the allegorical nature of the tale that advocates women's solidarity and emphasizes female subjectivity and integrity. While Zhang Jie scrutinizes the female self against a backdrop of love, career and marriage, Zhang Xinxin examines the difference in expectations and imbalance in power relations between men and women in her short story "How Did I Miss You?" (Wo zai na'er cuoguo le ni?) published in 1980. Through the moral crisis faced by a bus-conductress who finds herself caught in a love relationship that demands the negation of her self, Zhang Xinxin shows that a power imbalance between the sexes still perpetuates in contemporary China, leading to the need for a reconsideration of the self on women's part. Through the power struggle between the lovers, Zhang shows that women like the bus-conductress are not fully emancipated at the psycho-cultural or ideological level, as they fail to construct a coherent identity. It eventually dawns on the bus-conductress that she has no self of her own under her "unisex" uniform or behind her masculinized appearance in socialist China because she has never accepted herself as she is but has always adopted a pseudo-male identity in her daily interaction with the opposite sex.

What comes as a shock to her is her inability to bridge the gap between her social self at her workplace and her private self in her love relationship with a theatre director. Caught in a moral dilemma when her autonomy and integrity as a person are challenged by her theatre-director lover, who wants to "rewrite" her story and "direct" her life, the bus-conductress is forced to make a painful decision to leave her beloved director boy-friend in order to write her own "play" and run her own life. In the course of her struggle for self-expression and space, the bus-conductress comes to realize that her own double aspiration is not something imposed by men upon her. Instead, she has "accepted" and "internalized" these patriarchal values and prejudiced attitudes prevailing in society without her knowing. Zhang Xinxin makes it clear to the readers that the liberation of the self under socialism can easily become another form of self-confinement if it demands or results in the negation of the self, especially the female self, or denies the individual of his or her distinct identity.

Zhang's interest in equality and integrity is deliberated fully in her renowned novella "On the Same Horizon" (Zai tongyi dipingxian shang), in which she presents women at the crossroads. The complexity of Chinese women's lives in a rapidly changing society is depicted in vivid images. Alternating her narrative between the male and female protagonists, Zhang shows the tension between the husband and wife in the story, highlighting the female protagonist's psychological and emotional changes which the female protagonist undergoes. While playing the role expected of her as a traditional wife, the female protagonist is aware that such a compromise of her self does not guarantee happiness or security in her marriage. She fully understands that she does not enjoy equal status with her husband in the family. As she reflects on her marital situation:

Women are all the same. Where can I retreat? … Once I give birth to a baby, I will be trapped. Will he be happy and satisfied then? No. I will still lose him when I have nothing to offer, when I can no longer "meet" him in career terms or in spiritual terms! … From the very beginning, I have failed to strike a balance in the family. (Zhang, 1981, p. 177)

Though she is aware of her social role as a wife, Zhang's female protagonist finds it difficult denying her individual self with its aspirations. She abhors the subordinate position assigned to her by society and resists the passive role she is expected to play in marriage. Frustrations mark her life as she feels the pressure on her not only as a woman but more importantly as a career woman in contemporary China where a patriarchal mentality still reigns.

Zhang's narrative is significant as it epitomizes the concerns of a generation of Chinese women writers since the 1980s whose writings address not just the power relations between the sexes, but also women's conscious search for equilibrium and inner harmony. As revealed in their writings, women will no longer leave their happiness and future to chance, luck or "fate." Instead, they are determined to take full charge of their lives even if it means a life characterized by loneliness and incessant battles. The disparity between a woman's public social self that enjoys economic and political equality with men and her private self that suffers under unbalanced power relations and prejudiced gendered roles is highlighted in Zhang's story. Realizing that she can never meet her husband on the same horizon, that the society does not allow or expect her to meet men on equal terms, that such an imbalance in power and status will continue to haunt their relationship, the female protagonist chooses to take charge of her situation and demands a divorce from her beloved husband. Her decision reveals her determination to lead a life of her own, resisting all institutional claims upon her individual self, for they tend to unsettle the core of her self. That is to say, she refuses to play the role of the "generalized" other in a male-female relationship (Mead, 1934, p. 186).

Zong Pu's short story "The Tragedy of the Walnut Tree" (Hetaoshu de beiju) also addresses women's psycho-emotional independence and solidarity. Disturbed by the unwelcome visit of some youngsters to her huge walnut tree, which has served as her confidante since the departure of her lover thirty years ago, the aging female protagonist, Qingyi, uses all her might to chop the tree down. Through the single image of the walnut tree that symbolizes Qingyi's devoted love and her lover's promise, Zong Pu reveals the false hope of many women, who often place their own future in men's hands, naively relying on the latter to bring them happiness and fulfilment. In the story, Qingyi's emotional and psychological transformation is completed with the downfall of the tree. Having wasted half her life waiting for the return of her lover, who left her for self-betterment (overseas study) thirty years ago, the aging Qingyi is determined to an end to her suffering. As Qingyi admits, "The tree has not merely disturbed her; it has also cheated on her. She will no longer be cautious or weigh her situation carefully. Without hesitation and conflict, she goes ahead with one thought in mind: to chop the tree down" (Zong, 1991, p. 282). Her determination to "stand on her own feet" and take charge of her future is presented in vivid terms, showing not just a single woman's psycho-emotional independence but symbolizing a generation of enlightened women who took a decisive step forward in asserting their selves, a step characterized not by self-sacrifice and passive waiting but by self-affirmation and an active quest for self-fulfilment. Qingyi's act of removing the tree can thus be interpreted as her effort to displace her old connections in order to establish her new being defined by her autonomous self. The falling of the huge walnut tree in this case signifies, in a symbolic way, Qingyi's successful detachment and abandonment of her emotional past, with its socio-cultural shackles, that has weighed her down.

This need for self-reconstitution is a motif in Chinese fiction and it is often presented as an integral part of women's discourse. As revealed in the short stories discussed earlier, women's hope of redefining their gender roles reveals the increasing need for voice and identity in society. What they have yet to learn is to accept themselves as they are and guard against any form of compromise, "self distortion" or "colonization." It is only when women succeed in living in peace with themselves that they can reach out to meet their sexual other on equal terms. It is apparent from the selection of writings discussed above that there is an urgent need for Chinese women to recognize themselves as individuals with distinct selves and to see the importance of connecting with other women through mutual support and recognition. One of the major keys to Chinese women's liberation and happiness lies in their enhanced awareness of themselves as women and of their selves in both the public and private spheres. Under the socialist order and in the age of globalization, contemporary Chinese women feel an urgent need for a redefinition of the self, a reconsideration of stereotypical or gendered relations, as well as a close examination of the female self, including the female body in contemporary China. Writers have elucidated in their discourses the complexity and profundity of Chinese women's life with special reference to their quest for identity, defined not by Confucian ideology but by romantic individualism in the twentieth century. Mistakes and crises seem inevitable as Chinese women make moral choices in their resistance against patriarchal prejudices or in their struggle for self-definition. Many have paid a high price in the process and yet their efforts have been noted and registered as an integral part of Chinese fiction.

## REFERENCES

Chen Ying (1997). "Wujun" [The charming one]. In Chen Ningning, ed., *Aiqing de kaishi: Chen Ying xiaoshuo* [The beginning of love: Short stories by Chen Ying], pp. 38–44. Shanghai: Shanghai guji chubanshe.

Ding Ling (1990). "Shafei nüshi de riji" [Miss Sophie's diary]. In Ding Ling, *Ding Ling*, pp. 3–40. Hong Kong: Joint Publishing.

Erikson, Erik H. (1959). *Identity and the Life Cycle: Selected Papers*. New York: International University Press.

Garrett, Stephanie (1992). *Gender*. London: Routledge.

Giddens, Anthony (1991). *Modernity and Self-Identity: Self and Society in the Late Modern Age*. Cambridge: Polity Press.

Giver, Joan (1991). *Katherine Anne Porter: A Life*. Athens: University of Georgia Press.

Howe, Irving (1992). "The Self in Literature." In George Levine, ed., *Constructions of the Self*, pp. 249–267. New Brunswick, NJ: Rutgers University Press.

Ibsen, Henrik (1986). *A Doll's House and Other Plays* (1879). London: Penguin.

Kaplan, Randy (1988). "Images of Subjugation and Defiance: Female Characters in the Early Dramas of Tian Han." *Modern Chinese Literature*, Vol. 4, Nos. 1 & 2 (Spring & Fall), 87–98.

Kinkley, Jeffrey C. (1990). "The Cultural Choices of Zhang Xinxin, a Young Writer of the 1980s." In Paul A. Cohen and Merle Goldman, eds., *Ideas across Cultures: Essays on Chinese Thought in Honor of Benjamin I. Schwartz*, pp. 137–162. Cambridge, MA: Harvard East Asian Monographs.

Lu, Tonglin, ed. (1993). *Gender and Sexuality in Twentieth-century Chinese Literature and Society*. Albany: State University of New York Press.

Lu Xun (1989). "New Year's Sacrifice" (Zhufu) (1924). In Lu Xun, *Selected Stories of Lu Xun*, trans. by Yang Hsien-yi and Gladys Yang, pp. 125–143. Beijing: Foreign Languages Press.

Lu Yin (Huang Luyin) (1935a). "Hechu shi guicheng?" [Where would my destiny be?] (1927). In *Lu Yin duanpian xiaoshuo ji* [A collection of short stories by Lu Yin]. Shanghai: Nüzi shudian.

Lu Yin (Huang Luyin) (1935b). "Huoren de bei'ai" [The sorrows of a certain youth] (1922). In *Lu Yin duanpian xiaoshuo ji* [A collection of short stories by Lu Yin]. Shanghai: Nüzi shudian.

Mead, George H. (1934). *Mind, Self, and Society: From the Standpoint of a Social Behaviorist*. Chicago: University of Chicago Press.

Porter, Katherine Anne (1979). *The Collected Stories of Katherine Anne Porter*. New York: Harcourt.

Porter, Roy, ed. (1997). *Rewriting the Self: Histories from the Renaissance to the Present*. London: Routledge.

Shen Congwen (1996). *Xiaoxiao*. Taipei: Hongfan shudian.

Showalter, Elaine (1977). *A Literature of Their Own: British Women Novelists from Brontë to Lessing*. Princeton, NJ: Princeton University Press.

Tu, Wei-ming (1985). "Selfhood and Otherness in Confucian Thought." In Anthony J. Marsella et al., eds., *Culture and Self: Asian and Western Perspectives*, pp. 231–251. New York: Tavistock Publications.

Unrue, Darlene Harbour (1988). *Understanding Katherine Anne Porter*. Columbia: University of South Carolina Press.

Woolf, Virginia (1927). *To the Lighthouse*. New York: Harcourt Brace.

Woolf, Virginia (1993). *A Room of One's Own* and *Three Guineas*. London: Penguin.

Xie Bingying (1985). *Nübing zizhuan* [Autobiography of a girl soldier]. Chengdu: Sichuan wenyi chubanshe.

Ye Shaoxian (Terry Siu-han Yip) (1994). "Nüxing, ziwo yu quanli: Du Zhang Xinxin de 'Wo zai na'er cuoguo le ni?'" [Woman, self and power: A reading of Zhang Xinxin's "How did I miss you?"] In Chen Bingliang (Chan Ping-leung), ed., *Zhongguo xiandai wenxue yu ziwo* [Self and modern Chinese literature], pp. 148–163. Hong Kong: Department of Chinese, Lingnan College.

Yin Guoming, and Chen Zhihong (1990). *Zhongguo xiandangdai xiaoshuo zhong de zhishi nüxing* [The female intellectuals in modern and contemporary Chinese literature]. Guangzhou: Guangdong gaodeng jiaoyu chubanshe.

Zhang Ailing (1976). *Bansheng yuan* [Eighteen springs]. Taipei: Huangguan zazhishe.

Zhang Jie (1989). *Ai, shi buneng wangji de* [Love must not be forgotten]. Taipei: Xindi wenxue chubanshe.

Zhang, Jie (1993). *The Ark* (1986). San Francisco: China Books & Periodicals.

Zhang Xinxin (1980). "Wo zai na'er cuoguo le ni?" [How did I miss you?]. *Shouhuo*, No. 5, 91–105.

Zhang Xinxin (1981). "Zai tongyi dipingxian shang" [On the same horizon]. *Shouhuo*, No. 6, 172–233.

Zong Pu (1991). "Hetaoshu de beiju" [Tragedy of the walnut tree]. In Li Ziyun, ed., *Zhongguo nüxing xiaoshuo xuan* [Selected works in Chinese female fiction], pp. 272–284. Hong Kong: Joint Publishing. Originally published in the journal *Zhongshan*, No. 6 (1982).

## GLOSSARY

Amah Liu 柳媽

*Bansheng yuan*《半生緣》

Chen Ying 沉櫻

Ding Ling 丁玲

Eileen Chang 張愛玲

"Fangzhou"〈方舟〉

"Hechu shi guicheng?"〈何處是歸程？〉

"Hetaoshu de beiju"〈核桃樹的悲劇〉

"Huoren de bei'ai"〈或人的悲哀〉

Jiang Qing 江青

Lu Xun 魯迅

Lu Yin (Huang Luyin) 廬隱（黃廬隱）

Manlu 曼璐

Manzhen 曼楨

*Nübing zizhuan*《女兵自傳》

Qingyi 清漪

"Shafei nüshi de riji"〈莎菲女士的日記〉

Shanü 沙侶

Shen Congwen 沈從文

Wang Anyi 王安憶

"Wo zai na'er cuoguo le ni?"〈我在哪兒錯過了你？〉

Wujun 嫵君

Xianglin 祥林

Xianglin's Wife 祥林嫂

Xiaoxiao 簫簫

Xie Bingying 謝冰瑩

Yaxia 亞俠

"Zai tongyi dipingxian shang"〈在同一地平線上〉

Zhang Jie 張潔

Zhang Kangkang 張抗抗
Zhang Xinxin 張辛欣
"Zhufu"〈祝福〉
Zhu Hongcai 祝鴻才
Zong Pu 宗璞

## 2    Gender Construction, Stereotyping and Cross-Gender Writing

KWOK-KAN TAM

THEORIES ON FEMALE IDENTITY IN the past fifty years have become one of the several important debates between psychoanalysis and cultural anthropology, with the former emphasizing the inner workings of a woman's psyche and the latter stressing the effect of socialization, or materiality, on identity formation. Such a debate can be summarized as an argument over what Erik H. Erikson calls the "inner and outer space" of womanhood. Female identity can be seen both as a psycho-analytical awareness and as a social construct, which are two processes related to the female as a biological given and womanhood as a psycho-analytic reality. Most current studies on gender rely on the distinction between "sex" and "gender" as two opposed categories, with the former being considered as a biological given at birth, while the latter is culturally acquired in later life. Gender is therefore not something permanent and universal, and its definition and distinction vary from one community to another.

In anthropology, the study of gender plays a particularly important role in understanding culture and society, for it sheds light on the formation of gender concepts, gender initiation and gender stereotyping in relation to the dominant culture and patterns of human behaviour. Due largely to the insights and discoveries of anthropology, as well as the feminist critique of Freudianism, gender study has recently been focused on the cultural formation of gender, gender identity, and gender representation, knowledge of which will help enhance the understanding of gender identity and femininity and how they are constructed and shaped, as well as of their sociocultural significance.

## AN ANTHROPOLOGICAL VIEW OF GENDER

The belief that gender is culturally constructed and not biologically determined brings forth attacks on Freudianism, which ranges from

19

psychoanalytic theory on gender formation to its various descriptions of the relation between psychology and biology. In the interdependent tripartite structure of "biology/psyche/culture" suggested by Freud (Freud, 1965, pp. 416–418), only the cultural element remains of interest to cultural theorists, and for this reason most recent studies on gender have tended to develop along this line. However, as scholars focus their attention on the significance of cultural formation of femininity, recent studies in anthropology have led to a new perspective on gender formation. In her article, "The Cultural Constitution of Gender," Henrietta Moore re-examines the concepts developed by Sherry H. Ortner in "Is Female to Male as Nature Is to Culture?" and points out that the female enjoys a "universal secondary status."[1] In her study, Moore proposes that masculinity is a product of culture, while femininity is a product of nature. Such a thesis is apparently dependent upon the opposition between culture and nature as the basis of the opposition between masculinity and femininity, but not solely upon cultural formation, which is what the feminists and cultural theorists believe in. This thesis thus entails a contradiction, of which Moore is unfortunately unaware, and argues against the point that gender is solely culturally shaped. Although the thesis of Moore's study is to illustrate that culture plays a significant role in gender formation, it also brings forth the question, why do females have the same secondary status in different cultures? If culture were the sole determining factor in gender formation, then females in different cultures should have different statuses. In other words, cultural difference can explain differences in behaviour and values, but not their sameness. So how can the common lower status held by females in different cultures be explained by cultural difference? This contradiction in Moore's thesis suggests the possibility of a middle-road approach between psychoanalysis and culturalism in the study of gender formation. As far as gender identity in the unconscious is concerned, such a middle-road approach proposes that gender is formed as a result of the internalization of cultural behaviour. According to Moore's thesis, the biological given of sex is within the realm of nature, and so is the formation of femininity. Should one then argue that gender identity is based more on biological and psychical elements than on culture? Moore does not answer this question, and the question also falls outside the focus of anthropological research. An answer to it will probably have to be sought by reconsidering Freud's interdependent tripartite structure of "biology/psyche/culture."

## FREUD REVISITED

In his essay "Femininity" (1933),[2] Freud adopts an indirect approach to defining femininity by taking the Oedipal stage as the starting-point in the differentiation of gender identity. This indirect approach and the way it defines femininity are anti-culturalist in methodology and in definition, as it believes that the unconscious is formed at the Oedipal stage, with the mother being replaced by the father as a love-object. In his thesis, Freud gives numerous examples to argue that it is impossible to define femininity in a direct way. Dichotomies such as "activity/ passivity," "aggressiveness/inaggressiveness," and "independence/dependence," are not convincing ways of differentiating male from female, since there are many examples which can be used to prove the opposite stance—for example, in some cultures or among some animals the female is more "active, aggressive and rational" than the male. In other words, it is impossible to define masculinity and femininity by dichotomizing them according to external traits in cultural behaviour. So in what way can they be defined?

In any given culture, every member can be defined as male/masculine or female/feminine, and everyone knows what gender he or she is. Gender identity is thus transcultural in the human unconscious. But, as is well known to every cultural theorist, the attempt to arrive at a transcultural definition of gender identity is close to impossible, if not totally impossible. Since different cultures may define their cultural traits in different ways, how can "masculinity" and "femininity" be defined transculturally, though they exist as transcultural categories of (un)conscious identity? In his essay on femininity, Freud's major interest is to define gender for a given cultural community, which in this case is Western culture, and he does not claim universality for his ideas. It also seems impossible for the feminists and cultural theorists (including anthropologists) to draw any universal conclusion on "femininity," which is defined as a cultural construct. Thus Nancy Chodorow and Julia Kristeva also offer only an indirect argument in defining femininity (Kristeva, 1977, pp. 28–29). They argue that in different cultural communities all members, be they male or female, possess traits of both masculinity and femininity in their personality, and their difference in gender behaviour or gender identity is only a difference in the manifestation of these traits. This argument, however, still fails to give a direct account of what femininity is, although it does attempt to offer a transcultural definition. The best this argument can do is to say that femininity is "a fluidly defined" process (Gardiner, 1981, p. 352). This means that "masculinity" and "femininity" are unstable personality traits and are therefore indefinable as gender consciousness. Furthermore, such an argument also fails to account for the role the unconscious plays in the formation of gender identity. Gender identity is both cultural identity and unconscious psychical identity, which inevitably involves, at the personal level, the process of how the unconscious influences individuals in acting with other members of the same gender group.

It is, therefore, necessary to re-examine the concepts of "masculinity" and "femininity" in psychoanalysis, as well as the ways these concepts are related to self-identity in cultural theories. Freud considers masculinity and femininity as psychoanalytic processes of the unconscious, the former constructed on the basis of the Oedipus complex, the latter on the Electra complex (Freud, 1965, p. 418). Gender identification and the formation of gender unconscious are two different psychoanalytic processes. A boy has his mother as his first love-object, which remains so even until the stage when the Oedipus complex is formed. That implies that the formation of masculinity, as gender unconscious, in a boy is a continuous psychoanalytical process, which is uninterrupted and without the change of love-object. But in a girl the formation of femininity, as gender unconscious, is a process which undergoes a dual transition in the change of love-object and change of love-hate relationships. The first transition takes place in the change of the love-object from the mother to the father, while the other is the transition from love of the mother to hatred of the mother. The completion of this dual transition signals the emergence of femininity, which is a process of discontinuity in the psychoanalytic state. Although this theory of gender identity is not accepted by feminists, it offers an explanation for the psychical emergence of femininity and fills the gap in the relation between cultural formation and psychoanalytic formation at the personal level. After all, to have an impact on the individual, culture must be able to exhibit an effect on an individual's psychology.

On the basis of Freud's idea of the ego, Erik H. Erikson develops his psycho-culturalist theory of ego-identity, in which he argues that the changes which the ego experiences in its formation are a process of socialization. In this process, which Erikson calls "the life cycle," there is an interdependent relation in identification of the self with others, from whom the self also recognizes his own distinction.[3] Based on his theory of the ego, Erikson proposes treating the formation of the ego as a developmental process. His theory of ego-identity in the formation of the self has had a widespread impact on the psychoanalysis of the self, and has eventually become a dominant theory that lays the foundation for the view that identity is "a developmental process." However, his theory of "ego-identity" has been challenged since the 1970s by feminists who see it as male-based and male-biased.

## TWO MODELS OF GENDER CONSTRUCTION

From a cross-cultural perspective, Erikson's theory of the ego as a development of the Freudian psychoanalytic structure of identity is culture-specific in its application. To treat the constitution of the ego as the basis for the formation of selfhood is valid in the Western cultural tradition. However, in Chinese culture, the formation of selfhood is not treated as a psychoanalytic process, but has to be seen as a moralistic process of discourse, in which identity is defined according to external roles of identification, such as in the relationships of parent-son, ruler-subject, and teacher-student. The psychoanalytic approach to self-identity in Western culture does not seem to go along with the moralistic tradition in Chinese culture, and the theory proposed by Erikson fails to account for the role-identification process in the formation of selfhood in the Chinese tradition in particular.

In contrast to the theories proposed by Freud and Erikson, Nancy Chodorow, a feminist psychoanalyst, believes that after the formation of primary identity (which is a concept derived from Erikson's theory), the roles which both the male and the female experience during the process of formation of gender identity are opposite, and are different from what Freud has described.[4] A comparison of these two theories is summarized as follows (Figure 1):

Figure 1: Comparison between the psychoanalytical and social models

| Theory | Primary Identity | Gender Identity | Process of Identification |
|---|---|---|---|
| Freud/Erikson (psychoanalysis) | Oedipal ego-identity | *masculinity*: Oedipus complex (mother as the love-object remains unchanged) *femininity*: Electra complex (father replaces mother as the love-object) | psychical formation |

**Figure 1:** (Contd)

| Theory | Primary Identity | Gender Identity | Process of Identification |
|---|---|---|---|
| Chodorow (cultural theory) | Pre-Oedipal ego-identity | *masculinity*: distinguished from the mother and identified with the father (shift in role identification)<br><br>*femininity*: identified with the mother (continuity in role identification) | social formation |

Chodorow believes that the formation of female identity is a direct process, in which the mother provides the model for role identification, while the formation of male identity has to undergo a process of differentiation, in which the boy must be able to recognize the distinction between himself and the mother before he turns to the father as his model for role identification. In this theory, identity formation is seen as a process of socialization, but not as a psychoanalytic process. In actual fact, the theories proposed by Chodorow and Freud/Erikson are not in conflict with each other, and the difference lies mainly in their emphases. Both theories are based on the formation of the ego as primary identity, from which gender identity is developed through the process of socialization, while the effect on the psyche will be internalized as a psychical process. As demonstrated by Lacan's theory of psychoanalytic-linguistic formation, these two processes may occur concurrently. Only through these processes can selfhood for the male and the female be formed. The formation of selfhood is thus first based on self-distinction and later on the recognition of sameness with others.

## THE CHINESE TRADITION

In Chinese cultural thought, the formation of selfhood is not based on the construction of the ego as self-identity. The Chinese self, as described in Confucianism or Daoism, is a psychosomatic process of socialization and a form of personal cultivation, in which the self is a body self, not a psychoanalytic process. As demonstrated in the classic text *Great Learning* (*Daxue*), the process of "cultivating the person, regulating the family, ordering the state, bringing peace to the world" (*xiushen, qijia, zhiguo, ping tianxia*) prescribes a strongly communitarian way of living, in which the self is simply a relational role-self. In Confucianism, the self is always described in relation to others, but never as an independent category. Instead of according the self with the primacy of autonomy, relational selfhood is emphasized. This concept of selfhood thus entails a cluster of self-other relations, in which there is a dual process of identification and socialization. Since the self has no separate or autonomous status, it is never considered as an individual psychoanalytic process in the sense of a "subject." The following chart summarizes the process of socialization in traditional Chinese self-cultivation[5]:

**Figure 2: The socialization process of the Confucian self in the formation of the super-ego**

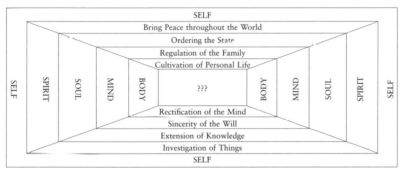

*Note.* There is no theory in traditional Chinese culture showing or discussing how the self is internally represented in its psychological state at the initial stage of the self-cultivation process. But the disciplining activities in the process strongly suggest that there is a super-ego that functions in the unconscious.

Within this framework of cultural formation of the self, there is no reference whatsoever to the psychoanalytic process that occurs in the formation of the Chinese self. The Chinese view of the status and function of the "ego" in the formation of "primary identity" therefore remains a mystery (and therefore in Figure 2, the central area is represented by a "?" that follows the "super-ego"). According to the relationships displayed in Figure 2, the traditional Chinese (or Confucian) self is a process of "self-realization," which entails the fulfilment of multiple roles as well. In this respect, the traditional Chinese concept of self is seen merely as a matter of cultural formation. However, during the process of self-realization, the "self" expands to become broader and broader, and its compass extends so far that the "self" ultimately becomes a "selfless self" (*wuwo*). The realization of the self is actually externalized into the fulfilment of roles. When the "self" is externalized and expanded into "roles," the ego is repressed into non-existence, and what remains, in psychoanalytical terms, is the super-ego:

| Theory | Primary Identity | Gender Identity | Process of Identification |
|---|---|---|---|
| Chinese Model | Super-ego identity (?) | *masculinity*: role identification<br>*femininity*: role identification | process of socialization |

In the absence of any theory on primary identity, gender identity in the traditional Chinese context does not follow what Freud or Chodorow describes in the process of formation, for it is not based on psychoanalytic formation and is simply reduced to the fulfilment of familial and social roles. So, is there anything similar to what Freud or Chodorow calls "gender identity" in the Chinese tradition? Or is there only "role identification" at the socio-moral level? If there is "gender identity," how will it be defined in the Chinese context?

In traditional Chinese culture, discussion of the gender identity of the male is scarce, not to mention that of the female. In the Confucian discourse, both the male and the female are defined merely by roles as governed by the "*sangang*" [the three cardinal guiding principles] and "*wuchang*" [the five constant virtues], in which the female is placed in a subordinate position. There is no theory of gender identity based on the concept of "the ego" as "primary identity" at the level of the unconscious. (Here, I may even postulate the thesis that the modern concept of "homosexuality" is not theorized in traditional Chinese culture, probably because gender is not defined as a psychoanalytic unconscious formed in ego-identity, but always in terms of socio-moral roles, which prescribe that the male must perform masculine roles, and the female feminine roles.)

## FEMALE IDENTITY AS A PROBLEMATIC IN CHINESE MODERNITY

As discussed by many scholars,[6] the search for individualism in the sense of liberation of the self is one of the characteristics of the Chinese movement towards modernization in the twentieth century. In this respect, one of the most important cultural elements that constitute Chinese modernity lies in the changing concept of the self, which must go beyond the sociocultural category to explore the psychoanalytic dimension that makes possible the formation of the new self. Yet in view of the lack of a psychoanalytic tradition in Chinese culture, this search for a new concept of self often remains as a problematic rather than as an illuminating understanding of the psychological workings that operate in the formation of the self in Chinese society. In the following, examples from Chinese literary writings will be discussed to illustrate the difficulties Chinese writers in the twentieth century have encountered in their search for a new concept of the self, gendered or not.

Lu Xun's story, "New Year's Sacrifice" (Zhufu), depicts a traditional woman, Xianglin's Wife, who encounters numerous difficulties in her quest for a self-identity which is defined by her social roles. Xianglin's Wife is a woman without a name; she does not have her own social status. She is recognized by other villagers only as the wife of Xianglin, or as the servant of a certain master. Coupled with her lack of "self-identity" is her inability to cope with changing roles imposed externally upon her as the wife to two men and later as the servant to her master. This is a tragedy of confusion of roles in the process of self-identification, which finally results in the complete loss of her senses, together with her self and identity:

> If you [Xianglin's Wife] had held out longer or knocked yourself to death, it would have been better. As it is, after living with your second husband for less than two years, you are guilty of a great crime. Just think: when you go down to the lower world in future, these two men's ghosts will fight over you. To which will you go? The King of Hell will have no choice but to cut you in two and divide you between them. (Lu Xun, 1989, p. 141)

What Xianglin's Wife faces is a dilemma. On the one hand, her identity and social recognition in the world are defined by her marriage to someone; but in the world after death she will be torn between her roles as wife to two men. This is exactly the tragic fate of a woman who does not have a self-identity. What remains in her is mere social identity, which is defined by her external roles. The plight delineated in "New Year's Sacrifice" is not necessarily restricted to the experience of the female; it may happen to the male too, for it is largely a cultural tragedy.

Xianglin's Wife is reduced to a state of non-existence as a result of finally being deprived of her external roles. In this story by Lu Xun, the tragedy of the traditional mode of role-identification in the formation of self-identity, which is particularly prescribed for women, is fully explored, with the implication that there is a need for a new mode of gendered identity for the female.

In Mao Dun's short story, "Creation" (Chuangzao), there is an attempt to experiment with the creation of a new identity for women. The story relates how a man tries to create an ideal wife against the background of the May Fourth era. This man finds it alarming that the roles of the female have changed after they have been influenced by the new way of thinking, and as a result of which the relations between the sexes are in great confusion. Therefore he decides to marry a self-less lady—someone who does not have any sense of identity—so that he can provide her with a list of readings, by which means he believes he can create the "ideal wife" he desires. The ending of this story shows his failure in the experiment. As the female protagonist reads more and more, she realizes that women can play many different roles from that of a wife. Hence, she decides to set herself free from the fixed role prescribed by her husband by leaving home to look for other new roles. In such a treatment of Chinese women's search for personal freedom and new roles, there lies a hidden dilemma, for which Mao Dun fails to provide a resolution. Since roles are changeable, they can hardly be used as an anchor point for the formation of gender identity. Breaking away from the confinement of externally imposed fixed roles does not necessarily "emancipate the self," for it does not mean the establishment of a new personal identity in a woman's mind. To redefine the identity of women by giving them new social roles can only mean restrictions or confinements of a new kind. It does not address the question: What is a woman other than her external roles?

In his second experiment with the identity of women, Mao Dun depicts a woman's search for a "new self" in the novel, *Rainbow* (*Hong*). If "Creation" can be read as a ridicule of men's attempt to re-define women, then *Rainbow* is no better, as it is a novel written by a male author about a woman. The female protagonist does not rely on the male to search for and create her "self." In her various attempts to define herself by her different social roles during the period of social turmoil, she first defies the role of a wife by escaping from a pre-arranged marriage, then becomes a school teacher, and finally decides to join the revolution and play a genderless revolutionary role. This new woman's journey in her search for a new self and a new identity is a process of choosing and fulfilling different roles. However, all these attempts cannot remove the uncertainty raised at the beginning of the novel: "What are the roles of a female?" "What is a female?" The question that should be asked is: "What is femininity?" Such questions are left unanswered in the novel because Mao Dun is not aware that these questions actually originate from women's attempts to redefine themselves.

In a similar vein, Xie Bingying's *Autobiography of a Girl Soldier* (*Nübing zizhuan*), is a further exploration into the social roles of the female, which are posited as a matter of the female's self-consciousness. Unfortunately, the answer Xie Bingying provides is again the replacement of the female roles by the male ones, so that the female can integrate into society and contribute to the nationalist cause of resisting the invaders during the Sino-Japanese war of the 1940s. As Lydia H. Liu has demonstrated in her study of Xiao Hong's *The Field of Life and Death* (*Shengsi chang*), the nationalist discourse, under which gender issues in the emancipation of the female self are subsumed, is a process of reducing the female to a status of non-existence, which again is the result of the ideological conflict between the female's social roles and her own gender definition.[7]

Unlike Mao Dun and Xie Bingying, who see the nationalist or social cause as the "great self" (*dawo*) for which the "little self" (*xiaowo*) of the female (and perhaps also of the male) must be sacrificed, Shen Congwen in the novel *The Border Town* (*Biancheng*) portrays the "little self" and its formation in a teenage girl, Cuicui, and shows how she comes to an awakening of her femininity. Cuicui is a motherless girl brought up by her grandfather. She is also isolated from her peer group of young girls, as she lives outside the town. In the course of her growth, she is confronted with many difficulties in her gender identity and fails to understand herself because of the absence of a mother who might have served as the model for identification of female roles. In the absence of a female model, Cuicui still knows that she is female and possesses a vague sense of femininity which remains mysterious and undefined to her. Shen's novel offers a counter example, showing that it is hard to explain femininity on the basis of socio-moral roles,[8] and that Cuicui comes to her sexual awakening through an encounter with her male suitor: "Glancing out of the corner of her eyes, Cuicui found that the young man [Nuosong] was watching her. She turned her head, pursing her lips without a word, and self-consciously set to work" (Shen,

1978, p. 263). Isolated in a male-dominated world, Cuicui is still able to overcome her difficulties in gender identification, not through female models, but through the love-object, as Freud has delineated. Such a story provides an example to confirm the universal significance of the psychoanalytic dimension in the formation of gender identity, which the Chinese seldom emphasize in their cultural tradition. Such a story also illustrates the difficulties Chinese writers, as well as theorists, are facing in their project of postulating a female identity without consideration of the psychoanalytic dimension involved in it. Is it possible to consider gender identity merely as a matter of external roles, and postulate a theory of gender without any reference to the psychical state of the gendered subject? As Chodorow has put it, "The conscious aspects of personality, like a person's general self-concept and, importantly, her/his gender identity, require and are dependent upon the consistency and stability of its unconscious organization" (Chodorow, 1974, p. 46). Added to the complexity of these issues is the theoretical dimension: Is it possible to construct a theory of Chinese feminism which does not have any reference to the specific psychological workings of gender identity in the Chinese context? The answer, perhaps, can only be provided by Chinese critics who claim to be feminists.

All the literary works discussed above demonstrate the strategy that Chinese writers have employed in probing gender identity, as well as the difficulties they have encountered. It further shows that it is impossible to define "gender identity" merely by external socio-moral roles, which are unstable and changeable. To define gender identity in the framework of unstable socio-moral roles is to put it under the scrutiny of the indefinable, and will only render it into a matter of changing subject positions, offering no clue to the understanding of gender identity as subjectivity.

### NOTES

1. Refer to Moore, 1994, in which she has borrowed the idea of the opposition between nature and culture as a binary concept in the distinction between the female and the male. Moore thinks that culture plays a very significant role in the constitution of gender. However, Moore seems to be unaware that her thesis proves just the opposite: that gender is not merely constituted by culture, as nature (including the human psyche as a part of human nature) also plays an undeniably significant role. See also Chodorow, 1974, p. 45.

2. Freud published this lecture in 1933, and in it points out that there is a

difference in behaviour between the male and the female, which is the result of the difference in gender identity as an unconscious in the psyche. His contribution to an understanding of the formation of gender identity lies in his theory of the formation of ego-identity.

3.  See Erikson, 1964, in which he has developed Freud's idea of the ego as a model for identity formation in relation to the shaping force of culture. It is also in this theory that for the first time identity formation is seen as a developmental process in life, hence the term "life cycle."

4.  See Chodorow, 1974 & 1978, in both of which she sees gender identity mainly as a psychological process of internalized role-identification. In so doing, Chodorow considers the cultural element as being of paramount importance in identity formation. However, Chodorow's theory fails to account for the female's identification with the mother and the male's with the father.

5.  Cf. Tu, 1994, p. 185, in which the realization of the Confucian self is described as a broadening process of the moral mind. In Tu's chart, there is no reference to the psychological state of the self in this broadening process of the Confucian moral mind.

6.  See the following for recent discussion of Chinese modernity in relation to the introduction of individualism to China, the changing concept of the self, and cultural change: Jin, 1996, pp. 20–27; and Tam, 1995, pp. 57–64.

7.  In her essay, "Chongfan *Shengsi chang*: Funü yu minzu guojia" [Revisiting *The field of life and death*: women and the nation-state], Liu He (Lydia H. Liu) argues that the body of the female is used as an illustration of the nationalist discourse on women, and thus renders women's own sufferings insignificant in the face of the nationalist cause.

8.  In her study "Body Politics and Female Subjectivity in Modern English and Chinese Fiction," Lo Man-wa cites Shen Congwen's *The Border Town* (*Biancheng*) as an example of the search for the female self, in which the female protagonist encounters tremendous difficulties in the absence of female models for role-identification. Interestingly, she also cites Ding Ling's *The Girl Ah Mao* (*Ah Mao guniang*) as an example to illustrate the lack of individuality in the female protagonist Ah Mao who identifies herself too closely with other women as her model. Both examples can serve as support for the argument for the lack of individuality or difficulty in the formation of Chinese womanhood.

## REFERENCES

Bem, Sandra Lipsitz (1993). *The Lenses of Gender: Transforming the Debate on Sexual Inequality*. New Haven, CT: Yale University Press.

Butler, Judith (1990). *Gender Trouble: Feminism and the Subversion of Identity*. New York: Routledge.

Butler, Judith (1993). *Bodies That Matter: On the Discursive Limits of "Sex."* New York: Routledge.

Chodorow, Nancy (1974). "Family Structure and Feminine Personality." In Michelle Zimbalist Rosaldo and Louise Lamphere, eds., *Woman, Culture, and Society*, pp. 43–66. Stanford, CA: Stanford University Press.

Chodorow, Nancy (1978). *The Reproduction of Mothering: Psychoanalysis and the Society of Gender*. Berkeley: University of California Press.

Chodorow, Nancy (1979). "Feminism and Difference: Gender, Relation, and Difference in Psychoanalytic Perspective." *Socialist Review*, No. 46 (July–August), 51–69.

Croll, Elisabeth (1995). *Changing Identities of Chinese Women: Rhetoric, Experience, and Self-Perception in Twentieth-century China*. Hong Kong: Hong Kong University Press.

Erikson, Erik H. (1964). "Inner and Outer Space: Reflections on Womanhood." *Daedalus*, Vol. 93, No. 2 (Spring), 579–606.

Freud, Sigmund (1965). "Femininity" (1933). In *New Introductory Lectures on Psycho-Analysis, Lecture 33*, pp. 412–432. New York: W. W. Norton.

Gardiner, Judith Kegan (1981). "On Female Identity and Writing by Women." *Critical Inquiry*, Vol. 7, No. 4 (Winter), 347–361.

Garrett, Stephanie (1992). *Gender*. London: Routledge.

Humm, Maggie (1989). *The Dictionary of Feminist Theory*. London: Wheatsheaf Harvester.

Jin Yaoji (Ambrose King) (1996). "Lun Zhongguo de 'xiandaihua' yu 'xiandaixing'" [On China's "modernization" and "modernity"]. *Beijing daxue xuebao* [Journal of Peking University], No. 1, 20–27.

Kauffman, Linda, ed. (1990). *Gender & Theory: Dialogues on Feminist Criticism*. Oxford: Blackwell.

Kristeva, Julia (1977). *About Chinese Women*. Trans. Anita Barrows. London: Marion Boyars.

Lacan, Jacques (1978). *The Four Fundamental Concepts of Psycho-Analysis*. New York and London: W. W. Norton.

Li Xiaojiang, Zhu Hong and Dong Xiuyu, eds. (1994). *Xingbie yu Zhongguo* [Gender and China]. Beijing: Sanlian shudian.

Li Zijian (1988). "Nüxing de zhuixun: Ershi shiji Zhongguo nüxing wenxue zongguan" [In search of femininity: An overview of women's literary writings in twentieth-century China]. In Zhu Weiguo, ed., *Zhongguo nüxing zuojia henluan xiaoshuo xuan* [A collection of love stories by Chinese women writers], pp. 798–811. Beijing: Zuojia chubanshe.

Liu He (Lydia H. Liu) (1994). "Congfan *Shengsi chang*: Funü yu minzu guojia" [Revisiting *The field of life and death*: Women and the nation-state]. In Li Xiaojiang, Zhu Hong and Dong Xiuyu, eds., *Xingbie yu Zhongguo* [Gender and China], pp. 63–77. Beijing: Sanlian shudian.

Lo Man-wa (1994). "Female Initiation in Modern Chinese Fiction." M.Phil. thesis, The Chinese University of Hong Kong.

Lo Man-wa (2000). "Body Politics and Female Subjectivity in Modern English and Chinese Fiction." Ph.D. thesis, The Chinese University of Hong Kong.

Lu Xun (1989). "New Year's Sacrifice" (Zhufu). In Lu Xun, *Selected Stories of Lu Xun*, trans. by Yang Hsien-yi and Gladys Yang, pp. 125–143. Beijing: Foreign Languages Press.

Mao Dun (1928). "Chuangzao" [Creation]. In *Mao Dun duanpian xiaoshuo xuan* [Short stories by Mao Dun], Vol. 1, pp. 17–34. Hong Kong: Yixin shudian.

Mao Dun (1935). *Hong* [Rainbow]. Hong Kong: Lingnan chubanshe.

Mitchell, Juliet (1975). *Psychoanalysis and Feminism*. New York: Vintage.

Moore, Henrietta (1994). "The Cultural Constitution of Gender" (1979). In *The Polity Reader in Gender Studies*, pp. 14–21. Cambridge: Polity Press.

Ortner, Sherry H. (1974) "Is Female to Male as Nature Is to Culture?" In Michelle Zimbalist Rosaldo and Louise Lamphere, eds., *Woman, Culture, and Society*, pp. 67–83. Stanford, CA: Stanford University Press.

Oskamp, Stuart and Mark Costanzo, eds. (1993) *Gender Issues in Contemporary Society*. Newbury Park, CA: Sage Publications.

Probyn, Elspeth (1993). *Sexing the Self: Gendered Positions in Cultural Studies*. London: Routledge.

Radtke, H. Lorraine and Henderikus J. Stam, eds. (1994). *Power/Gender: Social Relations in Theory and Practice*. London: Sage Publications.

Sass, Louis A. (1992). "The Self and Its Vicissitudes in the Psychoanalytic Avant-Garde." In George Levine, ed., *Constructions of the Self*, pp. 17–58. New Brunswick, NJ: Rutgers University Press.

Shen Congwen (1978). "Biancheng" [The border town]. In *Shen Congwen duanpian xiaoshuo xuan* [A collection of Shen Congwen's short stories], pp. 225–310. Hong Kong: Wenjiao chubanshe.

Smith, Paul (1988). *Discerning the Subject*. Minneapolis: University of Minnesota Press.

Tam, Kwok-kan (1995). "Self-identity and the Problematic of Chinese Modernity." *Humanities Bulletin*, Vol. 4, 57–64.

Tsui, Wanda Wing Yi (1994). "Female Identity in Virginia Woolf and Wang Anyi." M.Phil. thesis, The Chinese University of Hong Kong.

Tu, Wei-ming (1994). "Embodying the Universe: A Note on Confucian Self-Realization." In Roger T. Ames et al., eds., *Self as Person in Asian Theory and Practice*, pp. 177–186. Albany: State University of New York Press.

Walton, Jean (1995). "Re-Placing Race in (White) Psychoanalytic Discourse: Founding Narratives of Feminism." *Critical Inquiry*, Vol. 21, No. 4 (Summer), 775–804.

Xie Bingying (1985). *Nübing zizhuan* [Autobiography of a girl soldier]. Chengdu: Sichuan wenyi chubanshe.

Ye Shoaxian (Terry Siu-han Yip) (1994). "Nüxing, ziwo yu quanli: Du Zhang Xinxin de 'Wo zai na'er cuoguo le li?'" [Woman, self and power: A reading of Zhang Xinxin's "How did I miss you?"]. In Chen Bingliang (Chan

Ping-leung), ed., *Zhongguo xiandai wenxue yu ziwo* [Self and modern Chinese literature], pp. 148–163. Hong Kong: Department of Chinese, Lingnan College.

## GLOSSARY

*A Mao guniang*《阿巫姑娘》

*Biancheng*《邊城》

"Chuangzao"〈創造〉

Cuicui 翠翠

dawo 大我

*Daxue*《大學》

*Hong*《虹》

*Nübing zizhuan*《女兵自傳》

Nuosong 儺宋

ping tianxia 平天下

qijia 齊家

sangang 三綱

Shen Congwen 沈從文

*Shengsi chang*《生死場》

wuchang 五常

wuwo 無我

Xiao Hong 蕭紅

xiaowo 小我

Xie Bingying 謝冰瑩

xiushen 修身

zhiguo 治國

3  Feminist Literary Criticism in China since the Mid-1990s*

LIN SHUMING AND HE SONGYU

IF FEMINIST LITERARY CRITICISM IN the late 1980s is called the first wave in China's new era of reform, then the year 1995 can be regarded as the beginning of the second wave. It was in this year that the Fourth World Conference on Women was convened in China. As part of the activities for the World Conference on Women, several large-scale cultural exchange activities were held in Beijing around the theme "Equality, Development and Peace." These activities included such events as "Beijing 1995 World Women's Films Week," "Magical Women Variety Show," "Concert of Love, Friendship and Peace," "An Exhibition of Chinese Female Artists' Work," and the "Feminist Literary Symposium." Publishing houses, literary periodicals and scholarly journals devoted special publications to feminist literature and criticism, which promoted the study of feminism in China. The year 1995 can be regarded as a year of feminism in China.

In the field of publishing, feminist theories and literary works abound. The following are some of the book series that began publication in 1995: "The Red Poppy," "Female Talents," "Female Culture in Everyday Life," and "Modern Women." There were also books and monographs devoted to the study of feminist criticism, such as *Gender and China* (*Xingbie yu Zhongguo*) (edited by Li Xiaojiang et al., 1994), *Feminism and Literature* (*Nüxing zhuyi yu wenxue*) (Kang Zhengguo, 1994), *An Introduction to Western Feminist Studies* (*Xifang nüxing zhuyi yanjiu pingji*) (edited by Bao Xiaolan, 1995), *A History of Women's Literature in 20th-Century China* (*Ershi shiji Zhongguo nüxing wenxue shi*) (edited by Sheng Ying, 1995), *Biographies of Famous Chinese Women Writers in the 20th Century* (*Ershi shiji*

---

* Translated from the Chinese by Kwok-kan Tam and Terry Siu-han Yip, with the assistance of Jack Hang Tat Leong.

*Zhongguo zhuming nüzuojia zhuan*) (edited by Yan Chunde et al., 1995), *Beyond the Confine of the Patriarchal Tradition* (*Zouchu nanquan chuantong de fanlong*) (Liu Huiying, 1995), *A History of Women's Literature in Contemporary China* (*Dangdai Zhongguo nüxing wenxue shi lun*) (Lin Danya, 1995), *An Introduction to New Women's Literature* (*Xinchao nüxing wenxue daoyin*) (Huang Lin, 1995), *Feminist Literary Criticism in China* (*Nüxing zhuyi wenxue piping zai Zhongguo*) (Lin Shuming, 1995), *Seeing through the Myths* (*Shenhua de kuipo*) (Chen Huifen, 1996), and *A Study of New Chinese Prose by Women* (*Zhongguo xin shiqi nüxing sanwen yanjiu*) (Li Huazhen, 1996). The journal *Foreign Literature Review* (*Waiguo wenxue pinglun*) (No. 2, 1995) published a special section on the latest developments in Western feminist theories. Thus the year 1995 saw a sudden blooming of feminist literature and studies that were to have a long-lasting influence on the critical thinking of contemporary Chinese intellectuals.

By the end of the twentieth century, there were already great achievements in feminist literary criticism in China, which brought modern Chinese literary criticism to new heights. Influenced by feminist ideas, more and more critical studies on sex, sexual problems and gender began to emerge on the scene of contemporary Chinese cultural studies. Representative works include *Tang Goddesses and Venus* (*Gao Tang shennü yu Weinashi*) (Ye Shuxian, 1997), *Female Literature of the Song Dynasty* (*Songdai nüxing wenxue*) (Su Zhecong, 1997), *Beijing Opera, Stilts and Gender in China* (*Jingju, qiao he Zhongguo de xingbie guanxi*) (Huang Yufu, 1998), *Dunhuang Sex Culture* (*Dunhuang xing wenhua*) (Shi Chengli et al., 1999), and *A History of Female Ci Poetry* (*Nüxing ci shi*) (Deng Hongmei, 2000). In the last decade of the twentieth century, there was further diversification of Chinese feminist criticism into gender studies and critiques of Chinese cultural traditions.

## WESTERN FEMINISM IN CHINA

The first obvious characteristic of the second wave of Chinese feminism is that, as theories of Western feminism continued to pour into China, there was a growing interest in Western feminist literary criticism. A review of the feminist literary criticism of 1980s shows that many Chinese scholars at that time had little understanding of feminism and gender concepts. This situation only began to improve around the time of the World Conference on Women.

The book, *Gender and China* (*Xingbie yu Zhongguo*), edited by Li Xiaojiang, Zhu Hong and Dong Xiuyu, is a collection of essays, either translated or originally written in Chinese, presented at the international conference, "Engendering China: Women, Culture and the State," held at Harvard University, Wellesley College and MIT in 1992. Covering a wide spectrum of subjects and adopting various perspectives, these essays tend to "integrate the study of women with that of history and culture" so as to arrive at a "re-visioning of Chinese history" (Li et al., 1994, p. 2). Some topics in this collection provide fresh insights for Chinese scholars. For example, in her essay "Learned Women in the Eighteenth Century," Susan Mann gives her thoughts on how women were treated as inferior in traditional Chinese society and points out that Chinese female intellectuals began to be accepted into literary circles only after the eighteenth century, establishing themselves through the means of writing. In her essay, "Rethinking Van Gulik: Sexuality and Reproduction in Traditional Chinese Medicine," Charlotte Furth takes issue with Van Gulik and points out that "it is easy to recognize Van Gulik's androcentrism, and to see that the reader is being offered a familiar Orientalist fantasy of an exotic, eroticized 'other' woman of the East…. He claimed to be correcting stereotypes of Chinese sexual mores as 'depraved' and 'abnormal'—negative Orientalist representations which were the mirror image of his own positive ones, and like them a product of the modern culture of colonialism" (Feixiali, 1994, pp. 326–327; English original in Furth, 1994, p. 128).

In *Gender and China*, there are other essays that discuss specifically how Chinese women have been depicted in the nationalist discourse and become ungendered. Many of these essays reflect the unique views of Western scholars on gender issues in China. Just as Mary Ann Burris, one of the organizers of the conference puts it: "Although Chinese women is a topical issue, in the past there was little space for such a topic in Western academic circles. The study of Chinese women in Western academe has never been introduced to Chinese readers. This Harvard-Wellesley conference aimed at providing an opportunity for the exchange of opinions between individuals and organizations" (Baimei, 1994, p. 20).

The Chinese interest in Western scholarship on feminism can be seen in the information provided in the essay, "Western Feminist Theories and Modern Chinese Literary Studies in the West" (Xifang nüxing zhuyi lilun yu Xifang Zhongguo xiandai wenxue yanjiu) by Zong Xueping.[1] In the essay, Zong outlines the history and current studies of contemporary Chinese literature in Western academe, and discusses how they have been indebted to feminist theories. Most of the major works are discussed in Zong's essay, among them Rey Chow's book *Women and Chinese Modernity*, Tonglin Lu's edited volume, *Gender and Sexuality in Twentieth-century Chinese Literature and Society*, and Yi-tsi Mei Feuerwerker's *Ding Ling's Fiction: Ideology and Narrative in Modern Chinese Literature*.

In the essay, Zong points out that it was in the late 1980s that the study of modern Chinese literature from feminist perspectives began to appear in North American academic circles, and that most of the scholars involved were females from mainland China and Taiwan. These scholars advocated a re-reading of contemporary Chinese literature in terms of gender ideology, such as gender and patriarchy, the relationship between female readers and patriarchy, the changing status of modern Chinese women and reflection of social problems in literary works. The adoption of feminist perspectives in the study of Chinese literature has opened up a new field of enquiry. Because many of these scholars are from the Third World, they feel the need to find a new orientation in feminist studies so that they can go beyond the confines of Eurocentrism. Scholars in the field of Chinese studies also propose to re-examine Chinese society and its problems from new perspectives that can take into consideration the local politics in China. Feminist studies of China and Chinese literature thus have to break new ground in two areas: one is the need to have new perspectives, and the other to challenge the limits of Western theories.

In Rey Chow's *Women and Chinese Modernity*, there is a critique of Julia Kristeva's superficial understanding of Chinese women, which is not only a product of Western bias, but also a view that entrenches the hegemonic position of Western theories. Kristeva's view makes Chinese women "the other," denying them as subjects and their complexity as women. Such a critique of Western theorization of Chinese women provides inspiration to many scholars in China, especially in relation to the need to remain critical about Western theories. What should be pointed out is that not many of these debates have been brought to the attention of scholars in China. There has not been systematic translation or introduction of original works in the field, such as Kristeva's *About Chinese Women* and Rey Chow's *Women and Chinese Modernity*. As a result of the lack of knowledge about what is currently happening in the debates on feminism in the West, scholars in China are not prepared to engage in a dialogue between East and West. The current efforts Chinese scholars have made in promoting feminism in China are limited to a national dialogue, and they have not been able to take advantage of the achievements of scholars in the West. The insightful observations made by Kristeva, such as those concerning the relationship between the Chinese feudal economy and gender, the female roles of the Chinese farming culture, the patriarchal implications of Dayu's creation myths and the significance of foot-binding to Chinese women, cannot be fully understood if her works are not read in the original, but only in a summary produced by critics.

A second characteristic of contemporary Chinese feminist criticism can be seen in the timely introduction of the latest developments outside China, such as theories on ecological feminism, materialist feminism, feminist narration, feminist body theory, the dialogue between Bakhtin's theory and feminism, and the influence of feminism on children's literature.

Ecological feminism believes that the construction of feminist culture is a way to solve problems in the current ecological crisis. It promotes respect for differences, advocates pluralism, and emphasizes the relations between humans and nature. It also deconstructs the binary assumptions behind the opposition between men and women, culture and nature, mind and body, and reason and emotion. It attempts to break down all dualistic and hierarchical thinking (Guan, 1996). Ecological feminism is sure to exert a great influence upon Chinese literary and cultural studies, as the latter puts so much emphasis on the interrelatedness between nature and humans.

Materialist feminism is concerned with the original motivation of social development that is based not on the relationship between female and female, but between female and male. It believes that the female and male are ideologically related. Materialist feminism thinks that social conflicts have to be dealt with in terms of the materiality of social life, and the male should not always bear the blame for social inequality. To materialist feminists, the feminist movement is not the ultimate goal and it cannot be a substitute for the social ideal. Women should be allowed to develop their unique roles in society so that a new relationship between men and women can be formed, and society can be developed in a healthy way. Such a theory is undoubtedly welcomed by the less radical feminists in mainland China.

As a result of the impact of feminism, there have been a growing number of publications in the West that attempt to do away with sexual discrimination in children's literature by discarding the old popular formula of "the prince saves the country." It has become a new practice for scholars to consider the author's sex and the role of the female in books when selecting textbooks. The feminist rewriting of fairy tales by Angela Carter has also been introduced to China (Zhang, 1994). In the West, there have also been studies on the implications of Bakhtin's theory for feminism. The feminist advocacy of pluralist criticism opens up a dialogue with Bakhtin's dialogism.

The latest trend in studying narrative from the point of view of feminism has also been introduced to China recently. This strand of feminist studies makes a connection between narrative and ideology and attempts to uncover how ideology works within a narrative framework. Chinese critics will benefit from the new discoveries concerning how ideology is narrated and concretized in literary works. In the field of comparative literature and culture, such studies will shed light on the transcultural elements in gender construction.

## CHINESE FEMINIST CRITICS

Since the mid-1990s there has been further development of feminist criticism in China. Feminists in China are eager to re-examine the significance of Western feminist criticism with a view to seeking inspiration for their own work in China. Much work has been done on reviewing feminist literary productions in China (including Taiwan) since the 1990s, and the contribution of feminist critics is beginning to be recognized. Tao Jie, a retired professor from Peking University, has pointed out that the aim of the development of women's literature in China is not to start a new literature, nor to shock the reader. It does not aim at causing trouble in society, but at addressing the reality of life. In today's China, the belief that men are superior to women is still prevalent. Such a belief has existed for more than a thousand years and cannot be changed simply by legislation or new policies. What is needed is education, so that people will have new views on gender. This is the purpose and task of women's literature. Tao Jie believes that Chinese feminists may learn a great deal from American feminists and China needs its own *The Color Purple* and *Sula*, which call for solidarity among women (Tao, 1995).

In her book, *Narration and Gender in Contemporary Chinese Literature* (*Zhongguo dangdai wenxue de xushi yu xingbie*), Chen Shunxin clearly points out that the study of contemporary Chinese literature can be inspired by ideas of Western feminism. According to Chen, "critical re-reading" is an important strategy in Western feminism. "Critical re-reading" can unravel gender constructions in history and show how gender is constructed as effects of discourse, enabling people to understand better the society they live in. Chen affirms that female writing is not a product of the female sex, but female identity. Hence, knowledge of feminism will help the Chinese understand how female writing comes about. Chen also believes that it is necessary to rewrite literary history from the perspective of feminism. The gender perspective in feminist criticism can provide the key to gender codes in history and thus will open up a new field of enquiry in history and subvert male hegemony in historical writing (Chen, 1995, p. 28). With regard to feminist literary criticism in China, Chen points out that it faces three difficulties: (a) problems in inappropriate use of feminist theories in criticism, (b) misunderstandings about and resistance against feminism among male critics, and (c) lack of theoretical sophistication among female critics which leads to the lack of methodology in criticism (Chen, 1995, p. 29).

Liu Huiying shows in her book, *Beyond the Confine of the Patriarchal Tradition* (*Zou chu nanquan chuantong de fanli*), that China needs a more radical feminism than what it had in the 1980s, and she declares that the purpose of her books is "to construct a new feminist literary criticism" in China (Liu, 1995, p. 8). Liu thinks that the introduction of Western literary criticism and a re-examination of traditional Chinese literature have in effect established a new feminist vision in China. By criticizing the patriarchal culture, Chinese critics have contributed to the development of a new type of criticism, which is based on a theory-driven re-examination of contemporary Chinese literature and literary history (Liu, 1995, pp. 6–8).

Compared to Liu Huiying, the critic Chen Huifen is a little less optimistic about the achievements of feminism in China. She believes that Chinese women have become less spirited in their struggle for a feminine voice in China and many of them feel confused by different ideas of feminism. Unlike the West, there has never been a "women's movement" behind the feminist movement in China, and therefore the problems confronted by Chinese women are not the same as those in the West. Chen believes that there is no harm in borrowing theories from the West so that feminist criticism can be established in China (Chen, 1996, p. 14).

No matter how Li Xiaojiang rejects the label "feminist," and no matter how much she declares herself a Marxist, just like the French critic Hélène Cixous, she stands firm on her idea that feminism has to be established in its rebellion against patriarchal culture. Such a view is fairly obvious in her works. Commenting on feminism in the West, she thinks that Western critics have never asked for more than women's rights and space for personal development. Instead, Western feminists have made a great contribution to the modern world by uniting women and revitalizing the study of culture from new perspectives (Li, 2000b, p. 282). Li further sees the recent social and political changes in China as a golden opportunity for women to develop themselves so that they can have their own cultural space. Feminism in China, as Li sees it, is a movement of empowerment for women.

A striking feature of recent Chinese literary criticism has been the wide use of feminist ideas since the mid-1990s. For example, in 1995 when there was a "culture fever" in China, which many people saw as a celebration of women's rising status, the critics Dai Jinhua and Chen Huifen warned that behind this celebration of women was women's loss of direction in their struggle for self-empowerment. As Dai Jinhua puts it, while the Fourth World Conference on Women provided an opportunity for Chinese women, it also revealed men's desire in show-casing Chinese women. On such a desire, she further comments that in China men always think of women as creatures born to be seen, and that their beauty has to be recognized by men. Behind the flourishing of feminist literature is the manipulation of men. Thus, there is a male editor in every book of feminist literature and the significance of female writers can only be established by the authority of male critics (Wang and Dai, 1996). Dai Jinhua sees the commercialization of literary production in China as a threat to women, with female writings, especially autobiographies, being packaged for business purposes (Wang and Dai, 1996).

Chen Huifen insists on the importance of having a distinctive feminist position. With regard to the reader's enthusiasm for women's writings in the 1990s, she asks, "Who are the editors? Who are the publishers? Who are the decision makers? Who are the readers?" It is obvious that several of the major book series on women are edited by men. These publication projects were not initiated by women, and such projects actually revealed women's lack of self-motivation. The publications resulting from these projects fall into the trap of "exhibiting women for commercial purposes." The World Conference on Women of 1995 did provide an opportunity for Chinese women to be packaged for exhibition. The self-assertion of Chinese women, unfortunately, has to be realized by male manipulation and by the demands of the market (Chen, 1996, pp. 240–243).

Feminism in China today is marked by two distinct characteristics. Firstly, it attaches importance to literature as a historical development and much work has been done in charting the history of feminist writings. Secondly, critics are becoming more aware of the differences between China and the West. They believe that it is necessary to take into consideration the peculiarities of Chinese culture and society when they practise feminist criticism. In her essay "Adventures and Breakthroughs: Female Writings in the 1990s" (Qiyu yu tuwei: Jiushi niandai nüxing xiezuo), Dai Jinhua identifies the features of Chinese female writings by studying the works of Wang Anyi, Xu Lan, Meng Hui, Xu Kun, Chi Li, Hai Nan, Tie Ning, Lin Bai, Chen Ran and Xu Xiaobing. She believes that one common characteristic of these writers is the theme of gender identity and gender awareness. Women writers today no longer put their hope in male heroes and no longer think that women have to be saved by men. Their characters do not need men's praise of being "progressive" and do not want to be a part of "men's drama." Instead, they are depressed and haunted by the "ghosts" of despair (Dai, 1996).

The critic Huang Lin has also written on the historical development of women's writings in the 1990s. According to her, the development of women's writings can be divided into three stages. The first stage is marked by Dai Houying's *Man, Oh, Man* (*Ren, a ren*) and Zhang Jie's "The Ark" (Fangzhou), through which the Chinese feminists express their concern about the emancipation of women as human beings. Many of the writers of this stage believe that women should be represented differently from the way they have been represented in history. The second stage is marked by an emphasis on the relationship between the sexes. The novels by Can Xue and Wang Anyi represent such views in the second stage. Contrary to the usual method of writing history from a temporal point of view, these writers probe into the dreams and the unconscious of women, and are attempting by this means to promote the female discourse. The third stage is a turning toward representation of an individualized voice in women. A feature of this stage of women's writings is the awareness that a writer has to express the living experience of the female through that of individuals. Women writers such as Lin Bai and Chen Ran believe that writing is an expression of a personalized discourse. Women's writings in this stage are full of voices yearning for freedom and space for women. But how to reach a certain level of depth in the depiction and representation of reality is still a problem which many women writers face (Wang and Huang, 1997).

The critic Chen Hong thinks that women's literature in China today should be defined by a feminine consciousness. The rise of a feminine consciousness can be seen in the development from Zhang Jie, who knows little about feminism, to Zhang Xinxin, who has begun to relate feminist ideas to her particular experience, and to Wang Anyi who believes in theory but holds independent views. Writers of the younger generation, such as Lin Bai and Hai Nan, who are aware of feminist issues, may be said to represent the maturity of Chinese feminist writings (Chen, 1995).

Among scholars, there have been various attempts at re-presenting the history of women's writings in China. Examples are Sheng Ying's edited volume, *A History of Women's Literature in 20th-Century China* (*Ershi shiji Zhongguo nüxing wenxue shi*), Lin Danya's book, *A History of Women's Literature in Contemporary China* (*Dangdai Zhongguo nüxing wenxue shilun*), Ren Yiming's two articles, "Modern Developments in Taiwan Women's Literature" (Taiwan nüxing wenxue de xiandai yanjin) and "An Overview of Women's Literature in Hong Kong" (Xianggang nüxing wenxue gaiguan), Xiao Han's "Lingering under the Big Tree of Civilization: A Comparative Study of the Femininity in mainland China and Taiwan" (Paihui zai zhe uo wenming dahsu zhixia: Haixia liang'an nüxing wenxue zhong nüxing yishi de bijiao kaocha), and Fan Luoping's "A Study of New Taiwan Feminist Literature" (Taiwan xin nüxing zhuyi wenxue xianxiang yanjiu). All these studies attempt to chart the historical development of women's literature in Taiwan by comparing it with that on the mainland.

Some critics in China have devoted their efforts to the study of differences between Chinese women writers and critics and their Western counterparts in terms of their different responses to feminism. This is a new development in China's feminist studies that cannot be found in the 1980s. For example, in Chen Huifen's analysis of Wang Anyi's works, she makes a connection between gender consciousness and racial identity, thus putting Wang Anyi in the context of "Third World women's writings." She points out that an awareness of the differences between Western feminism and the social reality in China will not pose an obstacle to a true feminist's work. Although Wang Anyi declares that she is "not a feminist writer," her works are examples of Third World women's literature, which is based not on any theory, but on particular problems which women find in their lives, such as the loss of self, conflicts between the two sexes, and gender biases experienced by women. In China today, the social and cultural issues as reflected in women's writings in the 1980s are concerned not just with patriarchy, but also with sexual conflicts in the age of globalization and the changing market economy. To women in the Third World, the problems they face are more often social and racial than sexual, and gender perspectives are often important critical tools in the analysis of social and racial problems (Chen, 1996).

Li Hui points out that materiality has become an aspect of gender enquiry in many Chinese women writers who are concerned with the social and racial existence of women. Writing that follows this line of inquiry is gender related, but may also serve as a record of women's social existence (Li, 1996). Li Xiaojiang believes that women in contemporary China would rather give up all they have, including their families, than relinquish their "social rights," which are their last territory. They would not regard families as shelters, as most traditional women did. What differentiates them from Western feminists is that they do not ask for rights from society, from the authorities, from men, or from the family, but from tradition. It is important to note this because it is a fundamental point in understanding the problems of modern Chinese women (Li, 1996). Li Xiaojiang reveals her views on feminism in the West in her preface to the book *Female?ism* (*Nüxing ? zhuyi*). As she says, feminism comes from the West; it is mainly a Western product. No matter how well intended it is and how influential it is, it is Western-centred, and the cultural hegemony behind it makes it difficult for Chinese women to identify themselves with it. Chinese women are facing a dilemma in the reception of feminism from the West, a dilemma which may involve many issues that are cultural, political, historical, or practical (Li, 2000b). Such a view shows that studies on Chinese women must take into consideration the particularity of women's existence and the uniqueness of the feminist discourse in China. Women of abstract and universal identity do not exist. Gender identity, sexual discrimination and sexual oppression are always closely linked with race, class, history and religion. Li Xiaojiang's position points to the fact that feminists in China, unlike their counterparts in the West, do not think that the plight of women is merely a result of patriarchy. This represents the gradual shift of Chinese feminism from its anti-patriarchal position in the 1980s.

A phenomenon that can be found since the 1990s is that there had appeared a critique of feminists in China. Some critics find that both

Dai Jinhua and Wang Fei read feminism into the works of writers, such as Tie Ning, who were not feminists. Such a reading may expand the horizons of the reader, especially the male reader. The difference between Wang Fei and Dai Jinhua lies in the fact that the former is more concerned with the rights of women, while the latter focuses on the femininity of women. Dai is able to probe the multiple levels of meaning in Tie Ning's works. On the one hand, both Wang and Dai seem to have mastered the techniques of feminist reading, but on the other they also seem to feel their limitations in filling in the "gaps" and "blind spots" in Chinese feminist criticism (Yi, 1995). This comparison is useful. However, I have the feeling that Dai Jinhua's "feminist criticism" is more militant than Wang Fei's. Dai, like Li Xiaojiang, does not claim that she is a feminist, so that she can have more freedom in her work of deconstructing patriarchy.

## CONTROVERSIES OVER FEMINISM IN CHINA

Accompanying the second wave of feminist criticism that has emerged in China since the 1990s are controversies and debates over issues of its validity and applicability. Some critics assert that it is dangerous for Chinese feminists to borrow feminism from the West without any adaptation. They argue that Western feminist literary theory is only a critique of patriarchal beliefs, and it does not propose a new set of beliefs for the feminists. Some even say that from the very beginning women's liberation in the world has been a movement that denies women their identity (Zhao, 1997). Feminist ideas borrowed from the West may not stand the test of critical scrutiny. In China, women's liberation has been a movement that develops along the somewhat unusual line of "material/human/non-women" (masculinization of women). Hence, feminism is something that needs to be rethought in China. The point of departure for Chinese feminism is the idea of gender differences derived from Western feminism, which ignores the rich content of Chinese women's writings.

At the beginning of the new millennium, it has already been pointed out that the unitary perspective of Western feminism puts the Chinese feminists in a de-historicized position in the study of Chinese feminist literature. Some Chinese critics believe that Chinese feminism seems radical but in fact is submitted to the hegemony of Western culture. They attack it as a new form of colonialism, in which Chinese feminism undoubtedly plays the role of being feminized in the face of a powerful

Western discourse (Zhao, 2001). In the West, the second wave of feminism developed in the 1970s as a result of discrimination against women, who were supposed to have equality in society. In China, women in the 1970s had already achieved equal status with men. In this respect, even Western feminists are surprised at the achievements of Chinese women (Zhao, 2001).

In recent years, there has arisen an idea that men and women are opposed to each other in binary relations. The overemphasis on gender and its opposition, which, as some critics worry, may lead to conflicts, and is considered biased for it ignores the fact that there could be harmony between the sexes. The interest in women's issues aroused by the Fourth World Conference on Women has given "feminism" an opportunity to become a hot topic in China. However, it may not be unreasonable to warn against any excessive emphasis on gender opposition, which might lead not just to a new battle of the sexes, but also to female chauvinism and female-centredness (Wang, 1995).

Critics in China believe that such a tendency in Chinese feminist criticism is caused by the desire to be "new," to be "unorthodox." Such a desire will make literary criticism a pursuit of things new at the expense of criticism per se. In contemporary Chinese feminist literary criticism, there is the practice of treating the text merely as a text about sexual differences and ignoring its politics. On the one hand, this approach is critical of the fact that the text has been subjected to the discourse of power in history; on the other hand, it attempts to depoliticize feminist literary criticism. Such a practice brought about undesired effects upon women's writings in the 1990s, such as those by Chen Ran, Lin Bai, Wei Hui, and Mian Mian (Zhao, 2001).

This is a tendency in criticism which has just begun and many issues are still to be debated. In my view, a text on gender is necessarily a political text, and the two can never be separated in gender politics. The separation of politics from gender issues, as seen in China, results from male-centred thinking. The view which regards feminist criticism as a deviation from humanism is, in my opinion, also problematic. Human existence can be concretized as relations between men and women, between oppressors and the oppressed, between Easterners and Westerners. Viewed from a gender perspective, the "human race" and the "natural, harmonious, beautiful and ideal human state" between both sexes are all problematic terms and in themselves dubious. The so-called true, general values of art are just objects to be deconstructed by feminist criticism. The framework that supports the idea of "true, general values" is artificially produced and is not based on anything universal and unchangeable. Practices and beliefs have been taken for granted as truth, but they are simply constructions of language. In China, one can find contradictions among some so-called "feminist" critics. It is problematic to say that Chinese feminism has been influenced in an undesirable manner by Western feminism because Western feminism has a "unitary perspective" on gender. Feminism in the West is an extremely complex phenomenon. As Hélène Cixous has pointed out, the masculine and the feminine are inseparable concepts that form an intricate web of social and cultural relations. To isolate the feminine and consider it separately from the masculine is to fall into the trap of ideological debates. In her article, "The Difficulties Facing Chinese Feminism" (Zhongguo nüxing zhuyi de kunjing), Zhao Xifang affirms the position taken by Kate Millett in her book *Sexual Politics*, in which Millet proposes to examine gender from multiple perspectives that include views of ideology, biology, sociology, class, economics, education, power, anthropology and psychology (Zhao, 2001). However, Zhao is too optimistic about Chinese women when she compares them with their Western counterparts. Zhao thinks that women in the West are not truly liberated, even though they have property and voting rights, and women in China are more fortunate because both sexes are equal in society. This, however, does not seem to be the situation in China today, as there are still people who think that men are superior to women and in many jobs women do not receive equal pay. Zhao cites Julia Kristeva to support her view, but she has forgotten that Kristeva is problematic in her description of Chinese women, particular when Kristeva considers foot-binding as a form of recognition of Chinese women in the "symbolic order."

## NOTE

1.  Zong Xueping teaches at Boston College. His essay first appeared in *Shanghai Culture* (*Shanghai wenhua*), No. 2 (1995) and is collected in the Chinese book *An Introduction to Western Feminist Studies* (*Xifang nüxing zhuyi yanjiu pingjie*).

## REFERENCES

Baimei (Burris, Mary Ann) (1994). "Shengyin de jiaoji" (A Polyphony of Voices), trans. by Li Wenjing. In Li Xiaojiang, Zhu Hong and Dong

Xiuyu, eds., *Xingbie yu Zhongguo* [Gender and China], pp. 17–20. Beijing: Sanlian shudian.

Chen Hong (1995). "Zhongguo dangdai wenxue: Nüxing zhuyi, nüxing xiezuo, nüxing wenben" [Contemporary Chinese literature: Feminism, feminist writing and feminist text]. *Wenyi pinglun* [Literary and arts criticism], No.4, 42–47.

Chen Huifen (1996). *Shenhua de kuipo: Dangdai Zhongguo nüxing xiezuo yanjiu* [Seeing through the myths]. Shanghai: Shanghai shehui kexue chubanshe.

Chen Shunxin (1995). *Zhongguo dangdai wenxue de xushi yu xingbie* [Narrative and gender in contemporary Chinese literature]. Beijing: Beijing daxue chubanshe.

Chow, Rey (1994). *Woman and Chinese Modernity: The Politics of Reading between West and East*. Minneapolis: University of Minnesota Press.

Cixous, Hélène (1976). "The Laugh of the Medusa." Trans. Keith Cohen and Paula Cohen. *Signs: Journal of Women in Culture and Society*, Vol. 1, No. 4 (Summer), 875–893.

Dai Jinhua (1996). "Qiyu yu tuwei: Jiushi niandai nüxing xiezuo" [Adventures and breakthroughs: Female writings in the 1990s]. *Wenxue pinglun* [Literary criticism], No. 5, 95–102.

Ding Fan et al. (1997). "'Nüquan' xiezuo zhong de wenhua bolun" [Cultural subversion in feminist writings]. *Wenyi zhengming* [Literary voices], No. 5, 12–17.

Fan Luoping (1996). "Taiwan xin nüxing zhuyi wenxue xianxiang yanjiu" [A study of the new feminist literary phenomenon in Taiwan]. *Beijing shifan daxue xuebao* (Sheke ban) [Journal of Beijing Normal University (Social sciences edition)], No. 1, 106–111.

Feixiali (Furth, Charlotte) (1994). "Zhongguo chuantong yixue li de xing yu shengji: Dui Gaolopei de fanxi" (Rethinking Van Gulik: Sexuality and Reproduction in Traditional Chinese Medicine), trans. by Zhao Hong. In Li Xiaojiang, Zhu Hong and Dong Xiuyu, eds., *Xingbie yu Zhongguo* [Gender and China], pp. 323–347. Beijing: Sanlian shudian. English original in Christina K. Gilmartin, Gail Hershatter, Lisa Rofel and Tyrene White, eds. (1994), *Engendering China: Women, Culture and the State*, pp. 125–146. Cambridge, MA: Harvard University Press.

Feuerwerker, Yi-tsi Mei (1982). *Ding Ling's Fiction: Ideology and Narrative in Modern Chinese Literature*. Cambridge, MA: Harvard University Press.

Guan Chunling (1996). "Xifang shengtai nüquan zhuyi yanjiu zongshu" [A synopsis of Western ecological feminism]. *Guowai shehui kexue* [Foreign social sciences], No. 2, 25–30.

Kelisiti, Huo'er (Hall, Christine), Mike Suangdesi (Mick Saunders) and Wu Xuexian (1996). "Dangdai Yingguo ertong wenxue gaishu: Jiantan jizhong liuxing lilun dui ertong wenxue de yingxiang" (Contemporary British Children's Literature: Also on Some Popular Theories That Have an

Influence on Children's Literature). *Waiguo wenxue pinglun* [Review of foreign literature], No. 1, 130–136.

Kristeva, Julia (1977). *About Chinese Women*. Trans. Anita Barrows. London: Marion Boyars.

Li Hui (1996). "Geren, xingbie, zhongzu: Jiushi niandai nüxing xiezuo" [The individual, gender and race: Female writings in the 1990s]. *Shanghai wenhua* [Shanghai culture], No. 2, 46–56.

Li Xiaojiang (1994). "Xu" [Preface]. In Li Xiaojiang, Zhu Hong and Dong Xiuyu, eds., *Xingbie yu Zhongguo* [Gender and China], pp. 1–7. Beijing: Sanlian shudian.

Li Xiaojiang (1996). "Beifuzhe chuantong de fankang: Xinshiqi funü wenxue chuangzuo zhong de quanli he yaoqiu" [Shouldering the resistance against tradition: Rights and demands in women's literature in the new era]. *Zhejiang daxue xuebao* [Journal of Zhejiang University], No. 3, 118–121.

Li Xiaojiang (2000a). "Nüxing shenfen: Yanjiu yu xiezuo" [Female identity: Research and writing] (Transcript of interview with Zhang Kangkang, February 2, 2000; February 13, 2000). In Li Xiaojiang, *Wenxue, yishu yu xingbie* [Literature, arts and gender]. Nanjing: Jiangsu renmin chubanshe.

Li Xiaojiang (2000b). *Nüxing ? zhuyi: Wenhua chongtu yu shenfen rentong* [Female? ism: Cultural conflicts and identity]. Nanjing: Jiangsu renmin chubanshe.

Li Xiaojiang, Zhu Hong and Dong Xiuyu, eds. (1994). *Xingbie yu Zhongguo* [Gender and China]. Beijing: Sanlian shudian.

Liu Huiying (1995). *Zouchu nanquan chuantong de fanlong* [Beyond the confine of the patriarchal tradition]. Beijing: Sanlian shudian.

Lu, Tonglin, ed. (1993). *Gender and Sexuality in Twentieth-century Chinese Literature and Society*. Albany: State University of New York Press.

Man, Sushan (Mann, Susan) (1994). "Shiba shiji de Zhongguo zhishi nüxing" (Learned Women in the Eighteenth Century), trans. by Ren Xiaojin. In Li Xiaojiang, Zhu Hong and Dong Xiuyu, eds., *Xingbie yu Zhongguo* [Gender and China], pp. 187–212. Beijing: Sanlian shudian. English original in Christina K. Gilmartin, Gail Hershatter, Lisa Rofel and Tyrene White, eds. (1994), *Engendering China: Women, Culture and the State*, pp. 27–46. Cambridge, MA: Harvard University Press.

Maiqiante, Kaluolin (Merchant, Carolyn) (1999). *Ziran zhi si: Funü, shengtai he kexue geming* (The Death of Nature: Women, Ecology and the Scientific Revolution). Trans. Wu Guosheng et al. Changchun: Jilin renmin chubanshe.

Ren Yiming (1995a). "Taiwan nüxing wenxue de xiandai yanjin" [Modern developments in Taiwan women's literature]. *Xinjiang shifan daxue xuebao* (Sheke ban) [Journal of Xinjiang Normal University (Social sciences edition)], No. 4, 67–71.

Ren Yiming (1995b). "Xianggang nüxing wenxue gaiguan" [A overview of women's literature in Hong Kong]. *Xinjiang shifan daxue xuebao* (Sheke ban) [Journal of Xinjiang Normal University (Social sciences edition)], No. 4, pp. 18–23.

Shen Dan (2000). "Meiguo xushi lilun yanjiu de xiao guimo fuxing" [A small revival of studies in narrative theories in the United States]. *Waiguo wenxue pinglun* [Review of foreign literature], No. 4, 144–148.

Tao Jie (1995). "Meiguo nüxing wenxue gei women de qishi" [Inspirations of American feminist literature]. *Wenxue ziyou tan* [Random thoughts on literature], No. 3, 89–95.

Wang Fengzhen (1995). "Nüquan zhuyi piping shumianguan" [Aspects of feminist criticism]. *Wenxue pinglun* [Literary criticism], No. 5, 149–156.

Wang Gan, and Dai Jinhua (1996). "Nüxing zhuyi wenxue yu gerenhua xiezuo" [Female literature and personalized writing]. *Dajia* [Great writers], No. 1, 193–203.

Wang Guangming, and Huang Lin (1997). "Liangxing duihua: Zhongguo nüxing wenxue shiwu nian" [Dialogue between two sexes: Fifteen years of Chinese women's literature]. *Wenyi zhengming* [Literary voices], No. 5, 4–12.

Wang Kan (1997). "Dangdai ershi shiji Zhongguo nüxing wenxue yanjiu pipan" [A critique of contemporary Chinese feminist literary studies]. *Shehui kexue zhanxian* [Social sciences front], No. 3, 156–163.

Wang Ning (1995). "Nüquan zhuyi lilun yu Zhongguo dangdai nüxing xian-feng wenxue" [Feminist theories and contemporary avant-garde Chinese literature]. *Shehui kexue zhanxian* [Social sciences front], No. 5, 106–112.

Xiao Han (1995). "Paihuai zai zheguo wenming dashu zhixia: Haixia liang'an nüxing wenxue zhong nüxing yishi de bijiao kaocha" [Lingering under the big tree of civilization: A comparative study of femininity in mainland China and Taiwan]. *Shandong shifan daxue xuebao* (Sheke ban) [Journal of Shandong Normal University (Social sciences edition)], No. 6, 80–84.

Yi Guang. (1995). "Fei nüquan zhuyi wenxue yu nüquan zhuyi piping" [Non-feminist literature and feminist criticism]. *Dangdai wentan* [Contemporary literary scene], No. 5, 12–16.

Zhang Zhongzhai (1994). "Anjiela kate qi ren" [Angela Carter]. *Waiguo wenxue* [Foreign literature], No. 1, 29–31.

Zhao Rong (1997). "Huaiyi yu zhuiwen: Zhongguo de nüxing zhuyi nengfo chengwei keneng?" [Doubts and questions: Is Chinese feminism possible?]. *Wenyi zhengming* [Literary voices], No. 5, 18–24.

Zhao Xifang (2001). "Zhongguo nüxing zhuyi de kunjing" [The difficulties of Chinese feminism]. *Wenyi zhengming* [Literary voices], No. 4, 74–79.

Zong Xueping (1995). "Xifang nüxing zhuyi lilun yu Xifang Zhongguo xiandai wenxue yanjiu" [Western feminist theories and modern Chinese literary studies in the West]. *Shanghai wenhua* [Shanghai culture], No. 2, 36.

## GLOSSARY

Can Xue 殘雪
Chen Ran 陳染
Chi Li 池莉
Dai Houying 戴厚英
"Fangzhou" 〈方舟〉
Hai Nan 海男
Lin Bai 林白
Meng Hui 孟暉
*Ren, a ren* 《人啊！人》
Tie Ning 鐵凝
Wang Anyi 王安憶
Xu Kun 徐坤
Xu Lan 須蘭
Xu Xiaobing 徐小斌
Zhang Jie 張潔

## 4  Food, Body and Female Subjectivity

*Reading between Western and Chinese Perspectives*

JESSICA TSUI YAN LI

FOOD NOT ONLY PROVIDES NOURISHMENT for the body, but also carries messages in the construction of female subjectivity across cultures. Female subjectivity can be considered as "the conscious and unconscious thoughts and emotions of the individual, her sense of herself and her ways of understanding her relation to the world" (Weedon, 1997, p. 32). In both Western and Chinese culture and literature, the construction of female subjectivity is strongly connected to food and body.

In discussing the relationship between food, body and female subjectivity, some feminist critics point out that women are victimized by various patriarchal discourses that reduce women's subjecthood to a relation between body and food, which is an attempt to restrict women's self to domestic roles that are consumable. For instance, in the gender-based division of labour, women are expected to perform domestic duties, such as food preparation and washing the dishes, that limit their space for personal development. Women are also subjected to commercially idealized images of the female body, thus being forced to control their appetites and exhaust their energies. All such restrictions and images may hinder women from achieving power and developing a positive self-identity.

These views help reveal the social victimization of women in relation to food and body, but they may neglect the positive aspect of women's self-assertion through food and body. For example, women may regard food nurturing and sharing as a medium of communication, a form of mutuality, and an expression of love and desire. They may also connect food provision and preparation to creativity and motherhood. In conforming to social codes, women may be restricted in their ideas about body shape and clothing, but they may also achieve a sense of community, commitment and security.

In this essay, I would like to argue that in the literary works studied, the female protagonists, through liberating themselves from over-determined denotations upon food and women's body, generate an ambivalent and ambiguous attitude of both rejection and assertion toward food and the female body in the construction of a non-essential, multiple, fluid and contradictory subjectivity. I have two main objectives in this essay. First, I aim to reassess the current Western and Chinese theoretical and social studies of food, body and female subjectivity. Second, by reading selected texts in contemporary Western and Chinese literature, I will re-examine the development of women's liberation in relation to the construction of female subjectivity encoded in food and body.

## FOOD AND FEMALE SUBJECTIVITY: WESTERN PERSPECTIVES

The signification of food, body and female subjectivity has been widely studied in the Western world. Nutritionists, for example, adopt a highly instrumental view of food and eating, associating habits and preferences with the anatomical functioning of the human body. The nutritionist's perspective advocates a specific diet in order to achieve good health: "Today nutritional scientists in Western countries are again stressing the importance of the relationship between food and health. They are setting standards of 'good food' and advising the public to keep to a 'prudent diet' which will maintain health" (Mennell, Murcott and Otterloo, 1992, p. 36). According to nutritionists, food tastes, habits and preferences are regarded as important mainly in shaping the body, which is secondary to the nutrition that contributes to body functioning and development. While nutritionists are mainly concerned with the physical functioning and state of health of the human body, anthropologists and sociologists argue that the symbolic nature of food and body, shaped by a wide variety of geographical, social, psychological, religious, economic and political factors, is far more significant in revealing people's social and cultural selves, as well as our individual subjectivity.

With the rise of structuralism in the 1960s, the anthropologist Lévi-Strauss considered food and its taste to be culturally shaped and socially controlled. His structuralist perspective takes food practices as a language with symbolic and metaphorical meanings. In *Structural Anthropology* (1968), Lévi-Strauss argues that "[l]ike language, it seems to me, the cuisine of a society may be analyzed into constituent elements, which in this case we might call 'gustemes,' and which may be organized according to certain structures of opposition and correlation" (Lévi-Strauss, 1968, p. 86). By examining the code underlying food, one can understand the culture, philosophy and psychology of a society: "If we find these structures to be common to several spheres, we have the right to conclude that we have reached a significant knowledge of the unconscious attitudes of the society or societies under consideration" (Lévi-Strauss, 1968, p. 87).

In his book *The Raw and the Cooked* (1986), Lévi-Strauss analyses food practices in relation to binary concepts in culture, such as the raw and the cooked, and food and non-food. According to Lévi-Strauss, cooked food represents a cultural transformation of the raw, signifying the transformation from nature to culture in people's everyday life. Lévi-Strauss' works highlight the relationship between food practices, language and social life. However, it is problematic to over-generalize complex daily life in the form of binary oppositions between nature and culture, or between the raw and the cooked.

Similar to Lévi-Strauss, Roland Barthes also perceives food as analogous to language. By analysing its codes and structures, one can understand its signification in social consciousness. In "Towards a Psychosociology of Contemporary Food Consumption," Barthes points out:

> food serves as a sign not only for themes, but also for situations; and this, all told, means for a way of life that is emphasized, much more than expressed, by it. To eat is a behavior that develops beyond its own ends, replacing, summing up, and signalizing other behaviors, and it is precisely for these reasons that it is a sign. What are these other behaviors? Today, we might say all of them: activity, work, sports, effort, leisure, celebration— every one of these situations is expressed through food. (Barthes, 1975, p. 51)

Barthes contends that food signifies the meanings of social systems in the world. His anthropological work that points out the social significa- tion of food remains influential and important, though it is sometimes criticized as essentialist and static.

Some structuralist feminists believe that the subordination of women may be due to certain social factors, such as the social structure of gender and the family, that affect patterns of food consumption and preparation, the relationship among women's dietary practices, their body shape and size, and the construction of femininity. They pay particular attention to women's major responsibility in preparing food according to the preferences of their family members, their deprivation of food consumption in favour of men's preferences, and social pressures relating to women's body size and shape that may cause women to develop eating disorders.

Anne Murcott, for example, claims in her "Cooking and the Cooked: A Note on the Domestic Preparation of Meals" (1983) that domestic cooking and feeding activities are generally understood as women's work. They reflect "the gender-based domestic division of labour" (Murcott, 1983, p. 179) and they are social sources for the production and reproduction of gender. By feeding the family well, a woman considers herself properly feminine: "Cooking is securely anchored as the responsibility of women as wives and as mothers. Informants all affirmed that conventionally this is so. They also reported that they did the cooking. For all informants the kitchen was their domain, shopping and stocking their responsibility, routine planning and daily oversight of meals their work" (Murcott, 1983, p. 181). Murcott's research examines the meaning people attach to cooking and feeding as "womanly" work which reflects the social relationships involved in a gender-linked division of labour. In such relationships, men are mainly responsible for breadwinning, women for house-keeping.

In a similar vein, in *Women, Food and Families* (1988), Nickie Charles and Marion Kerr discuss the way in which food practices contribute to the reproduction of the social order—family, gender and class. They reach the conclusion that "food practices reproduce the patriarchal family, characterized by the authority of the father and the subordination of the mother and, at the same time, the authority of both over the children" (Charles and Kerr, 1988, p. 225). Also, the gender division of labour defines women as the servers and providers of food for men and for children within the family; it is women's way of expressing love and affection. "In this process women's own tastes and preferences are subordinated and those of men are privileged" (Charles and Kerr, 1988, p. 229). Since food practices vary across the class structure, they reflect not only patriarchal structure, but also class divisions.

On the relationship between food and body image, Susie Orbach in *Fat Is a Feminist Issue* (1997) argues that in Western societies, the social norms of appropriate feminine body size limit women's food intake, thus causing women to be more likely to adopt weight-reducing diets and develop eating disorders such as anorexia than men: "Being fat isolates and invalidates a woman. Almost inevitably, the explanations offered for fatness point a finger at the failure of women themselves to control their weight, control their appetites and control their impulses. Women suffering from the problem of compulsive eating endure a double anguish: feeling out of step with the rest of society, and believing that it is all their fault" (Orbach, 1997, p. 21). Social pressures relating to women's body size and shape indeed occupy many women and absorb their energies.

Structuralist approaches tend to adopt an essentialist perspective, with the assignment of a single meaning to food-as-text, often failing to fully recognize the dynamic contextual and contradictory meanings food has. Structuralist feminists focus on the subordination of women caused by the socialization of food and body, neglecting the aspect of women's self-assertion. Poststructuralists, on the other hand, explore the broader knowledge and political contexts in which a patterned system of language and practices around food and eating produces and reproduces knowledge and meanings (Lupton, 1996, p. 10). In recent research on food and eating, poststructuralists and postmodernists investigate patterned systems of language and practices around food and eating in dynamic and multiple social and political contexts. They believe that such systems produce knowledge and reinforce meanings upon the physical health, shape and size of the body, thus contributing to the construction of social structures, through which female subjectivity is formed.

In *Sweetness and Power: The Place of Sugar in Modern History* (1985), Mintz argues that "[f]ood choices and eating habits reveal distinctions of age, sex, status, culture, and even occupation" (Mintz, 1985, p. 3). He clearly explains in his work how the control of sugar production and consumption contributes to class hierarchy and colonial dominance. In his "Introduction" to *Food and Gender: Identity and Power*, Counihan points out that though Mintz neglects gender consid-erations, a photograph presents the implicit message of male control. The caption reads "Etienne Tholoniat, a great French sugar baker, puts the finishing touches on a life-size chocolate nude with spun-sugar hair. She is lying on a bed of six hundred sugar roses" (Mintz, 1985, p. 184). In Counihan's own words, "the active, powerful male literally defines the female as a supine, passive object of consumption—a food symbol for cultural practice mirroring male-female power relations" (Counihan and Kaplan, 1998, p. 3).

Marjorie L. DeVault argues in *Feeding the Family: The Social Organization of Caring as Gendered Work* (1991) that gender construc-tion is not only an individual performance, but also an interactive, collaborative and ongoing process of production and recognition of women and men through concerted activities, such as feeding, which are closely associated with one gender, thus appearing as "natural" expressions of that gender. She says:

> This observation does not imply that all women engage in such activity. Some choose not to do feeding. Others improvise and negotiate, developing idiosyncratic versions of this "womanly" work. And of course, some men do feeding work and remain recognizable men. But as long as feeding is understood, collectively, as somehow more "womanly" than "manly," the work stands as one kind of activity in which "womanliness" may be at issue. (DeVault, 1991, pp. 118–119)

Accordingly, many couples divide housework on the basis of what society assumes to be "properly" masculine or feminine behaviour. DeVault's work recognizes the dynamic, multiple and interactive social forces of gender construction embedded in food practices.

Similar to DeVault's approach, Carole M. Counihan in *Food and Gender: Identity and Power* (1998) analyses the social power that society allocates food to men and women. She points out that "[m]en's and women's ability to produce, provide, distribute and consume food is a key measure of their power. This ability varies according to their culture, their class, and their family organization, and the overall economic structure of their society" (Counihan and Kaplan, 1998, p. 2). She also examines the personal power of men and women in relation to food and its meanings in the formation of gendered subjectivity: "Men's and women's attitudes about their bodies, the legitimacy of their appetites, and the importance of their food work reveal whether their self-concept is validating or denigrating" (Counihan and Kaplan, 1998, p. 2). Counihan addresses the differences and demands of marginalized, diasporic cultures in which food practices contribute to gender construction, thus disproving the structuralist argument of hegemonic and universal oppression of women.

In poststructuralist perspectives, meanings are produced through discourse in interaction with experience, senses, emotions, the conscious and the unconscious. In his essay "Technologies of the Self" (1988), Michel Foucault argues that individuals internalize modes and rules of behaviour, emotion and thought and apply them to everyday life, thus consciously and unconsciously constructing their subjectivity.[1] According to Foucault, internalized ideas regulate and mould the body and subjectivity. Through food habits and preferences, individuals take control over the body in order to present themselves and communicate with others.

In a similar approach, Judith Butler suggests in *Bodies That Matter* (1993) that bodies are regulated by social norms and practices through materialization, reiteration and performance, producing the idea of normativity of gender relations and individuals' subjectivity. According to Butler, "'sex' is an ideal construct which is forcibly materialized through time. It is not a simple fact or static condition of a body, but a process whereby regulatory norms materialize 'sex' and achieve this materialization through a forcible reiteration of those norms" (Butler, 1993, pp. 1–2). Though the contours and movements of bodies will be continuously materialized and governed, they never quite conform to the norms imposed. Butler continues to argues that "it is the instabilities, the possibilities for rematerialization, opened up by this process that mark one domain in which the force of the regulatory law can be turned against itself to spawn rearticulations that call into question the hegemonic force of that very regulatory law" (Butler, 1993, p. 2). The contradictions between ideology and reality, therefore, create opportunities for the body to be constructed by social norms.

Julia Kristeva states that the female body itself and the feelings associated with it have emerged historically in connection with the social constitution of women, the nature of women's experience and their social marginalization and representation. According to Kristeva, femininity is conventionally defined as marginal and women exist negatively through their refusal to be categorized. In Kristeva's own words, "In 'woman' I see something that cannot be represented, something that is not said, something above and beyond nomenclatures and ideologies" (Kristeva, 1981, p. 137). Radically deconstructing the identity of the subject, Kristeva refuses to define female subjectivity and claims that there is no essential female subjecthood, not even a repressed one, and that feminist practice cannot be directed at recovering the essential state of woman (Weedon, 1997, p. 66). Kristeva's theory of the subject as unstable, in process and continued in language "presents a radical alternative to the humanist view of subjectivity in which it is self-present, unified and in control [and] offers the possibility of understanding the contradictory nature of individuals" (Weedon, 1997, p. 68). Kristeva's theory opens up ways to see female identity as changeable, for it argues that female identity is historically and culturally constructed, and not solely biologically determined.

The idea of a non-essentialist, dynamic and contradictory female subjectivity has been further elaborated by Chris Weedon in *Feminist Practice and Poststructuralist Theory* (1997). As Weedon states, "In making our subjectivity the product of the society and culture within which we live, feminist poststructuralism insists that forms of subjectivity are produced historically and change with shifts in the wide range of discursive fields which constitute them," and "the individual is always the site of conflicting forms of subjectivity" (Weedon, 1997, p. 32). According to her, feminist poststructuralism aims at transforming the hegemonic structure of masculinity by establishing an alternative knowledge that does not marginalize or subordinate women (Weedon, 1997, pp. 121–122). As a feminist poststructuralist, Weedon intends to deconstruct the concept of the essentialist, unified and rational subjectivity within the liberal humanistic tradition and propose a non-essentialist, multiple, dynamic and contradictory subjectivity. This highlights the multiplicity of choice in different situations and between different discourses, thus opening up new possibilities for positioning the self. Feminist poststructuralism, however, brings the question of the opportunity for resistance when female subjectivity is culturally and historically constructed. Weedon contends that, though the female subject is constituted by discourses, she still exists as "a thinking, feeling and social agent capable of resistance and innovations produced out of the clash between contradictory subject positions and practices" (Weedon, 1997, 121). Weedon argues for the fluidity of female subjectivity.

In *Postfeminisms: Feminism, Cultural Theory and Cultural Forms* (1997), Ann Brooks defines postfeminism as a body of theory and politics engaged with earlier feminist discourses and other social movements for change. She says:

> Postfeminism expresses the intersection of feminism with postmodernism, poststructuralism and postcolonialism, and as such represents a dynamic movement capable of challenging modernist, patriarchal and imperialist frameworks. In the process postfeminism facilitates a broad-based, pluralistic conception of the application of feminism, and addresses the demands of marginalized, diasporic and colonised cultures for a non-hegemonic feminism capable of giving voice to local, indigenous and post-colonial feminisms. (Brooks, 1997, p. 4)

Postfeminism challenges the hegemonic assumptions of patriarchal and imperialist oppression as a universally experienced oppression held by second-wave feminists. Instead, a new range of temporal, political and cultural relations in a process of ongoing transformation and change is emphasized.

## FOOD AND FEMALE SUBJECTIVITY: CHINESE PERSPECTIVES

The theme of food, body and female subjectivity, though it has not been theorized, can also be found in Chinese culture. It reflects the Chinese view that female subjectivity is historically and culturally constructed. The history of Chinese alimentary culture demonstrates the important role of food in life, in which the physical body and the social body join and shape each other in a dynamic relation. The proverb, "people revere food as if it were Heaven" (*min yi shi wei tian*), emphasizes the centrality of food and eating in traditional Chinese life, and explains the reverent attitude the Chinese have toward food.

Wide-ranging food choices, painstaking preparation of cuisine and the concern with the excellence of food are prevalent in society and reflected in the common form of Chinese greeting: "Have you had your meal?" (*Ni chiguo fan meiyou?*) It shows that food is not only a necessity to the Chinese, it also carries social meaning in that eating means enjoyment and the pursuit of a harmonious relationship among people which is created through eating together.

In Chinese society, food and eating are marked as a crucial way of socialization. Family and religious events, as well as social transactions, will be completed by sharing a meal. As Sun points out in *The Deep Structure of Chinese Culture* (Zhongguo wenhua de shenceng jiegou, 1983), food and eating are an important means of reaching harmony in Chinese society:

> According to the Chinese, *chi* [eating] is related to *hehexing* [the state of harmony]. *Yin* [lewdness] is the worst of all vices because it disturbs the harmony of the community. On the contrary, if *chi* [eating] is used as a social function, it can promote the feeling of *hehe* [harmony]. The tension among people can be released because of happiness produced after having a libation together around a fire. (Sun, 1983, p. 40)

The dialectic interaction between the physical body and the social body can be shown in the harmonious atmosphere generated through the means of eating together, something which is crucial in the Chinese concept of human relationship.

Apart from the proverb and the common greeting mentioned, the Chinese character, *chi* [eating], also demonstrates the dynamic interplay of various discursive boundaries, such as the economic, political, social and cultural embodiment. The Chinese ideogram *chi* [eating] presents "a mouth" followed by "beg." In "Wangbuliao chi" [Can't forget about eating, 1997], the Chinese writer Mo Yan describes the character *chi* [eating] as "the begging of the mouth, the begging mouth" (Mo, 1997, p. 92) because it signifies the meaning of starving and the low social status of the person who begs for food. This interpretation of the character shows that hunger and the suffering of the body are thematically related in modern Chinese culture.

Numerous compounds and configuration of the Chinese character, *chi*, comprise a broader semantic and discursive field than its English counterpart. As suggested by Gang Yue in *The Mouth That Begs: Hunger, Cannibalism, and the Politics of Eating in Modern China*,

> After a baby is born, one of the first instincts he or she follows is *chi nai* [eat milk, or suck the breast]. If the mother doesn't nurse her or him well, the baby has to *chi li* [eat with strength, or make an effort]. When he or she still cannot suck milk, the baby may *chi jing* [eat with shock, or be startled]. He or she may then fall ill and in that case has to *chi yao* [eat medicine]. If the baby is the only son in the traditional household, the grandma might scold the mother for making him *chi ku* [eat bitterness, or suffer]. Even if the mother has good reasons, say, she does not yield much milk, she is normally not supposed to retort but instead *chi yaba kui* [eat the mute's loss, or keep quiet despite ill treatment]. Suppose the mother is a concubine, while the first wife of the family doesn't have a son, then she will be able to *chi lao ben* [eat old capital, or rest on the fact that it was she who gave life to the only son, the sole heir in the patriarchal genealogy]. The first wife, without the grace of having a son, might then *chi cu* [eat vinegar, or become jealous]. (Gang, 1999, p. 18)

The above figurative meanings generated by the compounds of *chi* and other Chinese characters show the broad and flexible semantic field of the Chinese character, *chi*. Gang has contextualized the word *chi* in a manner that indicates the gender-specific discourse on women, especially mothers, as victims of traditional culture, which however might lead to an overgeneralization of the oppression of Chinese women disregarding their assertion in the discourse of *chi*.

Food in Chinese culture is also encoded with enormous metaphorical significations of the female body and subjectivity. For example, the Chinese linguistic terms for *lianzi* [lotus seeds] and *nian zi* [year son] have similar pronunciations. Because of this, when a couple is newly wedded, lotus seeds will be placed under the pillow of the wife, expressing the wish that she should give birth to a son every year, known as *niansheng guizi*. The phonetically similar capacity of the signifier and the signified in *lianzi* [lotus] and *nian zi* [year son] produces the metaphorical meaning of delivering a son every year. It signifies the traditional thought of the superiority of men over women and women's gaining of power through giving birth to a son.

Chinese people also tend to treat food as medicine or treat medicine as food in order to strengthen or build up the health of the physical body, showing the emphasis on the virtues of the balance, order, harmony and human relationship in Chinese subjectivity. In *The Food of China* (1988), E. N. Anderson points out that humoral theory is widely practised in China, "The humoral theory, in its most general form, holds that the human body is affected by heat, cold, wetness, and dryness. These 'qualities' or 'calences' must remain in balance if the body is to remain healthy" (Anderson, 1988, p. 189). Such a theory shows that for the sake of bodily health, the qualities contained in food must remain in balance, an important virtue in traditional Chinese thought.

According to traditional Chinese medical and nutritional beliefs, foods are classified as warm, mild, cool and cold. This classification is not determined by the actual temperature of the food, but by its medicinal effects on the body. For example, water-melon is cold by nature and therefore should not be consumed by pregnant women; otherwise, the fetus might die. Ginger is hot in nature, and therefore, women who have become weak and cold after childbirth should have a soup made of ginger in vinegar in order to regain their strength. Interestingly, "the honey of Szechuan is 'mild,' of Fukien and Kwangtung 'hot'; of the South-west 'cool'" (Lai, 1978, p. 13). If consumed by pregnant women, the mild honey would make the skin of the baby smooth, while the hot one would cause pimples on the baby's face, and the cool one might weaken the baby's health. As a result of such beliefs concerning harmony in the concept of food, Chinese people, especially pregnant women and new mothers who are largely responsible for the health of infants, have to observe the balance of "hot" and "cold" qualities in food in order to keep their bodies in good health.

The Chinese are particularly concerned with building up bodily health through nourishing food or tonics, known as *buyao* [tonic]. *Buyao* is widely consumed by Chinese people even if they are in a healthy state. Diet therapy is often integrated into herbal medicine. For instance, swallow's nests and shark's fin, considered to have the medicinal effect of nourishing the skin, are often made into soup and consumed by women, who usually pay more attention to their appearance than men do. As pointed out by Sun:

These types of medicinal materials are not for curative purposes, but for preventive and recuperative functions, thus often mixed up with the functions of food. Therefore, a more common phenomenon is to use food for building up bodily health. The food and drinking practices of the Chinese, besides satisfying the desire of the stomach, are particularly concerned with the function of *jinbu* [building up one's health]. The Chinese often believe that a particular kind of food can strengthen a particular part of the body. (Sun, 1983, p. 39)

The concept of *jinbu* is generated by the interaction of empirical truth and psychological construction. As mentioned by Anderson, "In the traditional Chinese worldview, bodily energy, spiritual energy, and the flow of energy in the natural world are all part of one great system" and the Chinese believe that "people can draw on natural energy flow by eating creatures that have a great deal of energy or even by positioning themselves in places that are appropriately located to take advantage of the flow of *chi* [energy]" (Anderson, 1988, p. 193). As a result, powerful creatures, such as eagles, pangolins, raccoon-dogs and sexually hyper-potent deer, would be precious food wit sources of energy. Some foods that are strikingly analogous in appearance with certain parts of the body are also considered as "strengthening and supplementing" (*bu*). For instance, red jujubes and port wine have a reputation for strengthening the blood because they are red (Anderson, 1988, p. 192). They are particularly favoured by women who have lost a great amount of blood during childbirth.

The major reason for the emphasis on the concept of "building up one's health with nourishing food" (*jinbu*) is that Chinese people tend to transform individual psychological problems into physical problems. As a result, they are particularly concerned with the health of their bodies, which is culturally regulated by harmonious human and social relationships and considered as a very important virtue of the Chinese.

Chinese people usually use the word *shen* [body] to refer to a person's self, showing the tendency to use the body as a metaphor for selfhood, and self is also a matter based on life and existence. As Sun argues, "Chinese people seldom suffer from psychological illness. In the case of psychological problems, they will be taken as physical diseases, such as dizziness, aching waist and back, feeling weak in the four limbs, etc." (Sun, 1983, p. 38). The Chinese believe that psychological problems can be regulated by human and social relationships. As Sun continues:

Indeed, the Chinese seldom have psychiatric problems compared with Westerners. It is not only due to the tendency of embodiment (*shenti hua*) of psychological problems, but also the super-stable (*chao wending*) personality of the Chinese—the body (*shen*) of Chinese people is regulated by the heart (*xin*) of human and social relationships, but not the individual. Therefore, the Chinese are always situated in the enclosure of a cozy magnetic field of human relationships. It would be easier for them to maintain a psychological balance compared with those people who encounter the world individually. (Sun, 1983, p. 38)

Chinese philosophy, governing principles and morality that give guidance to women's roles and behaviour are sometimes represented through the symbolic meaning of food and body. For instance, a restrictive moral code of conduct on Chinese women is presented in "To die of hunger is a trifling matter, to lose chastity is grave" (Chow, 1993, p. 60). Such an ideological and political signification of food and eating practices suggests that women's chastity is valued much more than their lives. In the Chinese tradition, the concept of women's marriage to one man only and their constancy in love and loyalty is a pretext invented by men for binding the wife for life to one man. This idea is expressed in the slogan: "A good horse will not serve two masters; a good woman will not marry two husbands" (Chiu, 1966, p. 59). It clearly shows the high moral standard imposed on women, but not on men who are generally permitted to possess more than one wife and concubine. It signifies the relative superiority of men and the dependency of women.

The traditional Chinese convention of female subordination is attributed to the Confucian ethics of "the three obediences and four virtues" (*san cong si de*) described in *The Book of Ceremonies and Rites* (*Yili*) and *The Rites of Zhou* (*Zhouli*) and women's education described in *The Book of Rites* (*Liji*) respectively. In setting moral rules for women, the "three obediences" establish that a woman has to obey her father before marriage, her husband after marriage, and her son after the death of her husband. The "four virtues" are to be morally good, to be discreet in your speech, to be tidy and to be diligent in your work. Moreover, among the Confucian canons, *The Book of Rites* prescribes that a girl needs to educate herself to perform domestic duties:

A girl at the age of ten ceased to go out (from the women's apartment). Her governess taught her (the arts of) pleasing speech and manners, to be docile and obedient, to handle the hempen fibres, to deal with the cocoons, to weave silks and form filets, to learn (all) women's work, how to furnish garments, to watch the sacrifices, to supply the liquors and sauces, to fill the various stands and dishes with pickles and brine and to assist in setting forth the appurtenances for the ceremonies. (Confucius, 1967, p. 479).

Under Confucian ethics, women, who are confined to the domestic domain and a life of subordination, have difficulty in developing an independent identity apart from their familial roles. As a result, "Chinese women, for lack of gender awareness, could not sufficiently resist their reductive roles as representations of masculinist ideology" (Lu, 1993, p. 18).

## FOOD IN WESTERN LITERARY REPRESENTATIONS OF WOMEN

Female subjectivity has been historically and culturally constructed through the symbolic meanings of food and body, not only in theories, but also in literature. In Western culture, women have often been associated with food. In "The Succulent Gender: Eat Her Softly" (1988), Eira Patnaik points out that one of the significant alimentary and culinary symbols is the edible commodity represented by women. The reason is that "women, when garnished, are comely to the eyes, smooth to the touch, fragrant to the nose and, with strawberry-flavoured lipstick, sensuous to the tongue" (Patnaik, 1988, p. 63). This parallels the characteristics of food that appeal to four of the five senses: sight, touch, taste and smell. Also, as providers of milk for infants, women are inseparable from the origin of nourishment (Patnaik, 1988, p. 65).

Food and women, therefore, become inseparable in people's minds and this is often reflected in Western culture. For instance, the Elizabethans often compared women's "complexion with whipped cream, her cheeks with ripening peaches and her lips with red cherries" (Patnaik, 1988, p. 59). In the seventeenth and eighteenth centuries, women's bodies were subjected to men's fantasies. For example, in Ben Jonson's *Volpone*:

> Volpone: Now torment on me! Squire her in;
> For she will enter, or dwell here forever:
> Nay, quickly. [retires to his couch]. That my fit were past! I fear
> A second hell too, that my loathing this.
> Will quite expel my appetite to the other
> Would she were taking now her tedious leave.
> Lord, how it threats me, what I am to suffer! (Jonson, 1993, pp. 25–31)

For the Victorians, both women and their kitchen functions were sanctified, seeing cookery as beguiling as women themselves (Patnaik, 1988, p. 61). The conjoining of women and food, as well as women and cookery, not only stresses women's socially constructed domestic role, but also their consumable qualities. The long-established assumptions about women's consumable and domestic roles in Western society were challenged by Mary Wollstonecraft in A *Vindication of the Rights of Woman* (1792). Since most women at that time were deprived of the right to education and were easily led by their emotions, Wollstonecraft encouraged them to be guided by reason. In her own words: "I may be allowed to infer that reason is absolutely necessary to enable a woman to perform any duty properly, and I must again repeat, that sensibility is not reason" (Wollstonecraft, 1993, p. 123). She believes that it is social conditions such as education and professional opportunities that have affected women's mindset on their social roles, and made them submissive in their behaviour. Her views are recognized as the early voice of women's rights and were considered radical at a time when women had no proper political, social and legal rights.

The roles of women in Victorian life were further questioned and changed as a result of the political and industrial revolutions, as well as the amendments to laws in favour of women in respect to education, property and the right to vote. The explosive growth of the textile industries brought hundreds of thousands of lower-class women into factory jobs with gruelling working conditions. In its disruption of family life and in its similarity to male labour, women's factory work presented an increasing challenge to traditional ideas about women's place being in the domestic sphere. In the political arena, it was abundantly evident that women continued to rank as second-class citizens. In early twentieth-century England, a law was passed to allow married women to possess property. The Factory Acts were also passed to protect working women by limiting their working hours to sixteen a day. Feminists, moreover, worked to enlarge educational opportunities for women. In 1848, the first college for women was established. By the end of the Victorian age, women could take degrees at twelve universities or colleges. There was also agitation for improved employment opportunities for women.

In spite of the numerous political and social revolutions, it took centuries for the social roles and positions of women to be improved. Upper- and middle-class Victorian women, married or unmarried, suffered painfully from the boredom of being restricted to the domestic sphere, as reflected in the experiences of Caroline Helstone in Charlotte Brontë's *Shirley* (1849). Living in her uncle's home, she finds no outlet for her energies, and her boredom becomes so intense that she longs for death. Some unmarried educated middle-class women became governesses. However, a governess expected no security of employment, and had an ambiguous status somewhere between a servant and a family member, as the humiliation of Sarah in John Fowles' *The French Lieutenant's Woman* (1969) illustrates. Although millions of middle- and lower-class English women in the Victorian age were employed as domestics, seamstresses, factory workers, or farm labourers, most of these jobs were onerous and low paying. Poor working conditions, therefore, drove thousands of women into prostitution, as depicted by Bernard Shaw in *Mrs. Warren's Profession* (1893). Driven by poverty and hunger, Mrs. Warren turns to prostitution. In her own words: "Do you think we were such fools as to let other people trade in our good looks by employing us as shopgirls, or barmaids, or waitresses, when we could trade in them ourselves and get all the profits instead of starvation wages? Not likely" (Shaw, 1993, pp. 1733–1734).

In the twentieth century, more female writers attempted to develop new notions of female identity and ideology by transgressing the traditional gender stereotypes and suggesting new types of thinking through the symbols of food and eating in literature. For instance, Virginia Woolf in *To the Lighthouse* (1927) advocates wholeness in personality through the signification of the dinner. In the novel, Mrs. Ramsay is the unifying power and the nurturing maternal force that provides understanding, sympathy and compassion to all the family members and friends who can experience a sense of sharing and belonging, especially during the evening meal: "They all sat separate. And the whole of the effort of merging and flowing and creating rested on her" (Woolf, 1927, p. 126). Mrs. Ramsay realizes the androgynous character of her marriage, in which she and her husband, characterizing femininity and masculinity respectively, join and form a unified whole. Lily, regarded as an inheritor of Mrs. Ramsay, steps beyond her accomplishments by developing an androgynous mind within herself, which is signified by drawing a tree in the middle of her painting. To remind herself to move the tree, she puts a salt-cellar on a budding flower in the pattern of the tablecloth. The tree represents an axis, while the salt represents a purifying force—it is used in the ritual of baptism and spells spiritual nourishment, promoting fraternity and communion (Knapp, 1988, p. 32). In the novel, Woolf breaks the masculine and feminine hierarchical opposition by advocating androgynous female subjectivity, which demonstrates the capacity of women to transcend the limitation of sexual difference and discrimination.

In *The Summer Before the Dark* (1973), Doris Lessing depicts Kate Brown's journey of self-examination and transformation. It reveals the social regulations of her subjectivity and her effort to refuse her socialization as sex-object, wife, woman-in-love and mother encoded in food and body. For example, she refuses to dye her white hair as a way to retain more control over her appearance. She also refuses to do some of the housework, which is always assumed to be a mother's duty. Through gaining more autonomy of the self and at the same time respecting social conventions, she maintains the balance between the private desire and public expectations.

## FOOD IN CHINESE LITERARY (RE/)CONSTRUCTION OF WOMEN

Female subjectivity has also been a theme in Chinese literature. For example, the conjoining of women and cookery is significantly presented in "The Newly Wedded Bride" (Xinjia niang), a Tang poem, by Wang Jian:

> Cooking on the third day after wedding,
> Wash the hands and make the soup;
> Not knowing the taste of mother-in-law,
> Let sister-in-law try it first. (*Poems and Pictures: Three Hundred Tang Poems*, p. 234)

This poem describes the newly wedded bride performing the duty of cooking. She delicately prepares the food and asks her sister-in-law to try it before serving. This poem not only shows the wife's domestic duty of cooking, but also her careful and conscientious manner in serving the husband's family, especially the mother-in-law, who embodies the discipline of women's code of conduct.

In modern Chinese literature, there has been a conscious attempt to reconstruct female subjectivity. During and after the May Fourth Movement of 1919, in which salvation of the silenced and subordinated woman was advocated, some female writers struggled to escape from the domestic realm by displaying a lack of appetite for food or indifference towards cooking and feeding babies. Resistance against food was presented as a means of resisting the traditional roles imposed upon women, and hence it was an attempt to construct a new independent female subjectivity. For example, in "Miss Sophie's Diary" (Shafei nüshi de riji) (1928), Ding Ling depicts Sophie as the most controversial image of "new woman" by explicitly displaying her female sexual desire in her diary. Sophie attempts to transgress the domestic sphere simply by developing a distaste for food. Performing the tedious act of boiling milk three or four times a day but never drinking it, Sophie rejects the doctor's advice to rest and eat more. The phrase "boiling milk" (re niunai) used by Sophie can, according to some critics, be interpreted as a "reference to masturbation" (Barlow and Bjorge, 1989, p. 359, note 1). The act of heating milk without drinking it is analogous to masturbation as a form of gratification. The metaphorical cross-reference between eating and sexuality signifies the female protagonist's incompetence in dealing with the outside world. As pointed out by Gang, "Sophie's lack of appetite can be seen as an apt metaphor for the empty routine of the everyday in which she is mired and from which she struggles to break free" (Gang, 1999, pp. 62–63).

In the upheaval of national crisis and social revolution in mainland China in the 1930s and 1940s, modern Chinese female writers often reflected in their writings an evolving female consciousness suffering from intense hunger. For instance, in *Market Street (Shangshijie)*, Xiao Hong depicts the anguish of the female protagonist who cannot bear the pain suffered by her husband, their sole breadwinner. When her husband says to her "Baby, you must be terribly hungry," she responds by saying "Not really." She was unable to tell her husband the truth that she was hungry when she saw that her husband's "clothing was frozen stiff from his search for something to eat" (Xiao, 1986, p. 12). This moving episode not only shows the reinforcement of the bond of love between the couple, but also the desire of the female protagonist to earn a living independently.

*Market Street* also describes the female protagonist's ambivalent feelings toward cooking. Being brought up in a wealthy family with maids attending to the daily housework, the female protagonist learns to cook only after getting married. In her first cooking experience, she finds herself transformed into a young housewife with ambivalent feelings. On the one hand, a well-prepared meal brings her pleasure: "By the time the rice was cooked, the potato slices were fried and ready. I opened the window and looked outside. Some puppies were playing in the courtyard" (Xiao, 1986, p. 37). On the other, any enthusiasm she feels for cooking is easily destroyed by the daily routine: "After the breakfast my time was spent washing the dishes, scrubbing the pot, cleaning off the stove top, and tidying up the shelf" (Xiao, 1986, p. 38). Through the description of the young housewife's daily life and experience, Xiao Hong vividly expresses the ambivalent attitude, of both enthusiasm and resentment, with which 1930s women regarded cooking.

After the establishment of the Communist state in China in 1949, greater equality between men and women was advocated, and this is reflected in Mao Zedong's well-known slogans: "Women uphold half the sky," and "What men can do, women can also do." However, in *Gender and Sexuality in Twentieth-century Chinese Literature and Society*, Tonglin Lu claims that since the old gender hierarchy has not been truly changed, women still encounter difficulties in handling demanding tasks in both the public and private spheres, while men only need to fulfil their duties in society, but not in the family (Lu, 1993, p. 7). In *Emerging from the Surface of History (Fuchu lishi dibiao, 1993)*, Meng Yue and Dai Jinhua maintain that the women's liberation has made little progress because women are displaced in a new order of collectivism. Women are not truly liberated in contemporary China and men are deprived of their privileges. Under the Communist ideology, both men and women lose their selves as individuals and have difficulty in establishing their gender identities (Lu, 1993, p. 8).

In the post–Cultural Revolution era, women generally have faced a crisis of identity when they tried to pursue an independent life and retain their dignity in mainland China. After the Communist Party took over China in 1949, women had a collective identity imposed on them. Before women had fully abandoned their Confucian relational roles, they had to adopt new revolutionary and productive roles of the Communist collective identity. These multiple role-identities therefore became a double burden to women trying to assert themselves. The ten-year Cultural Revolution destroyed most people's belief in traditional values as well as Communist ideology. The post–Cultural Revolution era then became an age in which people were lost in their search for identity, in defining themselves and looking for the meaning of life. Having been burdened with multiple roles and suffering from the loss of self, women were particularly bewildered in the assertion of their female subjecthood, making their voices "problematic, dispersed and disturbing" (Lu, 1993, p. 11).

In "The Ark" (Fangzhou) by Zhang Jie, the three female protagonists are examples of modern women who encounter enormous social pressure, especially in the conflict between career and family commitments. In order to realize their potential, they all have to reject traditional familial roles by ending their marriages and earning a living independently. They show the same ambivalent feelings towards housework as those expressed in Xiao Hong's *Market Street*:

> A large pile of dirty dishes had collected in the sink over the past two days, and not a single clean bowl remained in the cupboard. If they were to have breakfast Jinghua would have to do washing-up first, a job which none of them enjoyed. (Xiao, 1986, p. 119)

The female protagonists unconventionally refuse to do the traditionally feminine task of dishwashing. Also, although they think cooking is "much more pleasant and creative" (Xiao, 1986, p. 119), they make everything filthy and never do it properly. Their unenthusiastic attitudes towards the domestic duties of cooking and cleaning reflect their rejection of traditional female familial roles and desire to break free from the domestic domain in order to have more room for personal development.

In conclusion, I would like to restate my argument that through discarding the over-determined signification upon food and body, the female protagonists in these works generate an ambiguous and ambivalent attitude of both resentment and assertion toward food and body in the construction of a non-essentialist, multiple, and dynamic female subjectivity. The meanings attached to food, body and female subjectivity have been discussed in both Western and Chinese contexts. While Western theories focus on language and symbols, Chinese theories concentrate on moral regulations and the social roles of women. In modern English and Chinese literature, there has also been an attempt to construct female subjectivity through advocating an androgynous personality, refusing the socialization of women as sex-object, wife and mother, and displaying a lack of appetite for food or indifference towards cooking and feeding babies, thus opening more space for women to develop themselves.

## NOTE

1. To illustrate this idea, Foucault cites Christianity as an example: "The duty to accept a set of obligations, to hold certain books as permanent truth, to accept authoritarian decisions in matters of truth, not only to believe certain things but to show that one believes, and to accept institutional authority are all characteristic of Christianity" (1988, p. 8).

## REFERENCES

Anderson, E. N. (1988). *The Food of China*. New Haven, CT: Yale University Press.

Barlow, Tani E., and Gary J. Bjorge, eds. (1989). *I Myself Am a Woman: Selected Writings of Ding Ling*. Boston, MA: Beacon Press.

Barthes, Roland (1975). "Towards a Psychosociology of Contemporary Food Consumption." In Elborg Forster and Robert Forster, eds., *European Diet from Pre-Industrial to Modern Times*, pp. 47–59. New York: Harper & Row.

Brontë, Charlotte (1981). *Shirley* (1849). Oxford: Oxford University Press.

Brooks, Ann (1997). *Postfeminisms: Feminism, Cultural Theory and Cultural Forms*. London: Routledge.

Butler, Judith (1993). *Bodies That Matter: On the Discursive Limits of "Sex."* New York: Routledge.

Charles, Nickie, and Marion Kerr (1988). *Women, Food and Families*. Manchester: Manchester University Press.

Chiu, Vermier Y. (1966). *Marriage Laws and Customs of China*. Hong Kong: The Chinese University of Hong Kong.

Chow, Rey (1993). "Against the Lures of Diaspora: Minority Discourse, Chinese Women, and Intellectual Hegemony." In Tonglin Lu, ed., *Gender and Sexuality in Twentieth-century Chinese Literature and Society*, pp. 23–45. Albany: State University of New York Press.

Confucius (1967). *Liji* [The Books of Rites]. Trans. James Legge. Vol. 1. New York: University Books, Inc.

Counihan, Carole M. (1999). *The Anthropology of Food and Body: Gender, Meaning, and Power*. New York: Routledge.

Counihan, Carole M., and Steven L. Kaplan, eds. (1998). *Food and Gender: Identity and Power*. Amsterdam: Harwood Academic Publishers.

DeVault, Marjorie L. (1991). *Feeding the Family: The Social Organization of Caring as Gendered Work*. Chicago: University of Chicago Press.

Ding Ling (1982). "Shafei nüshi de riji" [Miss Sophie's diary] (1928). In Ding Ling, *Ding Ling wenji* [Writings of Ding Ling], pp. 43–82. Changsha: Hunan renmin chubanshe.

Foucault, Michel (1988). "Technologies of the Self." In L. H. Martin, H. Gutman, and P. H. Hutton, eds., *Technologies of the Self: A Seminar with Michel Foucault*, pp. 16–49. London: Tavistock Publications.

Fowles, John (1998). *The French Lieutenant's Woman* (1969). Boston, MA: Back Bay Books.

Gang, Yue (1999). *The Mouth That Begs: Hunger, Cannibalism and the Politics of Eating in Modern China*. Durham, NC: Duke University Press.

Jonson, Ben (1993). *Volpone* (1606). In M. H. Abrams et al., eds., *The Norton Anthology of English Literature* (6th ed.), Vol. 1, pp. 1129–1217. New York: W. W. Norton.

Knapp, Bettina (1988). "Virginia Woolf's 'Boeuf en Daube.'" In David Bevan, ed., *Literary Gastronomy*, pp. 29–36. Amsterdam: Rodopi.

Kristeva, Julia (1981). "Woman Can Never Be Defined." Trans. Marilyn A. August. In Elaine Marks and Isabelle de Courtivron, eds., *New French Feminisms: An Anthology*, pp. 137–141. New York: Schocken Books.

Lai, T. C. (1978). *Chinese Food for Thought*. Hong Kong: Hong Kong Book Centre.

Lessing, Doris May (1973). *The Summer Before the Dark*. New York: Knopf.

Lévi-Strauss, Claude (1968). *Structural Anthropology*, Vol. 1. Harmondsworth, England: Penguin.

Lévi-Strauss, Claude (1986). *The Raw and the Cooked*. Trans. John Weightman and Doreen Weightman. Harmondsworth, England: Penguin.

Lu, Tonglin (1993). "Introduction." In Tonglin Lu, ed., *Gender and Sexuality in Twentieth-century Chinese Literature and Society*, pp. 1–22. Albany: State University of New York Press.

Lupton, Deborah (1996). *Food, the Body and the Self*. London: Sage Publications.

Meng Yue, and Dai Jinhua (1993). *Fuchu lishi dibiao: Zhongguo xiandai nüxing wenxue yanjiu* [Emerging from the surface of history: The study of modern Chinese female literature]. Taipei: Shibao wenhua chuban shiye youxian gongsi.

Mennell, Stephen, Anne Murcott and Anneke H. van Otterloo (1992). *The Sociology of Food: Eating, Diet and Culture*. London: Sage Publications.

Mintz, Sidney W. (1985). *Sweetness and Power: The Place of Sugar in Modern History*. New York: Viking.

Mo Yan (1997). "Wangbuliao chi" [Can't forget about eating]. *Tianya*, No. 5, 92–96.

Murcott, Anne (1983). "Cooking and the Cooked: A Note on the Domestic Preparation of Meals." In Anne Murcott, ed., *The Sociology of Food and Eating: Essays on the Sociological Significance of Food*, pp. 178–185. Aldershot, England: Gower Publishing.

Orbach, Susie (1997). *Fat Is a Feminist Issue: The Anti-Diet Guide for Women*. New York: Galahad Books.

Patnaik, Eira (1988). "The Succulent Gender: Eat Her Softly." In David Bevan, ed., *Literary Gastronomy*, pp. 59–74. Amsterdam: Rodopi.

Shanghai cishu chubanshe (1997). *Shi yu hua: Tangshi sanbai shou* [Poems and pictures: Three hundred Tang poems]. Shanghai: Shanghai cishu chubanshe.

Shaw, Bernard (1993). *Mrs. Warren's Profession* (1893). In M. H. Abrams et al., eds., *The Norton Anthology of English Literature* (6th ed.), Vol. 1, pp. 1714–1754. New York: W. W. Norton.

Sun Lung-kee (1983). *Zhongguo wenhua de shenceng jiegou* [The deep structure of Chinese culture]. Hong Kong: Jixianshe.

Weedon, Chris (1997). *Feminist Practice and Poststructuralist Theory* (1987). Oxford: Blackwell.

Wollstonecraft, Mary (1993). *A Vindication of the Rights of Woman* (1792). In M. H. Abrams et al., eds., *The Norton Anthology of English Literature* (6th ed.), Vol. 1, pp. 101–126. New York: W. W. Norton.

Woolf, Virginia (1927). *To the Lighthouse*. New York: Harcourt Brace.

Xiao Hong (1986). *Shangshijie* [Market street: A Chinese woman in Harbin]. Trans. Howard Goldblatt. Seattle: University of Washington Press.

Zhang, Jie (1993). *The Ark* (1986). San Francisco: China Books & Periodicals.

## GLOSSARY

bu 補

buyao 補藥

chao wending 超穩定

chi 吃

chi (qi) 氣

chi cu 吃醋

chi jing 吃驚

chi ku 吃苦

chi lao ben 吃老本

chi li 吃力

chi nai 吃奶

chi yaba kui 吃啞巴虧

chi yao 吃藥

Ding Ling 丁玲

"Fangzhou" 〈方舟〉

hehe 和合

hehexing 和合性

jinbu 進補

lianzi 蓮子

*Liji*《禮記》

min yi shi wei tian 民以食為天

Mo Yan 莫言

nian sheng gui zi 年生貴子

nian zi 年子

san cong si de 三從四德

"Shafei nüshi de riji" 〈莎菲女士的日記〉

*Shangshijie* 《商市街》

shen 身

shenti hua 身體化

"Wangbuliao chi" 〈忘不了吃〉

Xiao Hong 蕭紅

xin 心

"Xinjia niang" 〈新嫁娘〉

*Yili* 《儀禮》

yin 陰

Zhang Jie 張潔

*Zhouli* 《周禮》

## 5 Women as Human vs. Women as Women

### *Female Consciousness in Modern Chinese Women's Literature**

QIAO YIGANG

MODERN CHINESE WOMEN'S LITERATURE CAME into being during the New Culture Movement of 1919 and it has matured over the past century amidst the upheavals which have occurred in Chinese society. With its quest for an intellectual re-orientation, this literary movement has contributed to the modern development of Chinese literature through its transformation of an earlier style of women's writing, which embodies patriarchal values and is constrained by a narrowly defined literary view. This essay aims to take a broader perspective in examining the intellectual progress and orientations of modern Chinese women's literature by relating them to historical and social developments.

In its history of a hundred years, modern Chinese women's literature has gone through a series of transformations that are closely related to changes in women's lifestyles in modern China. The variety and psychological depth of traditional women's literature are comparatively restricted. These writings express mainly personal emotions within confined spaces, such as life within palace walls, boudoirs and gardens. Under the confinement of patriarchal culture, traditional women rarely had a rich and free life of their own. It was therefore difficult for them to develop profound perceptions of life and intellectual pursuits, and so most traditional women's writings show a strong tendency towards being personal and thematically confined, and the aesthetic principles employed are relatively monotonous.

Modern Chinese women's literature arose in the midst of social revolution and developed in the process of subverting tradition. A precedent was set for the new orientation of women's literary activities with the works of Qiu Jin, a female poet and key figure in the democratic

---

\* Translated from the Chinese by Katrine Wong and Kwok-kan Tam; revised by Yomei Shaw and Terry Siu-han Yip.

revolution at the beginning of the twentieth century. Qiu Jin instils into her works the realization of a new feminine consciousness. In her writing, she reveals the great impact of social changes on the emergence of a new mentality in Chinese women intellectuals, whose modern identity is marked by the pursuit of new ideas. Beginning with Qiu Jin's works, the sentimentalism that traditionally characterized women in Chinese literature started to give way to a concern for society, with a greater sense of political awareness. To be creative is no longer a matter of simply being productive within one's personal space, rather, artistic creativity takes place within a broad socio-historical realm that makes literary activity a sophisticated process of social engagement. In this sense, May Fourth women writers and their successors have expanded the space for women's literature through their achievements in constantly breaking out of both personal and social confinements. Such progress reflects the history of twentieth-century literature. The political implications of modern Chinese women's literature can be seen in the growth of a new female awareness that calls for independence, resistance against patriarchal culture, and a heightened self-awareness.

Chinese women's literature over the past hundred years is often characterized by the optimistic desire for the social liberation of women. Among the cultural issues, gender ranks as the most crucial in different historical contexts and it manifests itself in various ways, some more explicit than others. The most characteristic of the age's concerns is women's redefinition of themselves as human beings first, and women second.

Being confined for millennia in a patriarchal society, not only did Chinese women lose their dignity and rights as human beings and become slaves to men's greater political, social and economic power, they also lost the opportunity to pursue their own intellectual interests. They were not encouraged to have their own ideas, and had to follow practices of the phallocentric society. Such a situation began to change substantially with the May Fourth women writers in 1919. As a new creative force, May Fourth women writers broke through the tiny circle of traditional women's literature for the first time, and developed a new humanistic way of understanding their female identities. They filled their works with a new awareness and passionate desire for the awakening of a female identity. In different literary genres such as poetry, novels, essays, and drama, they not only articulated their dissatisfaction with the lack of status for women in traditional society, they also displayed an intellectual horizon which was different from that of women scholars of ancient times. On the whole, they showed a strong desire for more participation in social life, and demanded to have their own voice.

A growing sense of social responsibility can be found in many modern Chinese women writers, who have adopted a new attitude towards writing and see it as a way to fulfil their historical mission. The scope of their writing is greatly expanded, and is filled with a strong passion for social progress. Whether in works dealing with specific socio-political issues in the 1930s and 1940s through to the 1960s, or in works which explore issues of human dignity, values, rights, responsibilities, and weaknesses in the 1980s and 1990s, all of these writers show their concern for women's self-awareness and self-realization. Modern Chinese women writers are deeply concerned with opening up a new space for women's participation in social life; their yearning for independence, dignity, and self-empowerment is a crucial aspect of modern Chinese female consciousness.

During the May Fourth period, the quest for a self-identity was displayed in women's writing that expresses a strong desire for freedom in love and marriage, freedom of the self, and economic independence. After the 1930s, women's writing began to merge with revolutionary literature and became alienated from concerns of feminine identity and power. It exhibited women's growing awareness of themselves as members of society, which was a trend that implicitly called for women's self-denial by urging them to immerse themselves into the mainstream of the age. Women writers of the new era since the 1980s, however, are able to reach new heights in their examination of life. After all the difficulties the women's movement in China has experienced, Chinese women writers now have come to understand that changes in the socio-political system alone do not make Chinese women free. For Chinese women to be free, there must be a revolution in social consciousness together with women's awareness of the need to have spiritual independence. China's open-door policy and reform have given women a new opportunity for development: a new generation of Chinese women writers have emerged. These women writers have an even more intense desire for spiritual liberation and are eager participants in the search for meaning and value in women's lives.

In literary writings, when a woman's ideal comes into conflict with social reality and historical events, many women writers will let their characters be resolute in making a decision that defends female individuality, while others will portray the perplexity and frustration in their troubled female characters. And today, when one re-reads the significant novels about women that came out at the beginning of the new era in the 1980s, such as Zhang Jie's "The Ark" (Fangzhou) and Zhang Xinxin's "On the Same Horizon" (Zai tongyi dipingxian shang), one can still vividly experience the bitter struggle of Chinese women who fight for spiritual independence; the steps they have taken are only the initial steps necessary for women to become individual beings. As a matter of fact, what the female protagonists refuse in these works is never marriage itself, but the inferiority of women in patriarchal society, and what they prize is not just a career, but the value of each woman's being an independent individual. Modern women are no longer subordinate to the family or tied to men; though they still long for love, the love they hope for is a love of equality that promises to preserve social values. The ideal man from a woman's point of view is no longer the master of her soul, but a soul-mate who lives and walks with her. All in all, these women are looking for their other half and for fulfilment in life under the banner of independence.

## GENDER AWARENESS IN WOMEN WRITERS

At the same time, some women's writings explore women's experience, physical and spiritual, in their newly redefined roles as women in modern society. They write about corruption in society as well as political inequality between men and women. At the beginning of the Literary Revolution in the late 1910s, writers like Bing Xin already wrote on such themes, though not in an explicitly rebellious way. In later works by Ding Ling and Xiao Hong, a strong desire to resist patriarchal culture can be seen in the characterization of their heroines. In the new era of the 1980s, there is a growing awareness of gender issues in the new generation of women writers. They yearn for greater freedom in life, some of them even proposing to look at society, human relations and women's status from feminist perspectives. A large proportion of these works present themselves as challenges to phallocentric culture through the construction of a new feminine subjectivity that emphasizes female sensibility. These works have exerted a great impact in China and caused much controversy.

Just like women's liberation, a broad concept that can only be defined in relation to specific cultural contexts, the development of women's literature is inseparable from the existing literary tradition whose core values, in reality, are masculine. Traditional culture has the male as its centre, and has been developed in accordance with male needs and male psychology. In traditional Western literature, women are sometimes described as either Virgin Mary or whore. The chaste and beautiful goddess and the charming femme fatale are the two polarized possibilities. Other stereotypes of women include witches, jealous wives, cultured ladies, chaste martyrs and national heroines. Yet in examining the assumptions behind such stereotyping of women, the condemnation of promiscuity and the demand for chastity are reflections of male fantasies (Zhou, 2002). However, it matters little whether patriarchal standards worship or denigrate women. What is worth noting is that women have not only lost their true nature when they are vilified; they have also lost their selves when they are deified. Simone de Beauvoir points out in *The Second Sex* that "Few myths have been more advantageous to the ruling caste than the myth of woman: it justifies all privileges and even authorizes their abuse" (Beauvoir, 1997, p. 285). Eileen Chang (Zhang Ailing) sees very clearly that this strategy has been practised in the phallocentric society. As she points out in "About Women" (Tan nüren), Luoshen, the Chinese goddess, who has been described as "light as a frightened swan flapping into the air and fragile as a dragon swimming in water," is merely an ancient beauty; the much worshipped Bodhisattva/Guanyin is nothing more than a bare-footed ancient beauty; the half-nude big and muscular Greek statue is just a sportswoman, and the blonde Virgin Mary is simply a pretty grandmother who has been breast-feeding in public for more than a thousand years (Zhang, 1996).

Along with succinctly unveiling the masculine discourse behind such activities as the worship of the Virgin Mary, Chang has also critiqued the youthful and naïve romantic flavour commonly found in Chinese women writers during the early awakening years of the May Fourth Movement. When the May Fourth women writers were pursuing individual liberation under the banner of women's rights as humans, they were also creating illusions about the female sex by bestowing upon women the holiness of chastity. Chang bid farewell to these illusions in the 1940s, when she adopted the image of "Mother Earth" in her presentation of women.

Women's writings in China have faced unprecedented challenges from Western feminist ideas, which have come at the same time as social changes in the new market economy over the past twenty years. Many women writers, while continually carrying out new experiments in literature, remain conscious of the need to guard against the stance that women should be treated first and foremost as individual human beings.

On the one hand, they present women using a new aesthetics based on feminist thinking, lifestyle, disposition and feelings; on the other, they keep reminding themselves that they should not degrade themselves after they have broken away from the confinement of phallocentric culture. There is truly a great risk that women might fall into the trap of their newly acquired freedom and become corrupt. The most unfortunate development is that women's liberation seems to be fated in the sense that it has to be part of society's progress. Though authors may have different strategies in their writings, on the whole they have to fall within the limits of culture and history. This presents a problem for women's literature: history provides women writers with opportunities, but it also creates obstacles.

## GENDERED SUBJECTIVITY AND THE COUNTER-IMAGE OF WOMEN

Displaying and voicing the dynamics of gender oppression—including repression of social existence, psychology, sex, and emotion—that women suffer under a patriarchal culture has in itself been a theme in women's writings. The exploration of women's sufferings does not only deal with the hegemony of the other sex in social life, it also problematizes the predicament of women in terms of their self-understanding and relation to society. Embedded in this self-examination is an inward turn, which signifies Chinese women's growing consciousness of modernity.

During the May Fourth period of the late 1910s, female identity was realized mainly as an understanding of the relation between women as independent human beings and the outside world. Women writers at that time were concerned about the social oppression of women, yet they did not try to carry out a serious analysis of women's identity. Hence, women's writings in that period are mostly concerned with description of women's misery, protest against patriarchal (and Confucian) oppression, praise for personal liberation and freedom in marriage. Thirty years later, in the 1940s, the development of female identity fermented in silence when there were radical changes in the social and political realms of life. Some women writers would regard literature as a means of salvation for the country and incorporate nationalist themes in their pursuit of more humane treatment of women. Others continued in their belief in writing from a female perspective, focusing on women's experiences and portraying women's lives. Either way, women writers were concerned with how women's fate is predicated by the historical age. The former approach is doubtless common among many women writers whose works are infused with the spirit of the age and show less concern for women's distinct qualities. In such works, the portrayal of nationalist consciousness takes precedence over the portrayal of women. The latter approach, concerned with portraying the world from a woman's perspective, is less popular and is found mainly among writers living in the metropolis. For example, from the 1930s to early 1940s, writers like Ling Shuhua and Chen Ying wrote about the new problems faced by women who have gained freedom of marriage. In their works, the life of a *tai-tai*, or married woman, as the dependent of a man is questioned. Apparently, their writings, though inadequate and limited in critical vision, reveal the fact that women sense the danger of lacking self-identity, which they strive to build up by turning inward.

Eileen Chang, on the other hand, employs a cold and detached viewpoint to look at women. She knows very clearly that the culture in which women live is a male culture and that women "are a lot more miserable than men" in life. The phallocentric culture has inculcated in them "the virtues of a wife," a set of beliefs that springs from the roots of a deep-seated tradition. Nonetheless, women are partly responsible for their miseries: "It won't work if you just blame others." Although individuals are ineffectual in transcending the restrictions and limitations of society, they have "some degree of freedom" in their personal choice. Therefore apart from pronouncing aloud the weaknesses and flaws in women, Chang also intentionally exposes the spitefulness in women's lives. She believes that "putting all the blame and responsibilities on men" will not produce "a thorough answer" (Chang, 1996). The turn towards introspection of Chang's female characters indicates important progress in the growth of modern female identity. It also reflects Chang's negative view of women.

Eileen Chang's depiction of the frustrations of maternal love has attracted the attention of many critics and readers. The figure of Qiqiao in "The Golden Cangue" (Jinsuo ji) is an example of a mother who lacks motherliness in any idealized sense. Chang portrays Qiqiao's morbid state of mind, ruthlessly disclosing the inner reality in this character. In a sense, Qiqiao is a deconstruction and counter-image of the idealized mother figure that emerged after the May Fourth Movement. The acclamation of maternal love has seemingly ascertained and brought to light the significance of the value of women. However, the adoption of the image of "virtuous wife and good mother"—a notion that is pervaded with male values—produces a dilemma: the more women are praised for their maternal love, the harder it is for them to break away from the constraints of the traditional roles imposed by patriarchal discourse. The reconstruction of the female self therefore requires a deeper critique of the patriarchal discourse.

It is impossible for the May Fourth women writers to transcend historical limits in their struggle for self-autonomy. In many of them, there is a strong bent towards narcissism in their writings, which they have inherited from traditional values. However, after the 1930s, when women writers were able to expand their scope and delve into matters related to society, politics and even the bloodshed of the battlefield, they neglected the need to reflect on women's existence and the meaning of their lives. In their portrayal, the mother is presented as a social self, whose love is merged with that for the country and the nation. Writing from her unique background in the 1940s, Eileen Chang looked at women from a different perspective and held a different stance on the glorification of maternal love. "The Golden Cangue" and other stories in *Legend* (*Chuanqi*) depict the numbness, ignorance, and mental perversion of women in circumstances where they are enslaved, suppressed, and fatally mistreated in traditional society. In these works, readers are confronted with scenes of the bleak reality of being a woman, which are so shocking simply because they counter the commonly accepted image of the mother.

Chang's description of women's imprisoned soul and analysis of the female unconscious reveals the truth that although the lifestyle of urban women has been revolutionized, the mindset of many women has not undergone any significant change. She also shows that while ostensibly a woman may have transformed from being a slave, deep down she is still an accessory, like a vase, for men. Such a phenomenon is the result of traditional beliefs and women's lack of self-esteem. Whether they are old-fashioned women, like Cao Qiqiao, or new women, like Bai Liusu and Ge Weilong, women in Chang's works are "subjects with agency," albeit limited in their worlds. They live under the threat of traditional culture that drives them gradually into "a corner without light." Chang senses a crisis in the portrayal of women. She measures their lives not by the yardstick of their contributions to society, but by the inner reality of women's existence. In so doing, she avoids the Bing Xin–style "idealization of the mother," which is constructed on the endorsement of male values. Chang does not attack men for the sake of fighting for women's rights. In contrast to Ding Ling, who presents women as arrogant and wild (for example the character Sophie), Chang's works may not point to a way out for women, but they do show not only how suffocating a traditional lifestyle can be, but also that the traditional way of life leads only to a dead end. In Chang's writings, there is the suggestion of awakening to self-awareness in women, which can be seen as an important stage of modernity in the history of modern Chinese women's literature.

## FEMININITY IN MODERN CHINESE WOMEN'S CONSCIOUSNESS

It is not hard to see the close correlation between the feminist orientation and creative principles of Chinese women's literature. Women in the old days were in an inferior position and their sexuality and gender characteristics were misrepresented. As a result, the consciousness that women are individuals has been repressed. The genesis of modern female consciousness of individuality cannot be separated from its socio-cultural contexts. The advent of female individuality in modern China has gone through a series of obstacles, with women's literature developing amidst the conflict between two broad ideas, "women's social awareness" and "women's self-awareness." Needless to say, the rise of female individuality has had a great effect upon women's literary production. On the one hand, for a long time more outstanding achievements could be seen in women's works that deal with social life. This is a phenomenon that illustrates the historic liberation of women in terms of their participation in society and their achievements in aesthetic creativity after they have broken away from the confinements of women's traditional roles. It also shows that modern female consciousness itself embodies a social dimension. On the other hand, literary production that has a strong female self-awareness is equally indispensable in women's literature. It gives women's literature an authentic and unique position in the literary world. Experiments with new subjects, themes and artistic techniques have not only expanded the scope of women's literature, but also created an inner psychological space in the representation of women, which is vital to the modern development of Chinese literature.

Women's self-consciousness and gender expectations are historical formations, whose cultural meanings also evolve with history. In the late nineteenth and early twentieth century, when China was undergoing a cultural change inspired by Western ideas of individualism, the idea of "women as individuals" began to take shape in the newly emergent Chinese female consciousness. When the forerunners of the democratic revolution, such as Qiu Jin, were awakened to the significance of women's possessing identity as human beings rather than as females and when the idea of individuality first received recognition, female consciousness also witnessed changes in meaning. Female consciousness in the modern sense still embodies the idea of women being a natural/ biological formation, but the associations with women as social beings have actually changed. The most important of these changes lies in the recognition of women as individuals. Such recognition has the social significance of raising the status of women in society, because as human beings and individuals women are equal to men. With this recognition, an emphasis is placed on the struggle for women's social rights, that is to say, women's rights are seen as part of human rights. Hence, women, not just men, are part of the human race. After the late 1920s, when class struggles and national conflicts became matters of life and death in China, women writers began to take up various stances in society and held a variety of different opinions towards women's identity as individuals and collectively as women. Out of the need to resist the inferior position imposed upon women and their sense of commitment to social revolution, most contemporary women writers consciously depict characters who deviate from the traditional norm in their characterization. In so doing, they believe that women can go beyond the confines of the private self by integrating with the masses. These writers not only see humanity as the foremost important quality in women's new identity, they see it as their *only* quality. For these writers, the sufferings of women are considered part of the disasters the Chinese people experience in class struggles, or in national conflicts. They believe that the liberation of women cannot be achieved without the liberation of class and the nation. All such understandings of women and their roles are reflected in literature, resulting in a de-emphasis on sex/gender, and a growing emphasis on social consciousness, which is in effect an erasing of femininity.

Other women writers, who emphasize the idea of a collective feminine identity, think that equality between men and women does not have to mean the masculinization of women. Human individuality and femininity are not incompatible as part of women's identity. They highly value a woman's duty as a mother, which they consider the lifeblood of the continuity of the nation, but they stress that the recognition of women's feminine identity is indispensable to the completeness of women's personality, mental health, and lived experience. Believing in differences between the two sexes, they think that ignoring the feminine traits of women will lead only to an abnormal and incomplete life that is unfavourable to women's personal development. Taking this as the point of departure, they portray women with feminine personality traits, sometimes even in an artistically elevated manner. Their works contain images that do not just celebrate feminine charm, but also criticize the weaknesses of women. These are also powerful images that reflect in a realistic way the injustice done to women and their sufferings in traditional culture. Such a portrayal of women is filled with cries of protest.

From the 1930s and 1940s up to 1966, as a result of socio-political changes in China that demanded a reconsideration of women's identity, there was a tendency in literature to emphasize women's social roles. However, after the mid-1980s, with the changes in society and the resurgence of individualism in female consciousness, an emphasis on the female self was allowed to develop. While recognizing the importance of equality between men and women, some women writers place their emphasis on the differences between men and women. Others focus on the significance of sex in women's lives by probing the most private areas in women's psychology and physiology and exploring the deep-seated natural and social elements hidden in female consciousness. Among these, some, through narrating women's stories, tell of women's fate and their tragedy of being reduced to the sex objects of men. Some dig into women's lives and expose the rivalry and jealousy among women so as to examine the warped female soul and its repressed desires as a form of resistance. There are also women writers who depict private experience in the female body with scenes of sexual perversion. A different world of experience is thus exposed in this new female identity. Women are presented in their inner selves in the relations between soul and body and between the two sexes. Many of these works contain explicit descriptions of a new female consciousness, which points to a quest for the meaning of women's existence in the process of attaining their liberation. They reflect the ideal of merging female awareness with human consciousness. In this process, one can see the influence of Western culture and philosophical ideas not only in the struggle of Chinese women for their rights, but also in the writers' views on femininity. Chinese women writers have now moved beyond the basic demand for equality between men and women in their campaign for women's liberation. They deal with themes of female individuality, women's values and spiritual freedom. Some young women writers are deeply influenced by Western postmodernist thinking, and in their works they experiment with strategies in the subversion of phallocentric culture. The wide range of the above examples indicates that Chinese women's literature has begun to move into a new arena of international postmodern visions.

On the whole, Chinese women's literature is a process of experimentation with new identities of women in the private and social domains of life. It signifies a historical development in Chinese femininity, particularly in the recognition of women as individuals who are equal to men. Strong desires for individual liberation and self-realization can be seen in many works that present new images of women. The achievements of Chinese women writers in the twentieth century are, to a certain extent, part of the search for modernity in Chinese literature.

## REFERENCES

Beauvoir, Simone de (1997). *The Second Sex*. Trans. and ed. H. M. Parshley. London: Vintage. First English translation published in 1952 by Knopf, New York.

Zhang Ailing (Chang, Eileen) (1977). "Jinsuo ji" [The golden cangue]. In *Zhang Ailing duanpian xiaoshuo ji* [Collected short stories by Zhang Ailing], pp. 150–202. Taipei: Huangguan chubanshe.

Zhang Ailing (Chang, Eileen) (1996). "Tan nüren" [On women]. In *Zhang Ailing sanwen quanji* [Complete collection of essays by Zhang Ailing], pp. 102–113. Zhengzhou: Zhongyuan nongmin chubanshe.

Zhang Ailing (Chang, Eileen) (2000). *Chuanqi* [Legend]. Beijing: Zhongguo qingnian chubanshe.

Zhang, Jie (1993). *The Ark* (1986). San Francisco: China Books & Periodicals.

Zhou Zuoren (2002). "Bei gouyuan tongxin" [Letters from the northern trench] (1922). In Zhou Zuoren, *Tan hu ji* [Collection of essays on tigers], pp. 272–279. Revised by Zhi An. Shijiazhuang: Hebei jiaoyu chubanshe.

## GLOSSARY

Bai Liusu 白流蘇

Bing Xin 冰心

Cao Qiqiao 曹七巧

Chen Ying 沉櫻

*Chuanqi*《傳奇》

Ding Ling 丁玲

"Fangzhou"〈方舟〉

Ge Weilong 葛薇龍

"Jinsuo ji" 〈金鎖記〉

Ling Shuhua 凌叔華

Qiu Jin 秋瑾

"Tan nüren" 〈談女人〉

"Zai tongyi dipingxian shang" 〈在同一地平線上〉

Zhang Ailing (Eileen Chang) 張愛玲

Zhang Jie 張潔

Zhang Xinxin 張辛欣

# 6 Liberation of Femininity? Women's Poetry in Post-Mao China

LISA LAI-MING WONG

ALTHOUGH "LIBERATION" HAS BEEN ONE of the preoccupations of Chinese intellectuals in the last century, women's liberation remains an incomplete project. From the point of view of Tonglin Lu, "the ideological basis for the traditional patriarchy has not truly been shaken by the aborted women's emancipation in China" (Lu, 1993, p. 8). As the May Fourth reforms and the socialist revolution have done little to rock the formidable gender hierarchy, alternative ways to achieve equality between the sexes are explored. In the literary milieu, the corpus of women's literature produced in the post-Mao era has caught much critical attention and is considered exemplary of a liberation of femininity.

Collaborative efforts of editors and critics to bring about a new tradition of women's poetry are evident in the early 1990s. Cui Weiping sees two kinds of women: "The difference between women who write and those who do not is no less significant than that between women and men" (Cui, 1993, p. 7).[1] Women who write are considered progressive and free. This liberation of women poets is often portrayed in a metaphor of flight. For example, to Cui Weiping, women poets are a flying species. Similarly, quoting Shao Wei's metaphor, "Let us stay together, let us fly," Lin Danya envisages that young women poets of China will soar to new heights through language in the twenty-first century (Lin, 1995, pp. 343–344). Besides, social mobility and financial independence enable women to possess a private space. Depicting a woman's autonomy in her own room, Yi Lei's most controversial poem, "The Bedroom of a Single Woman" (Dushen nüren de woshi) is celebrated by Liu Qunwei (penname, Huang Lin) as an assertion of women's independence and liberation (Liu, 1995, pp. 104–112). Single women, as the "aristocrats" among women, possess a room of their own and thus enjoy the freedom to choose their desired way of life. Deeply concerned with the great socialist project, many critics' discussions of feminist poetics are orientated towards a bright future.

Described as independent intellectually and financially, the "liberated" women of post-Mao China are readily appropriated in another grand narrative of revolution. A typical example is Shen Qi's preface to an anthology of women's poetry, *The Scarlet Singing* (*Xianhong de gechang*). Shen's essay sounds like a communist manifesto for a poetry revolution that aims to eradicate gender differences in order to attain a genderless utopia for poetry. Women poets are highly commended for having cleansed their works of "feminine" traits and made their poetry "masculine" in style:

> This is in fact a universal change—female literature, including female poetry, rises from every corner of the world and has become a major legacy of human civilization in the twentieth century. This is exactly what the new women poets have contributed in the mainland—to let Chinese poetry participate fully in the historical progress of the modernist world poetry. (Shen, 1994, p. 2)

Despite his positive appraisal of women's poetry, Shen's comment displays a tendency towards oversimplifying gender issues in creative writing. The successive leaps from the "feminine," to the "masculine," and finally to the "genderless" are, according to him, an inevitable process in human civilization. Women's poetry is recognized in order that a national or international historical mission can be fulfilled.

What appeals to me as important in these critical evaluations of women's poetry is the emphasis on "liberation," which is frequently highlighted as an achievement of women writers since the late 1980s. In order to pit this new wave of liberation against its aborted predecessors, the iconoclastic edges of the word used in different periods are note-worthy. To the May Fourth generation, "liberation" means to be free from the traditional Confucian shackles. Conventionally, the virtues of women are defined by their service to men such as their fathers, husbands and sons, at different stages of their lives. In resistance to this suppression under the patriarchal system, new women refused to be chained by men to a homebound, subservient role. To liberate oneself begins with standing on one's own feet and being able to walk away as one likes. The abolition of foot-binding, physically and metaphorically, implied this rebellion against the confinement to a domestic space. In general, the new youth saw family as a miniature of the patriarchal system. The defiant act of leaving home thus opened a promising path to liberation and self-realization. As pointed out by Kwok-kan Tam, Ibsen's autonomous Nora was considered a model of the new woman for the Chinese in the 1920s (Tam, 1998, pp. 95–105). However, exploitations of women were then taken as a social evil to be solved by the new China. Subsumed under the nation-building project, women's liberation did not stand out as a gender issue.

Departure from home marks the emergence of the individual self. To position oneself in a public space so as to be seen and heard is a step towards individualism and equality. During the socialist revolution, such demands for a public representation seemed to be fully answered by another liberation of women. Mao Zedong implemented equality between men and women by designating women as co-upholders of the sky with men. In the communist propaganda, women and men were portrayed as comrades standing side by side clothed in a *uniform(ed)* identity. A collective self was thus constructed by class rather than by gender. Women were assigned an equal share of labour in the workforce: as Mao's slogan says, "What men can do, women can also do." Through this emancipation, new women acquired a genderless self that served the Party for a great national cause. Assuming a political role engaged with a clearly defined external world, women during the Mao years apparently enjoyed an unprecedented equal share of public presence.

Along with the economic and ideological liberation policies since the latter half of the 1980s, there has been a new surge in women's liberation known as the "Sex Revolution" or "Sex Emancipation" movement. Political and ideological censures of open discussion about sex are challenged. Free exposition of distinct features of the female body and sexuality is deployed by women writers as a means to denounce the collective, genderless self. Such discursive practice of sex is viewed as a liberating act. In this paper, these recent claims of "liberation of femininity" will be examined with reference to women's poetry written in the post-Mao period. The women poets selected are Zhai Yongming, Tang Yaping, Yi Lei and others, whose works have invited the label "women's poetry" that situates them in a special gendered position in poetry writing.[2] They are regarded as different from earlier women poets such as Zheng Min and Shu Ting for their conscious exploration of female traits. In the following discussion, issues about the liberation of femininity will be explored along three paths.[3] First is women's attempt to go home. To recover femininity, which has been suppressed by the uniformed collective self, women speakers in the poems seek a gender model from their grandmothers and mothers at home. Second is the direct, exuberant expression of exclusive female experiences, such as pregnancy and childbirth, which are biologically given. In this case, femininity is foregrounded by means of politics of difference. Third is the fashioning of feminine consciousness through the construction of voice and space for the autonomous "new women."

## RETURN TO THE MOTHER AT HOME

Different from male initiation, which necessitates a departure from home to confront the outside world, female initiation is closely linked to physical changes of the body. A girl's separation from childhood marked by menarche defines for her a woman's procreative role in motherhood. The conventional confinement of women to domestic and familial roles helps foster a path to identity through affiliations in a community. A collective awareness of the innate femaleness is shared and reinforced as "received wisdom" among women. Therefore, the generational mother-daughter bond plays an integral part in the formulation of a female identity.

In this third phase of liberation of the 1980s, the major tasks for new women are to uncover a female body that speaks for themselves and to recover the feminine traits from the pre-communist legacy of their grandmothers. However, recollection of the grandmother's era is remote and unreal as a play. The two poems by Zhai Yongming, "The Grandma's Hours" (Zumu de shiguang) and "The Kid's Hours" (Haizi de shiguang) give a binocular view of the experience of theatre-going (Men, 1997, pp. 74–79). During the opera performance, "Grandma is entranced with the song/ Recollecting her maiden years." However, "The full light from the moon fails to light up the aged and the child":

> A thousand years that elapsed on the stage
> Are no longer than a tea break off stage
>     —the true drama is played
>     The false drama is performed

The lost world now re-enacted is one inhabited by the beauty and the talented scholar, the patriot and the traitor, the good and the evil, as well as the sorrowful ghosts. There is no way for a child of seven to feel a deep affinity to what her grandmother cherishes. Yet "Strands of blue smoke rise/ Long silky sleeves fly/ Together they have entwined my vision of a lifetime." However enticing these images of feminine grace are, from the child's point of view, the grandmother's traditional mode of life remains like a trance, from which no live model can be derived.

Equally baffling is the identification with the mother. Unlike the May Fourth precursors' adoration of the ideal mother as a sacrificial figure capable of an all-forgiving and all-encompassing love, contemporary women poets have an ambivalent attitude towards the mother figure. On the one hand, they see in the early May Fourth glorification of women as uncomplaining, forbearing mothers a trap that perpetuates the patriarchal victimization of women. On the other hand, they find it difficult to emulate the way of life of their uniformed mothers in the socialist revolution. Sceptical of narratives of selfless sacrifice, whether at the maternal or national level, women poets scrutinize their relationship with the mother figure from a distance.

The dialogue between mother and daughter has been a recurring topic in Zhai Yongming's poems. Her recent work, "Fourteen Plain Songs—To Mother" (Shisi shou suge—Zhi muqin) is a most illustrative example of the daughter's ambivalence towards her mother (Men, 1997, pp. 161–178). In song no. 2, "Song of Construction" (Jianshe zhi ge), she writes:

My mother in military attire
Red flags and songs like tides
Dress her up
Yet I have to wait for years
For another hilarious era
To imitate the attire of my mother
As if I am going to a masquerade

The tone of the speaker is characterized by a wavering between attachment and estrangement. This hesitation reflects the identity confusion caused by the mutilated role model. In her military uniform, the mother represents the generation of women who are clothed in a collective genderless self. The female body is covered up. This coercive move to erase gender is awkward and pretentious to the daughter, who cannot but take it as a game, like dressing up for a masquerade. Conversely, the new generation's alternative of exposing the body causes feelings of awe and shame in the elders. Song no. 11 "Song of a Dancing Woman" (Wudao de nüren zhi ge) shows how the genderless, "selfless" crowd is amazed by the performance of the self—the movement of the female body in flame:

There I set my body on fire
And make them gasp with open mouths
They do not understand why

> The beauty of the body is so shocking
> So is the shame of the body
> They are used to that selfless sacrifice
> Set to the rhythm of faith

Nevertheless, the emotional attachment to the mother is reaffirmed despite ideological differences, which are always subject to change with historical contingencies. What is common to all is the "unchanging change" brought about by time that gnaws at the mother as well as the daughter. Song no. 13, "Song of Fragments in Black and White" (Heibai de pianduan zhi ge), shows that even though the speaker has chosen to use the pen instead of the needle, she still sees herself in her mother:

> When I am tapping on the black and white
> Keyboard of the typewriter, with my elbows on the desk
> ...
> Mother bends over her sewing machine
> Supporting old age with her elbows
> She taps her days, each getting simpler than the other
> From her posture
> To my posture
> What has never changed
> Is that miserable, that ultimate
> Posture of purity
> Not projected by an idea
> ...
> Finally, an unchanging change
> Slowly gets close to the essence of time
> At the place our elbows locate

From mother to daughter, the bond in the blood is beyond the "projection of an idea." While domestic space and household chores are often trivialized in or excluded from intellectual discourses in patriarchal culture, the concluding scene in Zhai's suite poem vividly paints a picture of a cosy home. Sheltered in a private space and no longer clothed in a uniform, women of different generations find their own art of living. By sewing and by writing, mother and daughter are bound together in unyielding tenacity to elbow their way through time, to experience the essence of time regardless of the ravages it has caused.

In addition to the talents of weaving the tapestry of life by needlework or by language, women are empowered to conquer the human fear of mortality by procreativity. In the face of the inevitable decay of the body, to have one's life renewed in one's offspring is a consoling thought. For women only, a young body can be regained in a baby. The speaker in section 5 of Zhai Yongming's poem, "The Body" (Shenti), finds her lost body in another (Cui, 1993, pp. 35–38):

> Our heads, have already been snow-capped
> For how many winters?
> The smiles pretend to be calm
> Our antique bodies change like weather
> The truth, who can really forecast?
> A mother embraces her daughter
> Let the body feel the new life,
>
> ...
>
> The pale skin, no longer breathes
> No longer recalls to which direction the blood flows
> The body disappears. To look for it elsewhere
> To look for another body perhaps

The poet further reinforces the mother daughter bond by connecting their female abilities of production and reproduction in a way as Hélène Cixous has suggested: "There always remains in woman that force which produces/is produced by the other" (Cixous, 1976, p. 881).

## BECOMING MOTHERS

As seen in many poems of the late 1980s, liberation in this third phase is an ironic reversal of its previous mode—to liberate oneself now is to undress this self of the genderless uniform, and related to it, a genderless role. The role a woman plays exceeds that of a comrade and her job is more than an equal share of labour in the workforce. The exclusively female productivity and sensibility in motherhood prove that the resourcefulness of women goes beyond the imagination of Mao's political slogan of making women do what men do. The abundant descriptions of pregnancy, childbearing and delivery in poetry manifest "What women can do, men cannot do." By a liberal writing about sexual differences, women poets reclaim the unique role and identity of their sex. The physiological and psychological conditions of motherhood become a popular theme in women's poetry.

To a mother-to-be, her maternal body may appear strange and loathsome. Fu Tianlin's poem "Pregnancy" (Yun) depicts the new biological experience that is alien to the other sex: "What should I say to him/ The way I vomit, the awkward ... vomit/ Is not an illness" (Fu, 1985, pp. 112–113). This exclusively female ailment makes a woman turn from her husband to her mother for support and understanding:

A distant bell
Melts into the pulse
Awakens the beginning of my beginning of maternal love
Maternal love, shy and sacred, wakes up

The feeling of fulfilment during pregnancy is often compared to the growth of crops. After almost a year's toil, a good harvest is the most comforting reward to farmers. With the same expectation, the speaker looks forward to the day of delivery:

The time I will become a mother is August
Apples are red
Crops are yellow
A red and yellow August
Now is the time to weave wicket baskets
I guess I ought to weave a cradle

Similarly, the speaker in Tang Yaping's poem, "I Want a Son" (Wo yao yige erzi), talks about childbearing in the voice of a contented housewife: "We both have a good name/ We are a loving couple, hoping to stay together till the end of time/ Whiling away our days with regular meals/ Disputes are a treat" (Shen, 1994, pp. 84–87). Like most traditional women, the speaker believes that a son will make her family complete. The joy of childbearing is described in terms of a tree bearing fruit:

I hang on the tree
A big red persimmon
A belly of messy sweet
Feeling like being half drunk, it makes the blood run wild
To drop is a favourable condition of life
To fall is another posture

Childbirth is often associated with a miracle in Mother Nature, and in parallel literary creation is as natural as the ripening of crops. Before the baby is born, a poem is made. Sometimes, the anticipation of a happy delivery is marred by worries about possible mishaps. Poems such as Zhang Zhen's poem "Miscarriage" (Liuchan) pointedly present the anguish shared by pregnant women (Cui, 1993, pp. 192–193). To them, procreation is both a gift and a risk. "In an imagined relationship/ Mother and Son/ I and you," the speaker makes plans for her first baby. Unfortunately, her dream is smashed in a miscarriage. The battle for life between mother and son is traumatic. "In sleep, I race with you/ At last, it is me who is saved." At the funeral, the speaker makes a vow to her lost son that "Your brothers and sisters will be informed/ You are the eldest son; you come before everything/ You are prettier than everyone/ For this, I am so proud of you."

Although women have an enviable chance to fulfil the wish for rebirth by becoming mothers, they are often ensnared in the patriarchal narrative of heritage. In Tang Yaping's poem, when the speaker confesses that "I want nothing/ I want a son" in the last two lines, this ultimate desire for a son, rather than a daughter, seems to betray her unconscious admission of the gender hierarchy. As conservative is the preoccupation with "the eldest son," in Lin Xue's poem, "The Eldest Son" (Zhangzi) (Cui, 1993, pp. 17–18):

This phrase shimmers at night like a river
My child, my only son
He makes use of what is fluid and unshaped in his body
To love us, to record us

Besides reciprocal love, what is most important of all in this parent-child relationship is the perpetuation of the family lineage, and this mission falls on the shoulders of the eldest son. The last phrase, "to record us," which explains the significance of the eldest son, exhibits the parental vanity, a desire for immortality through the son's inscription in the male-defined genealogy. Poignant here is the collective unconscious of internalized patriarchal values among women. The foregrounding of the female biological usefulness to the species and a woman's wish to be locked in a male text in which her own origin will be forfeited only condemn the female to a self-annihilating prison house of ancestry.

The resort to sexual differences is certainly an indisputable means to establish a distinct identity for women. However, the liberating act of presenting exclusively female experiences can, paradoxically, result in a form of repression on women, if one fails to resist a mindless relapse into the traditional familial-conjugal enterprise that preserves the patriarchal system.

## THE ROOM—WOMEN ON THEIR OWN

Writing back against the national collective self, women poets in post-Mao China seek liberation in a private space into which women can retreat from the external world and divest themselves of a public role.

This withdrawal into a room of one's own is a manifestation of autonomy and independence. The room becomes a base from which the female self sets off for her journey of discovery and to which she can return at will.

When a woman stays in her room, she may not be entirely free. Like the Queen's looking glass in *Snow White*, the mirror that censures in a masculine voice shows a woman what she is supposed to be (Gilbert and Gubar, 1979, p. 46). In "The Trap of a Mirror" (Jingzi de quantao) Hong Ying summarizes a female's life by contrasting a young girl "gazing at/ white moths, five in total, outside the window/ flying" with a woman who "owns a big mirror/ mounted on the wall, at five places on my [her] body painted/ dirty stains" (Cheng et al., 1996, pp. 49–50). Initially the free-flying moths soar with the girl's youthful dreams towards a bright future, but in the course of time she learns that experiences in the outside world bring only contamination. Brainwashed by values of purity and chastity, the speaker feels uneasy before the mirror and views her own body with distaste. Alone, she mixes alcoholic drinks and tries to figure out when the others will arrive. Life has betrayed the woman. She rebels by "standing in her boots on the five shadows" of the past with her back to the mirror. Yet it seems ironic that a woman finds liberation only by anti-narcissism, an act of self-denigration.

In Xiao Jun's "Tidy Up the Room" (Zhengli fangjian), the speaker's ardent pursuit of cleanliness echoes a similar internalized patriarchal stricture on female purity (Cui, 1993, p. 104). "White always symbolizes cleanliness." The speaker leaves the mundane realities of the outside world to enjoy her time and space in private. When time spent in a waking public life suggests contamination, to have a sound sleep in one's tidy room seems to be the "cleanest" way of life:

> All problems of mine
> Are to while away time
> Not seeking any means
> Not seeking help by any means
>
> To while away time
> Sleep is a very good way
> It can start from now
> Without complaint or regret

If to tidy up the room is to clear an autonomous space for an individual's private life, sleep is a further escape from time and space. The speaker's resolute tone of self-reliance seems to defy any comment and judgment from outsiders. Nonetheless, confined to a life of privacy and domesticity, the woman in Xiao Jun's poem is characterized in a conventional way by her home-making instincts and reticence. The sense of alienation and helplessness in her cloistered withdrawal shows that her self-made home does not truly rescue her from socio-cultural inhibitions.

A woman's self-determination with regard to her way of living is also a major theme in Yi Lei's famous poem, "The Bedroom of a Single Woman" (Cui, 1993, pp. 105–115). In contrast to the quietude and stillness in the tidy room of Xiao Jun's poem, the bedroom created by Yi Lei is the stage for the speaker's dramatic performance of sexuality and meditation. Time is the concern of all mortals and it seems to be particularly the case for a single woman. In section 5, "A Small Gathering" (Xiaoxiao juhui), the poet writes, "The time of a single woman is like a pork chop/ But you do not come to take a bite." Like a pork chop, the time of the woman speaker is to be devoured and savoured, not to be left to rot. "It is almost a century since I was born/ My visage crumbles; wrinkles reach the leg/A single woman has no good name/ Only because she is young no more." Common is the biased view that aging is a female agony but Yi Lei brings it back to a human destiny in section 11, "Birthday Candles" (Shengri lazhu):

> God's commandment: Happy Birthday
> Everybody proposes a toast and laughs
> Welcoming a year closer to death
> Since this is the fear for all
> No one fears at all

The way to while away time is an existential problem for all. Xiao Jun proposes "sleep" as an exit from time and space, but Yi Lei actively consumes time by lavish descriptions of the activities in the bedroom. In section 2, the bedroom is transformed into "The Turkish Bath" (Tu'erqi yushi) and the female speaker does not shy away from narcissism:

> I am a true customer of this bathroom
> Narcissistic
> Long limbs, a slender body
> Tight hips, slanting shoulders
> Bowl-like breasts slightly shake
> Muscles are all passion filled
> I am my own model
> I created art; art created me

...
Soft mattresses and cushions are everywhere
One can easily fall asleep in any corner
  You do not come and live with me

By concluding every section of her poem with the refrain "You do not come and live with me," Yi Lei alludes to Christopher Marlowe's famous pastoral lyric "The Passionate Shepherd to His Love," and attacks the hypocritical disguise of male desire in it. While the shepherd in Marlowe's poem takes his lass as an object for adornment subject to his elaborate flowery construction, his proposal points finally to love's consummation in "beds of roses." The conventional appraisal of this invitation to "Come live with me and be my love" is that it is romantic though unrealistic. Stripped of all decorative gimmicks, Yi Lei's counter-proposal is stunning imagistically and disturbing morally, but nonetheless, honest and direct to the bone. In this section, with limpid depiction, Yi Lei lays bare the erotogenic parts of the female body. More pragmatic than "beds of roses," soft mattresses and cushions carpet the bathroom. If the adornment of the lass is for the pleasure of the male gaze and tempts an affirmative answer to the invitation for the fulfilment of male desire, "The Turkish Bath" stays clear of guile and disguise. It challenges the man to face the female body in its nakedness. The chiasmus that shows the interdependence between art and I declares not only the speaker's autonomy, but also her self-determination. Her declaration "I am my own model" negates extrinsic sources for self-fashioning. Yi Lei's counter-invitation can be read as a conscious act of female resistance to male manipulation.

Yi Lei's plain statement of female sexuality is an example of "the true texts of women—female-sexed texts" (Cixous, 1976, p. 877). The single woman asserts her independence in every aspect of life. Self-sufficiency is metaphorically presented in auto-eroticism in section 3, "The Secrets of the Curtains" (Chuanglian de mimi). Like Cixous, who regards a woman's "passionate and precise interrogation of her erotogeneity" as a kind of artistic activity, Yi Lei describes corporeal jouissance as rich and inventive (Cixous, 1976, p. 876):

In daytime, I always have the curtains drawn
To let me imagine the evils in daylight
Or enter the kingdom of emotions
Feeling more secure than ever
Feeling freer than ever

Inspirations then rise like spirits
I mix with them to reach the pleasures of orgasm
A new baby is born at once
More intelligent than ever
If I need happiness, I draw the curtains
Pain turns into enjoyment at once
If I want to kill myself, I draw the curtains
Desire to live will be ignited
Draw the curtains and listen to a symphony
Romance will fill up every corner
    You do not come and live with me

Originated from sexual and aesthetic pleasures, the new baby here is a poem born from the head. Erotic passion, like intellectual vigour, is rendered as both creative and transgressive. This bold exposition of the deluge of female desire is obviously a conscious subversion of traditional feminine traits, which are supposed to be docility, gentleness and subtlety. The unrepressed flow of liberating energy mounts to a "rapture" that ruptures the conventional morality. So it is not difficult to imagine that the single woman's invitation to her room is left unanswered. The refrain, "You do not come and live with me," is sung over and over at the end of each section. Unsurprisingly, the refrain evokes a patriarchal reading of the poem: Is this not a modern version of a "boudoir lament"? Is this not a betrayal of a lack felt by an unmarried woman?

Although Liu Qunwei highly commends Yi Lei's works as the most courageous experiment in women's liberation by a female writer, some critics find her poems obscure, pornographic and immoral. For example, Zang Di regards the best of women's poetry as "confessional" but not artistic, so he strongly protests against making "poetry a tool for women to explore their sensuality." To him, the treatment of sexuality in women's poetry is a "flaw" or a "sickness" in creative writing (Chen, 1995, p. 66). Lin Qi considers Yi Lei's poems as products of "self caressing" resulting from her disappointment in failing to get a man.[4] These criticisms apparently fall within the poet's anticipation. In the concluding section of the poem, "A Hopeless Hope" (Juewang de xiwang), the speaker talks back to men as a strong equal. She hurls a list of questions at the face of "you":

I wait for you every night with this hopeless hope
Will there be a world war if you come?
Will the Yellow River overflow if you come?

Will the weather turn bad if you come?
Will the harvest of wheat be affected if you come?

While the speaker succeeds in reclaiming her body from socio-
cultural suppression, her addressee, men in general, are not ready to
meet this "liberated" woman. The final refrain "You do not come and
live with me" hammers at the hard truth that men will stay away from
her. As the farsighted poet would have predicted, the emancipation of
the long hidden text of female sexuality will be curbed and the truth of
female experiences easily channelled back to its secret corners.

Above all, the significance of poems like Yi Lei's does not lie in the
story of a woman's destiny, but in the gradual awakening of her
consciousness of being a woman. As Cixous puts it: "Almost everything
is yet to be written by women about femininity: about their sexuality,
about their eroticization ... about the adventure of such and such a
drive ... [about] discoveries of a zone at one time timorous and soon to
be forthright" (Cixous, 1976, p. 885). Looking back at the year of
1995, Zhai Yongming regretted that discussions on women's poetry
were of no avail: "When critics and poets meet, they have innumerable
problems to talk about. In this meeting, like in any others, the debate
always ends up in a kind of discursive violence. But all I care about are
those trifles in others' eyes" (Cheng et al., 1996, pp. 6–7). Wang Xiaoni
too finds "trifles" her main concerns: "My mind is most enlightened
when I am preoccupied by trivial household chores. Potatoes, knives,
vegetables, and water bring wonders to me. A housewife should never
muddle things up; poetry alights when the conscious mind is asleep in
her concentration" (Cheng et al., 1996, pp. 23–24). In a word, a
woman's discovery and exhibition of her own zone celebrates the beginning of an independent life for half of humanity.

## LIBERATION/FEMININITY INCOMPLETE?

In the post-Mao era, the quest for what is lost or suppressed by the
unisex communist uniform gives rise to an ironic regressive move,
resulting in a search for role models and feminine traits in the past. This
trend of recovery herds the women speakers home to examine their
gender role and position in a domestic space. Both the first and the
second paths, returning to the mother at home and becoming mothers,
are grounded on gender differences. While the female experiences in
body and sex are biologically given, the conventional feminine traits are

sometimes revived to create a deliberate contrast with the image of a genderless comrade in the previous decades. Women speakers are now free to tell the truth about female bodily experiences, and to discuss subjects such as ailments and household chores, which are conventionally dismissed as trifles and small talk. In spite of these ventures, the emphases on the collective female consciousness fostered by generational bonds, a rebound to gender differences and the reliance on familial relationships, easily fall back on internalized patriarchal values. To avoid these pitfalls, some talented women poets resume old roles with ambivalence, displaying their new sensibility and self-consciousness. To them, the complexity of femininity needs to be scrutinized with reference to historical realities. Readjustment and compromise are resorted to, when necessary, but with keen critical awareness. The third path seems to be more open and dynamic, and through it one can see female subjectivity in the making. The new "liberated" women are intellectually and financially independent. They dare to confront taboos about female sexuality and traditional morality. These avant-garde women speakers in the poems are valiant loners, posing threats and challenges to their male counterparts.

What is happening in post-Mao poetry writing and criticism, it seems to me, is a significant transitional state of affairs. Most women poets are conscious of their freedom to write, but not many have successfully engaged with issues of "liberation" and "femininity" in their writing. Prevalent internalized patriarchal values sneak through the back door from time to time, indicating a lack of critical resistance. The enthusiastic responses to women's poetry in contemporary literary discourse are encouraging. However, voices of women poets are sometimes drowned in the dominant ideological discourse or feminist poetics. Such national or international narratives in fact fail to rescue women's muffled voices from the fate of fertilizing the patriarchal ideology, both in politics and in poetics.[5]

Far from being liberated from fetters of patriarchal culture and moral convention, women poets are still exploring new roles and consciousness under constriction. The poems and commentaries studied in this paper show that some critics and poets are not ready to fly or to see new women soar to the heights of individual freedom. Rather than patronizing women poets by assigning them a major supporting role in the historical progress towards modernist world poetry or an international feminist movement, critics will do more to help if they try to address women's plight from their specific perspectives. What women poets need perhaps is not an enshrined, definitive role on the revolutionary agenda, but a democratic site for their artistic and intellectual inquiry into the related issues of liberation and femininity.

## NOTES

1. Unless stated otherwise, all the passages quoted from poetry and prose are my own translations.
2. The women poets quoted in these discussions are considered poets of the third generation or poets of the Pioneer School. Representative works by women poets such as Zhai Yongming, Tang Yaping and Yi Lei, are labelled "women's poetry" (*nüxing shige*) by Chinese critics, in order to distinguish them from works written by earlier female writers. See Chen, 1995, p. 63.
3. Different from femaleness as a biological given and feminism as a political position, femininity discussed in this paper refers to a set of acquired traits by which a person becomes a woman and a person's consciousness of being a woman. As suggested by Simone de Beauvoir, "To be feminine is to appear weak, futile, docile. The young girl is supposed not only to deck herself out, to make herself ready, but also to repress her spontaneity and replace it with the studied grace and charm taught her by her elders. Any self assertion will diminish her femininity and her attractiveness" (Beauvoir, 1997, p. 314). In a similar light, Chung Ling summarizes the characteristics of "feminine sensibility" as "gentle, docile, beautiful, bewitching, delicate, exquisite, and sad" (Chung, 1990, p. 79).
4. "Self caressing" is a label coined by Xie Mian to criticize women's poetry produced in the post-Mao era. Lin Qi's comment is quoted from Chen, 1995, p. 65.
5. On this issue, the question raised by Tonglin Lu is insightful: "Chinese women were already 'saved' at least twice in modern history—first, by the radical May Fourth intellectuals, and then by the Communist Party. Do we want to duplicate the same mistake by 'saving' them a third time through feminist theory?" (Lu, 1993, p. 14).

## REFERENCES

Beauvoir, Simone de (1997). *The Second Sex*. Trans. and ed. H. M. Parshley. London: Vintage. First English translation published in 1952 by Knopf, New York.

Chen Xuguang (1995). "Ningwang shiji zhi jiao de qianye: 'Dangdai nüxing shige—Taishi yu zhanwang' yantaohui shuyao" [Gazing at the eve of the new century: Synopsis of the conference on "Contemporary Women's Poetry—Trends and Prospects"]. *Shi tansuo* [Poetry exploration], No. 19

(September), 62–69.

Cheng Zhifang et al., eds. (1996). *Shiren kongjian* [The space of poets]. Kunming: Yunnan renmin chubanshe.

Chung, Ling (1990). "Sense and Sensibility in the Works of Women Poets in Taiwan." In Howard Goldblatt, ed., *Worlds Apart: Recent Chinese Writing and Its Audiences*, pp. 78–107. Armonk, NY: M. E. Sharpe.

Cixous, Hélène (1976). "The Laugh of the Medusa." Trans. Keith Cohen and Paula Cohen. *Signs: Journal of Women in Culture and Society*, Vol. 1, No. 4 (Summer), 875–893.

Cui Weiping, ed. (1993). *Pingguo shang de pao: Nüxing shi juan* [The panther on the apple: Selected works of women's poetry]. Beijing: Beijing shifan daxue chubanshe.

Fu Tianlin (1985). *Yinyue dao* [The music island]. Beijing: Renmin wenxue chubanshe.

Gilbert, Sandra M., and Susan Gubar (1979). *The Madwoman in the Attic: The Woman Writer and the Nineteenth-century Literary Imagination*. New Haven, CT: Yale University Press.

Hong Ying (1996). "Jingzi de quantao" [The trap of a mirror]. In Cheng Zhifang et al., eds., *Shiren kongjian* [The space of poets], pp. 49–50. Kunming: Yunnan renmin chubanshe.

Lin Danya (1995). *Dangdai Zhongguo nüxing wenxue shilun* [Studies on the history of contemporary Chinese women's literature]. Xiamen: Xiamen daxue chubanshe.

Liu Qunwei (1995). "Lun Yi Lei" [On Yi Lei]. *Shi tansuo* [Poetry exploration], No. 17 (March), 104–112.

Lu, Tonglin, ed. (1993). *Gender and Sexuality in Twentieth-century Chinese Literature and Society*. Albany: State University of New York Press.

Men Ma, ed. (1997). *Heiye li de suge: Zhai Yongming shi xuan* [Plain songs in the night: Selected works of Zhai Yongming]. Beijing: Gaige chubanshe.

Shen Qi, ed. (1994). *Xianhong de gechang: Dalu dangdai nüshiren xiaoji* [The scarlet singing: Selected works of contemporary women poets of mainland China]. Taipei: Erya chubanshe.

Tam, Kwok-kan (1998). "Ibsenism and Ideological Constructions of the 'New Woman' in Modern Chinese Fiction." *Tamkang Review*, Vol. 29, No.1 (Autumn), 95–105.

Wang Xiaoni (1996). "Wo zai yijiujiuwu nian" [My life in 1995]. In Cheng Zhifang et al., eds. *Shiren kongjian* [The space of poets], pp. 22–24. Kunming: Yunnan renmin chubanshe.

Zhai Yongming (1996). "Yijiujiuwu nian biji" [The notes of 1995]. In Cheng Zhifang et al., eds., *Shiren kongjian* [The space of poets], pp. 6–8. Kunming: Yunnan renmin chubanshe.

**GLOSSARY**

"Chuanglian de mimi" 〈窗簾的秘密〉

"Dushen nüren de woshi" 〈獨身女人的臥室〉

Fu Tianlin 傅天琳

"Haizi de shiguang" 〈孩子的時光〉

"Heibai de pianduan zhi ge" 〈黑白的片段之歌〉

Hong Ying 虹影

"Jianshe zhi ge" 〈建設之歌〉

"Jingzi de quantao" 〈鏡子的圈套〉

"Juewang de xiwang" 〈絕望的希望〉

Lin Xue 林雪

"Liuchan" 〈流產〉

Mao Zedong 毛澤東

nüxing shige 女性詩歌

"Shengri lazhu" 〈生日蠟燭〉

"Shenti" 〈身體〉

"Shisi shou suge—Zhi muqin" 〈十四首素歌——致母親〉

Shu Ting 舒婷

Tang Yaping 唐亞平

"Tu'erqi yushi" 〈土耳奇浴室〉

Wang Xiaoni 王小妮

"Wo yao yige erzi" 〈我要一個兒子〉

"Wudao de nüren zhi ge" 〈舞蹈的女人之歌〉

Xiao Jun 小君

"Xiaoxiao juhui" 〈小小聚會〉

Yi Lei 伊蕾

"Yun" 〈孕〉

Zhai Yongming 翟永明

Zhang Zhen 張真

"Zhangzi" 〈長子〉

Zheng Min 鄭敏

"Zhengli fangjian" 〈整理房間〉

"Zumu de shiguang" 〈祖母的時光〉

7   Gender Construction in the Novels of Zhang
    Kangkang and Liang Xiaosheng

SUYING YANG

IN THE PAST CENTURY, CHINA has experienced numerous social, political and economic vicissitudes, of which changes in the role of women formed a crucial part. Fighting for the rights of women was one of the central items on the agenda in a series of anti-feudalist, anti-imperialist revolutions and pro-democracy movements.

In the first few decades after the Communist Party came to power in 1949, the "liberation of women" was but one element taken for granted in the larger context of constructing socialist China and instilling into people the communist ideal: a perfect world without social hierarchy, discrimination or suffering. As part of the overall effort to raise the social and financial status of the "workers, peasants and soldiers," the government not only propagandized the idea of gender equality but also promulgated a series of policies and statutes to protect the rights of women. The propaganda, policies and statutes produced great changes in the life of women in China, and these changes even gave rise to the myth of "the liberated women of China" among feminists in the West. "All of a sudden, Chinese women became the embodiment of liberation for women in the West, who had to struggle hard for what they believed they were entitled to"[1] (Li, 1996, p. 3).

Later, in the 1980s, China entered a new era of reform and the open-door policy brought the people of China back into the world community. In this more liberal political atmosphere, people had a chance to reflect on the inhumane and disastrous happenings during the Cultural Revolution and felt an urgent need to call for respect for human dignity and humanistic ideals. At the same time, more exposure to different cultures outside China made a significant impact on the worldviews and values the government had tried to cultivate in its citizens. It was in such a social and political environment that educated Chinese women gradually realized that their liberation was superficial and incomplete. "The awareness of the superficiality of women's liberation arose from people's general awakening to human rights" (Sheng, 1995, p. 706). Based on Chinese women's new understanding of their situation, some scholars in the West discarded the old myth of "the liberated women of China" and adopted the new "myth of double oppression." Some even went as far as to conclude that "the fate of Chinese women has not really changed for the past forty years and it may be even worse than before" (Li, 1996, p. 21). However, as Li Xiaojiang (1996) points out, neither of these myths in the West truly reflects the reality in China. In order to truly understand the situation of Chinese women over the past few decades, one must know the special nature of the women's liberation movements in China.

Women's liberation movements in China after 1949 have been very different from the feminist movements in the West. Feminist movements in the West were spontaneous and initiated by women themselves, but women's liberation movements in China were basically top-down government activities, initiated mainly by liberal-minded men (Li, Zhu and Dong, 1994; Huang, 1995). We may well imagine that this peculiar top-down model could bring about changes at the public level, but might not reach the private level of the family and the individual. The traditional values and views of the old patriarchal society were not eradicated, although many of them, especially those concerning public life, were challenged and even changed by the introduction of the new socialistic ideology in the women's liberation movements. The changes at the public level and the lack of change at the private level led to a unique phenomenon: the split role of women at the two different levels. At the public level, women received due respect as members of society. Their rights were protected by government policies and, especially in the cities, women and men had equal rights to education and job opportunities. The implementation of the "same-job same-pay" policy also protected the financial status of women. In a word, the government policies and statutes put women on an equal footing with men at the public level, making it possible for women to become self-reliant workers, teachers, and government officials. However, at the private level, as daughters, wives, mothers and acquaintances, women were still fettered by the deep-rooted patriarchal ideology of traditional society. The general public's expectation of women's behaviour at the private level was not very different from before. Women were still expected to be obedient daughters, chaste wives, and devoted mothers. It was common in those years to see women work outside the home in the same way as men because they were expected to become the equals of men, but at the same time these women were supposed to do all the household chores and take care of children simply because they were women.

The changes at the public level received a great deal of attention, but the lack of change at the private level was quite often ignored, because individual interests were in general overlooked in a social system where both the feudal tradition and the communist ideology emphasized the importance of collectivism and nationalism. People in such a system were too much concerned with public-level affairs to notice the different experiences of men and women at the private level. The larger situation of "big collectivism and small individualism" led to a false belief in women who grew up in the 1950s to 1970s that they were treated as the equals of men, and "they never considered themselves as different from men" (Li, 1996, p. 20). "The myth of the liberated women of China" was thus generated in the West.

Ren Yiming (1997) uses the phrase "owning two worlds at the same time" to describe the women writers who grew up in the 1950s to 1970s. She argues that these women writers are not only concerned with the outside world, but also interested in presenting the inner world of women. To her, some works are typical depictions of the outer world and some others are typical embodiments of women's inner world. However, in my view, these women writers' outer and inner worlds are inseparable. More importantly, the two levels we have just discussed exist not only in the outer world but also in the inner world of the writers. The upper level, or the public level, accommodates the high-sounding principles of equality brought about by communist ideals and women's movements, while the lower level, or the private level, houses the traditional views fostered and maintained by the patriarchy for several thousand years. The co-existence of the two levels in both the outer and inner worlds is not only true of the women writers Ren Yiming (1997) discusses but also true of the general public of their generation.

The co-existence of the public and private levels means that only by looking at both levels can one gain a good understanding of the fate of women in the past few decades. In the present study, I will use the two-level model to study gender construction in the works of two writers, Zhang Kangkang and Liang Xiaosheng, with a view to showing that the two-level model provides the reader with a new perspective to understand writers who grew up in the 1950s–70s.

Both Liang and Zhang were born around 1949. During their school years, they were immersed in stories and propaganda about the first-generation women pilots, first-generation women tractor drivers, first-generation women train drivers, and so forth. During the 1960s and 1970s, the spirit of "men and women each holding up half of the sky" manifested itself to the fullest. In factories and in the countryside, images of the so-called iron female emerged. The "revolutionary model operas" featured great female heroes like Jiang Shuiying, Ah Qing Sao, Li Tiemei and Wu Jinghua. It was in such a social and political environment that Liang and Zhang stopped their schooling and went to the countryside with other young people to receive "re-education" from the peasants. When the Cultural Revolution came to an end in the late 1970s, Liang and Zhang began to make a name for themselves in literary circles. Their earliest works are all based on their experiences in the countryside as "educated young people." Liang and Zhang grew up in the same social and political environment and they both started their literary career by writing about their experiences in the countryside against the same historical background. The only major difference between them is that Liang is a man and Zhang is a woman. Does this gender distinction lead to any differences in their construction of gender in their works? To what extent do their similar educational and social backgrounds influence their construction of gender? These are the questions the present study aims to answer.

## ZHANG KANGKANG: MEN IN A WOMEN'S WORLD

In a conversation with Li Xiaojiang in February 2000, Zhang describes herself thus:

> In retrospect, I ask myself the questions: Why didn't I have a strong gender sensitivity when I wrote? Was it because there existed in me a sense of feminine inferiority or a lack of attention to women? Or was it because I had been submerged and totally swallowed by the patriarchal culture? Another possibility is: I have all the time believed, in my heart, in my mind and in my experience, that men and women are equal, that is "men and women are equally capable." Take my family for example; my father and mother treat each other as equals. They have two daughters, my sister and me. I never had the feeling of being ignored because I was a girl. When I grew up, I did not feel any sexual discrimination. My resistance to the old social system was greater than my resistance to men. Why was it like this? The reason might be: I seldom felt male oppression. I was a student leader in primary school and started to publish when I was in primary 5. I did not really suffer any sexual discrimination. Nothing

particularly bad happened just because I was a girl ... Analysing my own psychological development, I feel that food will be very important to a starving person but will not matter that much to a person who is full. I did not experience sexual discrimination, so I took it for granted that men and women were equal. During the years in the countryside, my personal life was disastrous. I got married at twenty and had a divorce soon after. However, in the whole process, it did not occur to me that the hurt came as a result of sexual discrimination, and I did not feel I had ever lived under the shadow of men. In everyday life, I was very feminine since the time when I was very small and I was psychologically precocious. Even during the 1970s, I was not an iron female. So, in a sense, I should say that I have believed for a very long time that men and women are different. (Li, 2000, pp. 7–8)

At the very beginning of this monologue, Zhang says that she has all the time believed that men and women are equal, but later on she says that she has believed for a long time men and women are different. On the surface she is contradicting herself. However, we will not find her statements contradictory if we try to interpret what she says from the two-level perspective. Equality lies on the public level, while inequality is rooted in the private realm. What she describes here is exactly what many women, especially educated women, experienced in those years. At the public level, women were, like men, members of society. They were financially independent and enjoyed equal opportunities for education and jobs of various kinds. Their ability and competence were recognized in society. However, at the private level, they felt gender inequality. Unfortunately, they tended to ignore this feeling of gender inequality at the private level because of their greater concern with society and the social system. That is the reason why women writers who grew up in that period of time often believe that their writing is gender neutral. Zhang once said, "I sometimes reflect on what I have written and I find a secret: If I change the gender identity of my heroines, the ideological and emotional conflicts described in my works will remain basically the same, because I am writing about humans, that is, I am dealing with problems and crisis all of us, men or women, have to face" (Zhang, 1999, p. 28). It is true that Zhang is very much concerned with the common problems of her characters; however, her writing inevitably reflects her experience as a woman.

In *The Invisible Companion* (*Yinxing banlü*), Zhang describes the life of the "educated young people" on a farm in Heilongjiang. In her own words, "the life of the 'educated young people' is only a vehicle for the theme of 'the invisible companion.' By 'the invisible companion,' I mean that everyone has an invisible and irrational self hiding under the rational self and controlled only by the subconscious" (Li, 2000, p. 21). In this novel, Zhang is indeed working on a major theme: human nature. However, a truly gender-neutral person does not exist. The concept of the human has to be embodied by either a female or a male. Zhang's protagonists are inevitably women or men, like the woman Xiao Xiao and the man Chen Xu in *The Invisible Companion*. At the public level, Chen Xu and Xiao Xiao are both "educated young people" working together in the fields. They have the same educational background, the same social status, the same income and the same level of social independence. The woman Xiao Xiao displays an even greater sense of responsibility and persistence than most of the male "educated young people" on the farm. However, Chen Xu and Xiao Xiao are not presented to the reader as gender-neutral individuals. They are presented as a man and a woman and their gender distinction is made clear at the private level in their relationship with each other, in their relationship with other people, in their language and in their different psychological conditions.

Although Xiao Xiao shows persistence and greater will-power in enduring the hardships of life on the farm, she exhibits a true image of a traditionally tender and obedient girl when she is with Chen Xu, who, by contrast, is a very assertive decision-maker. At the beginning of the novel, Chen Xu is interrogated by Supervisor Yu and Secretary Sun about his behaviour in a fight among the "educated young people." In order to clear his name, he decides to go back to his home city of Hangzhou to ask for a testimonial from the authorities at his secondary school. It never occurs to him that he should consult with Xiao Xiao about the trip, but takes it for granted that she should go with him. Xiao Xiao does not want to go without asking for permission from the farm leaders but in the end she goes along with Chen Xu's decision. They meet after sunset and after a brief exchange of information they have the following conversation:

> "Now. Let's go," he said, decisively.
> "Where?
> "Just follow me."
> "To Jiamusi to see movies? Or ...."
> "Mind you, don't ask so many questions." He pulled her closer to him impatiently and pushed her on the waist.
> [...]

"I must know why," she said.

He broke a grass root with force, threw it away and yelled: "They interrogated me this afternoon. Didn't you see it? You should know. You should have known long ago. Where shall we go?—South, to Hangzhou, of course. Do we have any other choice?"

She drew in a long breath.

"Back to Hangzhou? I, I haven't asked for leave!"

"Ask for leave?" he sneered, "Thank you for being so considerate."

She bit her lip without knowing what to say. After a while, she said hesitantly: "Then, they ... they would say that we are ... deserters!"

"You're afraid, aren't you?" Sparks came out from his eyes towards her. "I was foolish enough to think that you would stay with me even when everybody else had left me." He turned away from her and strode towards the main road. "To tell the truth, it is for your own sake that I have asked you to go with me. You will be in big trouble if you stay here by yourself. Deserters? This isn't Zhenbaodao...."[2]

The sound became distant, and then the footsteps stopped.

[...]

She quickly ran to him and held him tightly by the arm. (Zhang, 1988, pp. 4–5)

Over the past few decades, many linguists have studied how females and males use language in different language situations. They have found some general patterns. For example, females usually speak with a softer tone. They tend to make requests in a consultative manner, even when they speak from a more authoritative position (such as a doctor speaking to a patient). While women often resort to hedges and explanations to make their requests more acceptable, male language displays very different characteristics. Men are usually more direct in making requests and they usually do not make an effort to soften the tone of their requests (Lakoff, 1975; Jones, 1980; West, 1984). The above quotation is not real language-use data but Zhang's construction of a dialogue between a male character and a female character. However, we see in this constructed conversation patterns that have been identified by scholars in studying real gender speech. The man, Chen Xu, makes a decision without consulting the woman, Xiao Xiao, and he wants her to do whatever he has decided in a tone which will brook no opposition. Xiao Xiao is not comfortable with the decision, but she gives up under the pressure of Chen's strong will.

In constructing this dialogue, Zhang may not be intending to describe the distinctions between male speech and female speech; however, the dialogue undoubtedly reflects her experience of real language situations. The similarities between this constructed dialogue and real language use as described by the scholars mentioned above could not be mere coincidence. I would argue that the similarities reflect gender inequality that has been fostered and maintained in the patriarchal system over several thousand years. The inequality might not be very obvious at the public level in terms of job opportunities and public matters, but its existence is real at the private level in terms of personal relationships and private matters.

As a member of society and the community of "educated youths," Xiao Xiao commands respect and trust from fellow educated youths because of her commitment to the community and her toughness in enduring hardships on the farm. However, when she gets back to Chen Xu's home in Hangzhou, she faces disrespect and even contempt from Chen Xu's parents. Chen Xu's mother does not allow Xiao Xiao to stay in their house because she and Chen Xu are not yet married and the neighbours would gossip if she stayed with his family. One day, Xiao Xiao allows the rice to burn when she is cooking. Chen Xu's mother flies into a rage:

> "Cooking without paying attention to what is cooked. Walking around like someone without a soul ...," cackled the coarse voice. ...
>
> "One doesn't know how much fuel and food cost unless one looks after a family ..." Xiao Xiao's future mother-in-law banged the lid of the water vat and the kettle. Xiao Xiao knew that she and Chen's mother did not have much in common and it was difficult for them to carry on a conversation.
>
> Unable to hold back anymore, she said, "We could put some green onion in the burned rice."
>
> This polite suggestion enraged Chen Xu's mother. She threw the cooking pot to the ground and shouted, "... Shit! Where did this vampire come from? Dreaming of taking control of me already! What are you capable of doing? Whining in bed?"
>
> Xiao Xiao flushed, thinking to herself, "It's not you I'm marrying. It is because of Chen Xu that I broke up with my family." She drew in a long breath and tried to speak calmly, "Mother, you may have your own ideas about me ...."
>
> Her remarks were interrupted by even more vehement reviling.
>
> "... I thought our house was haunted. There's a noise at the back door every day. It turns out we have a vampire here that has seduced Ah Long [Chen Xu]. What do I dare to say ..." (Zhang, 1988, pp. 94–95)

Here we see something that is very common in a patriarchal society. When there is a relationship before or outside marriage, or when there is an unlucky incident or disastrous warfare, women are always blamed. Men are never blamed when something bad happens, as if male power and male authority play no part in disasters or unwanted events.

In another novel, *Love Gallery (Qing'ai hualang)*, Zhang describes how Chinese intellectuals seek freedom and love in the period of reform and opening-up. This novel seems to focus more on women's courage in fighting for freedom and love, but Zhang seldom describes the inner world of women. Instead, Zhang lets us see her women characters through the eyes of men. The main female character, Qin Shuihong, is a liberal-minded woman with a good education. She teaches arts theory at a university. She is talented and has a high social status. Even at home, she enjoys respect and freedom because her husband is very liberal-minded. However, she has to wear make-up to cover up her dazzling beauty whenever she goes out. In the classroom, she is a professor, but in the eyes of ordinary men in the street, she is only a sex object. She enjoys the freedom to teach at a university, but at the same time, she does not even have the freedom to show her true looks to people outside her home. The effort that Zhang makes in describing Qin Shuihong's plight as a beauty is a demonstration of the fact that beauty only increases a woman's chance of becoming a sex object and thus becomes a cause of her bondage.

*Aurora Borealis (Beiji guang)* has been regarded as a typical reflective work on human nature and human ideals (Sheng, 1995, p. 815). The main character, Cencen, is a woman in the era of reform and opening-up. She is not content with her life as an ordinary worker and her future marriage to another ordinary worker. To achieve something better, she runs away when having her wedding photographs taken, in defiance of her parents and her fiancé and the expectations of the people around her. Cencen may be considered as a representative of those who fight undauntedly for independence and dignity. Zhang uses Cencen as an example to argue that she is writing about "human" not "a human." She says "even young men see themselves in my works. One young man wrote to me after he had read *Aurora Borealis*, saying that he saw in Cencen his own persistence in pursuing higher goals" (Zhang, 1999, p. 28). It is true that pursuing higher goals is something common to all humans, but Cencen's pursuit displays something particularly true of women. Cencen is a part-time student on a university degree course, but she does not have much hope of changing her fate through her own efforts. In the process of enhancing her spiritual life, she looks up to other people, especially her male classmates, for support and inspiration. If the main character in *Aurora Borealis* were a male instead of a female, would he rely on his female classmates in his pursuit of higher goals?

Zhang has created several women characters who have the courage to pursue their life's goals, such as Xiao Xiao in *The Invisible Companion*, Qin Shuihong, Ah Ni and Shu Li in *Love Gallery* and Zhu Xiaoling in *Scarlet Cinnabar* (*Chitong danzhu*). These women know how to make use of their own rights to realize their ideals. Interestingly, the male characters close to these female characters are all very liberal-minded, for example Xiao Xiao's husband, Qin Shuihong's husband, and Zhu Xiaoling's father. All of these male characters, without exception, are well educated and open to liberal ideas. To a certain extent, Zhang's enlightened setting for her female characters makes it possible for her to avoid too much concentration on the suffering of women and focus more on her concern with human nature and societal problems. Nevertheless, she cannot totally avoid private-level matters and throughout her treatment of these issues, we see a distinction between women and men. This distinction is clearly displayed in Zhang's works, although she herself may not have created it intentionally. In fact, her frequent praise for the liberal attitudes of the male characters also shows that she somehow realizes the importance of the male enlightenment.

Zhang's female characters are all independent members of society, but at the same time they also show moral and psychological dependence on their male companions. We need to pay special attention to the fact that their dependence on men is not the same as the traditional women's attachment to men, because Zhang's female characters are no longer the property of men. They are financially self-reliant and enjoy a certain degree of freedom and respect. However, they still suffer gender discrimination in private-level matters and the traditional patriarchal society has left some tender spots in their heart that make them weaker and more vulnerable than men.

## LIANG XIAOSHENG: WOMEN IN A MAN'S WORLD

Liang's *Women's Mentality* (*Nüren xinqing*) consists of five short stories. At the beginning of each story, there are the following remarks:

> Women are details of history.
> In the little folds of the history book, which are quite often ignored

by men, we find that it is women who provide exact interpretations of many sub-themes of different historical periods...

If men have made history more and more theatrical, women, as details, please make history more literary and more poetic!

At least, try to make life more like MTV! (Liang, 1999, p.1)

These remarks can be said to truly reflect Liang's views about women. In his eyes, men are playwrights, directors and leading actors, while women are details and supporting actresses on the social stage. Women are not the centre of the drama, but are details enriching the plot, enhancing vividness and beautifying the scene. "In this respect, women prove their strength by their instincts" (Liang, 1999, back cover). We cannot say that Liang does not show respect to women because, as he himself claims, "in all my works, whether they are short stories, novels or plays, or essays, there flows my respect and warm loving feeling for women. My respect is sincere, so is my loving feeling" (Liang, 2001, p. 318). However, in his mind men and women are, undoubtedly, different. Men are the main personae while women are only dispensable supporting characters. This idea that man is the main character is also the product of the top-down women's liberation movements in China. In the top-down model, it is men who give women the right and the chance to play their parts on the same social stage. These men are happy to see what changes their generosity and liberal attitudes have brought about in women. They respect women in supporting roles, but they know at the same time that they are the ones in control. In the backs of their minds, patriarchal culture still influences what they expect of women. Young women should be tender and kind and their delicacy should help set off the mental and physical strength of the male characters, so that the male characters can play their parts better. Older women should "be capable of enduring hardship, know their place and have the ability to handle crises intuitively whenever necessary ..." (Liang, 2001, p. 318). Men's desire for dominance and power often gets them into conflicts. Whenever there are conflicts, there are also suffering and pain. As a result, men need mothers as their haven or shelter. Thus the women characters constructed by Liang are largely of two kinds: lovely, tender young girls and tough, loving mothers. These young girls and mothers are different from the traditional images of women, because they are no longer properties or accessories of men, but neither are they the main characters on the social stage.

Shun Sao, in "Abiding Affection" (Ci ai chanmian), one of the short stories in *Women's Mentality*, is a typical example of a modern mother.

She is the product of revolution, a female pioneer in the liberation movement:

> When she was 15, she was already a cadre in one of the revolutionary bases. She joined the Chinese Communist Party at 16 and became the village head and the village militia leader when she was 17. At the same time she was the youngest member on the County Committee. Then militia leaders were given the privilege of carrying guns, so she carried a small pistol at her waist, feeling pretty and full of life. She commanded the respect of men and was the idol of all the young women in the village. (Liang, 1999, p. 109)

However, this heroine in the women's liberation movement later goes to Beijing with her husband and becomes a housewife. In her position as an ordinary housewife, she does not do much for the country but her kindheartedness and her instinctive love for the true, the good and the beautiful bring colour to the life of the people around her. Even during the Cultural Revolution, when human dignity is trampled, her motherly love brings light and hope to the oppressed.

Liang's other novel *Destruction* (*Minmie*) describes the development of two male friends from the early 1950s to the reform years of the 1980s and 1990s. One of the two friends, Zhai Ziqing gives up his dreams of many years and becomes a slave to money in the torrent of economic reforms. The other, Liang Xiaosheng, keeps his integrity intact and becomes a writer. An important female figure in the novel is Zhai Ziqing's wife, Wu Yan, who comes from a family with a long history of scholarship and has a Bachelor's degree in Chinese and a Master's degree in history. Against the trend of materialism in the era of economic reform, she rids herself of the burden of history and traditional culture in pursuit of personal dignity. She is representative of the beauty of humanity and the embodiment of humanity and rationality. Her rationality is of the purest kind that has transcended worldly reason and can uplift the best parts of human nature. Possessing the virtues of mercy, love, forgiveness and self-sacrifice, she is capable of purifying souls soiled by lust and greed and healing the wounds of men who get hurt in their struggles in the cruel and materialistic world. She is not lustful but at the same time she refuses to be bound by traditional views about sex and love. Her instinctive and pure sexual love can purify the souls of men. We may say that Wu Yan materializes Liang's ideal of woman in her pure femininity and maternity. At the end of the novel, Liang lets two glorious women characters die in accidents, showing his grief over the disappearance of his ideal woman in an increasingly materialistic China.

As Liang himself admits, he does not think highly of the so-called "modern white-collar women" in the reform era (Liang, 2001, p. 318). Xiao Jing in *Women's Mentality* is a typical "modern white-collar woman," who goes abroad to make money and starts her own business upon her return to China. To her uncle, the first-person narrator of the story, Xiao Jing is too unconventional and does not live up to people's expectations of a young woman. As the story unfolds, Xiao Jing reinvents herself as a traditional mother figure, "caring, understanding and full of sympathy and love for other people" (Liang, 1999, p. 239), after she has experienced the pain of her sister's death and later the healing love of her sister's brother-in-law. Her uncle is very happy with the change in her. Here, again, we see the purifying and uplifting effects of pure love and the glory of a mother figure.

To sum up, the women Liang praises are not of the traditional type. They have their own ideas and are independent financially. They are not exemplars of the Confucian woman who has "three obediences" (to her father before marriage, to her husband after marriage, and to her son after the death of her husband) and "four virtues" (morality, proper speech, modest manner and diligent work). However, women are not supposed to fight with men for leading roles on the stage of the society. Ideal women, in Liang's mind, are those who enhance men's power through their delicacy and comfort men with their love. They do not crave the leadership roles of men, but they will spend their talents and energy to influence and uplift men.

## AUTONOMY OF THE NEW WOMAN

The Chinese women's liberation movements since 1949 have changed the social hierarchy, women's fate and many traditional ideas, but these top-down movements did not stir up the deep layers of historical sediment. As a result, both in society and in people's consciousness, there are two intricate levels of gender constructions. At the public level, we find new ideas and values brought forth by the liberation movements. At the private level, we see relics of patriarchal history. In a situation like this, the liberation of women cannot be complete. Everyone has his/her specific experiences as a man or a woman and these experiences will leave marks in that person's mind and lead to changes at both the public and the private levels. Zhang and Liang are not defenders of the traditional patriarchal ideology. They both believe in free will and independence. They both like to have their female characters play roles on the social stage. Nevertheless, they both exhibit the influence of traditional ideas in different ways. Zhang's female characters, however independent they are, all look to men for mental and psychological support. The most successfully constructed characters in her works are young girls who pursue independence and human dignity on the one hand and seek a strong male shoulder on the other hand. Liang's mother-like women may play their roles on the same stage as men and even serve as shelter for men but they cannot compete with men for leading roles. They should be diligent, courageous, caring, and understanding but they should not be totally independent business women or vain "white-collar women."

When there is still gender discrimination, gender-neutral literature is not possible. Everyone's gender experiences will leave marks in his/her works. Zhang and Liang grew up in the same historical background. They have both seen the changes brought about by the women's liberation movements and they have both been influenced by the unchanged deep layers of patriarchal history. As a result, we find two different levels, the new and the old, implicated in their works.

## NOTES

1. All quotations in this paper are translated by the author.
2. At that time China was at war with the former USSR in Zhenbaodao.

## REFERENCES

Huang Lin (Liu Qunwei) (1995). *Xinchao nüxing wenxue daoyin* [Introduction to new women's literature]. Changsha: Hunan renmin chubanshe.
Jones, Deborah (1980). "Gossip: Notes on Women's Oral Culture." In Cheris Kramarae, ed., *The Voices and Words of Women and Men*, pp. 193–198. Oxford: Pergamon Press.
Lakoff, Robin (1975). *Language and Woman's Place*. New York: Harper & Row.
Li Xiaojiang (1996). *Tiaozhan yu huiying: Xinshiqi funü yanjiu jiaoxue lu* [Challenge and reply: Lectures on women's studies in the new era]. Zhengzhou: Henan renmin chubanshe.
Li Xiaojiang (2000). "Nüxing shenfen: Yanjiu yu xiezuo" [Female identity: Research and writing] (Transcript of interview with Zhang Kangkang, February 2, 2000; February 13, 2000). In Li Xiaojiang, *Wenxue, yishu yu*

*xingbie* [Literature, arts and gender]. Nanjing: Jiangsu renmin chubanshe.

Li Xiaojiang, Zhu Hong and Dong Xiuyu, eds. (1994). *Xingbie yu Zhongguo* [Gender and China]. Beijing: Sanlian shudian.

Liang Xiaosheng (1994). *Minmie* [Destruction]. Beijing: Chunfeng wenyi chubanshe.

Liang Xiaosheng (1999). *Nüren xinqing* [Women's mentality]. Beijing: Zhongguo qingnian chubanshe.

Liang Xiaosheng (2001). *You liewen de huaping* [A vase with cracks]. Tianjin: Baihua wenyi chubanshe.

Ren Yiming (1997). *Zhongguo nüxing wenxue de xiandai yanjin* [Modern developments in women's literature in China]. Hong Kong: Qingwen shudian.

Sheng Ying, ed. (1995). *Ershi shiji Zhongguo nüxing wenxue shi* [A History of women's literature in 20th-century China]. Tianjin: Tianjin remin chubanshe.

West, Candace (1984). "When the Doctor is a 'Lady': Power, Status and Gender in Physician-Patient Encounters." *Symbolic Interaction*, Vol. 7, No. 1 (Spring), 87–106.

Zhang Kangkang (1988). *Yinxing banlü* [The invisible companion]. Beijing: Zuojia chubanshe.

Zhang Kangkang (1995). *Chitong danzhu* [Scarlet cinnabar]. Beijing: Renmin wenxue chubanshe.

Zhang Kangkang (1996a). *Beiji guang* [Aurora borealis]. Guiyang: Guizhou renmin chubanshe.

Zhang Kangkang (1996b). *Qing'ai hualang* [Love gallery]. Shenyang: Chunfeng wenyi chubanshe.

Zhang Kangkang (1999). *Nüren shuohua* [Women talk]. Nanjing: Jiangsu renmin chubanshe.

## GLOSSARY

Ah Ni 阿霓

Ah Qing Sao 阿慶嫂

*Beiji guang* 《北極光》

Cencen 岑岑

Chen Xu 陳旭

*Chitong danzhu* 《赤彤丹朱》

Jiamusi 佳木斯

Jiang Shuiying 江水英

Li Tiemei 李鐵梅

Liang Xiaosheng 梁曉聲

# 8 Feminist Critique

## *The Patriarchal Discourse of Chinese Male Writers\**

SHENG YING

EVERY SCHOOL OF THOUGHT, WHILE maintaining its self-esteem, always has to respect, appreciate, and acknowledge its position with respect to other schools, for progress does not simply occur with the lapse of time, but comes also from interaction with other schools. In cultural research, particularly in women's studies, an attitude of open-mindedness is necessary in approaching male writers and their works. However, when those with radically different value systems and cultural orientations confront each other, awkwardness and bitterness inevitably arise in the attempt to remain tolerant of opposing perspectives, and sharing sometimes leads to arguments. Recently, many readers have had the same experience as I have in reading works written by major contemporary male writers, and have found themselves caught in a state of irritation, confusion and indignation. Many women readers, including myself, feel a strong urge to start a dialogue that will probe the assumptions behind the flood of patriarchal language in China's literary writings.

## CHINESE MALE WRITERS' REPRESSED EGOS

One may note that the ego of contemporary Chinese male writers has been severely repressed politically, materially, mentally and sexually. This is not just a reflection of the lack of individuality in traditional Chinese culture; it may also be caused by the deep frustration male writers have experienced in contemporary Chinese society. It may even be caused by their desperate attempt to shrug off various personal and political crises in their lives when their ego cannot find full assertion and expression. At the same time, they struggle in a bid for individual dignity and independent development. However, in my opinion, they

---

* Translated from the Chinese by Kwok-kan Tam and Terry Siu-han Yip, with the assistance of Jessica Tsui Yan Li.

125

often disparage and damage women in their struggle against repression, political or personal. Many male writers are self-proclaimed worshippers of women and they even produce all sorts of "myths" concerning women to exhibit their admiration and love for women. What do these myths about women really mean? What position do male writers take in fetishizing women?

First of all, they have created myths about love and sex. Perhaps people still remember the heated debates in the literary world in the mid- and late 1980s over Zhang Xianliang's novels, *Mimosa* (*Luhua shu*) and *Half of Man Is Woman* (*Nanren de yiban shi nüren*), and Jia Pingwa's *Abandoned Capital* (*Feidu*). Male writers, including these two, express either uneasiness or indifference toward feminist critics. As Diao Dou comments (2000a, 2000b), most male writers are men who passionately admire women and they are not misogynists. They are simply not willing to admit that their views regarding womankind are no longer acceptable in the modern world.

From a superficially psychological perspective, the love which Zhang Yonglin, the protagonist, has for women like Ma Yinghua, Huang Xiangjiu and Bai Yanhua in the novel *Puberty* (*Qingchun qi*) is truly sincere. The feelings such a character harbours towards women are gratitude and indebtedness, not a desire to dominate. However, if we examine the psychology of the characters more closely, it is obvious that the Zhang Yonglin stories are disgusting: after men have found sexual relief in women, satisfied their desires and regained their sexual potency, they use such excuses as "the need to transcend themselves" and "the will to resist material temptation" to renounce women and then blame women for having given them warmth, enlightenment and whole-hearted devotion. The myth of women's love, which the author has created, is always associated with a mother's affection and care. When it serves men's existence, it is brought within the orbit of men's lives. When it is no longer needed, men will throw it off or let their women leave of their own accord. This kind of myth tries to propagate the idea that a woman will have no value unless she lives in the life cycle of a man, loving him and serving him. When the man no longer needs her, the woman will lose the meaning of her existence. When Zhang Xianliang imagines female sexuality, he always stresses the female's natural body shape and primitive sexual power, as if in eulogy for male worship of the female body, and sees sexual appeal as a kind of beauty and romance; but actually, the writer only regards women's sexual appeal as seduction, which is subjected to the male gaze and exists for the service of men. The "gaze" at the female body is seen as a stimulus to man's youthful lust and romantic imagination, and sex is a service that allows men to indulge in a gentle state of euphoria. But if sex hampers or threatens a man's official rank and promotion, he will resist and renounce his woman without hesitation. This kind of myth represents women as the embodiment of sex, sexual appeal, uncultivated nature and flesh, while men present the essence of spirit, will, consciousness and transcendence. Isn't the belittlement of women obvious? Is it really worshipping women when male writers treat the female body as their bodhi tree, as their source of inspiration? What sort of worship is this?

After Zhang Xianliang's *Getting Used to Dying* (*Xiguan siwang*) and Jia Pingwa's *Abandoned Capital*, the sexualized image of women created by male writers takes on new features: while craving for the female body, the male protagonists tend to treat sex as a panacea for redeeming their souls and healing their broken hearts. Diao Dou gloats over his creation of "the theory of nourishment." He directly addresses women as "the symbol of sex," and believes that a man can "grow strong" with the sexual nourishment of women (Diao Dou, 2000a, 2000b). He has modernized the Daoist theory of "extracting *yin* [the female] to invigorate *yang* [the male]." These male writers write about women's bodies as a means of asserting their male superiority. They seek sexual relief and comfort from women in the hope of achieving unity of body and soul. The male protagonist in *Getting Used to Dying* is in the habit of telling his lovers stories of starvation and death when making love. In the arms of women, he longs to piece together the fragments of his soul that have been crushed in the politics of hegemonic power. Zhuang Zhidie, in *Abandoned Capital*, also seeks comfort for his soul by making love with Tang Wan'er and Ah-Can in his "Seeking-Lack Room." Decadent merrymaking allows him temporarily to fill his inner need or emptiness. Women breathe life into him, allowing him to restore his rotten character. Maybe this is the reason why male writers often merge the theme of decadence with hedonism in their stories featuring women as sex goddesses. In another example, in the Three-Family Village in Yan Lianke's *The Day and the Year* (*Riguang liunian*), young virgins are selected to be prostitutes in the city in order to raise money to tackle the epidemic of incurable disease that has struck the village. Lan Sishi, the most beautiful woman, volunteers to prostitute herself for money in order to cure her lover, the village head Sima Lan, of his illness. She then gains the title of "sex queen," and causes outrage in the village. Yan Lianke deconstructs this myth by having both the village head and Lan Sishi die at the end of the story, showing that sex can neither save the life of the village head, nor cure the despair of the villagers. But the women in the novel are trampled and destroyed.

Chinese male writings often contain the myth of beauty. Jia Pingwa says in his famous work "About Women" (Guanyu nüren): "In men's minds, the purpose of a woman coming into the world is to bring beauty." The meaning of a man's existence is "to conquer the world" and "the meaning of a woman's existence is to conquer man," and "a woman's beauty" is what conquers man. He further states that regardless of women's beauty and power over men, "this world still belongs to men." So women should understand that beauty is "men's designated function for women." It is only in this designated realm that men are "willing to be conquered," and thus women should take good care of their beauty in order to give men a sense of novelty and to make their beauty last. The male writer's position with regard to women is clear: the sight of a beautiful woman is no more than a form of sexual enjoyment. It is obvious that the male writer values a woman for her beauty, and this is viewed from a male perspective. Zhou Guoping puts it in a more straightforward manner by affirming that it is impossible for a man to look at a woman without lust ("Women in Men's Eyes" [Nanren yanzhong de nüren]). In the past, there was the belief that men's appreciation of women's beauty was like a person's appreciation of art. Such appreciation was artificially cultivated. Zhou believes that it is wrong to make women the objects of men's gaze, for it signifies a denial and deprivation of the status and right women should have as creators and spectators of beauty. Is such a male gaze not a betrayal of men's desire of women as their possessions and playthings? Objectifying women by placing them on a pedestal is in itself a power play of inequality.

On the one hand, Jia Pingwa idealizes feminine beauty. He yearns for women who can "calm one's emotions" and "catch one's attention" (Jia, 1992)—women who are "like a vivid touch in painting" and "beyond description" (Jia, 1992), and who have a graceful temperament (Jia, 1993b, 1995b). On the other hand, he is unable to appreciate a successful career woman. A look at the beauties living in the "Seeking-Lack Room" (Jia, 1993c) and the "Seeking-Lack Pavilion" (Jia, 1993c) reveals that they are all simple-minded and superficial. Zhou Guoping also makes it clear that he does not admire "sophisticated women" (Zhou, 2003, p. 277) and cannot tolerate women who have any depth (Zhou, 1996a). He believes that a woman who thinks will lose part of her beauty and this is heartbreaking for him (Zhou, 1996c). By praising the beautiful woman in the way that a playboy might, or in the patronizing tone of a knight, many male writers try to fix women eternally in the system of demarcated gender roles. They perpetuate the polarization of men and women as the strong and the weak. In the story "Mud Door" (Tu men), Jia Pingwa brazenly asserts: "a woman is a woman only when she occupies the opposite pole to men," and he also repeatedly exaggerates "the feminine aura". Zhou Guoping thinks it is necessary for a man to ease his "rationality" with the female like using it as a scent. He even puts forward the notion that men "create culture in solitude" while women "propagate culture in collectivity," and that women are "the friends of male geniuses" (Zhou, 1996b). Such a division of gender roles already implies a hierarchy. As women's pursuit of individuality is related to the full realization of virtue, intelligence, love and beauty, they have to be educated and empowered so as to adapt to the needs of age. They must not fall into the male traps by subscribing to the ideology of women being tender, angelic and humble. I believe that in China today, the relation between men and women is moving in the direction of mutual support, complementarity and interaction. Women are striving for further improvements. If male writers continue to reinforce and support the polarization of the two sexes, they are ignorant of the women's movement in China.

It is interesting to note that Jia Pingwa also tries to deconstruct the myth of the beautiful woman in his long novel *Yubai and Yelang (Baiye)*. The model Yan Ming, who is extremely ugly at the beginning of the story, changes her facial features, and therefore her destiny, by means of plastic surgery. The birth of her child, however, uncovers the truth of this fake beauty. In this story, the writer ruthlessly deconstructs the myth, through the male protagonist Yelang's doubts about reality—"Is there anything true? Nothing is true but my mother." When Yelang divorces Yan Ming, the writer's compassion for the beautiful woman also disappears. While questioning the elusive and illusory world, the writer's misogyny also manifests itself. He finally subverts the myth of the beautiful woman he has created. In the patriarchal world, the construction and deconstruction of the female myths are all presided over and carried out by men, and the alternation between misogyny and worship of the female becomes a casual and arbitrary matter.

Mother worship is an interesting phenomenon that warrants investigation. In the 1980s and 1990s, the heyday of feminism in mainland China, some female writers began to deconstruct the myth of the mother-figure. As a matter of fact, male writers already regarded the contemporary period as the great age of women, and popularized the vogue of worshipping the female. This explains why characters with an Oedipus complex pervade their works. It should be noted that China remains a nation where ancestors are respected and ethics valorized, and the patriarchal clan system, which emphasizes blood relations, is deeply inscribed in everyone's heart. The Chinese believe that they have to repay their mothers' sacrifice in giving birth to them with filial piety, and mother worship has become part of the collective unconscious. Chinese writers do not curse their own mothers as bitches, as some Western writers did (Wang and Xu, 2000). However, the emphasis of the clan system on ancestry and family is after all an ancient feudalist ideology. Its distinction between the sexes and the hierarchy of the old and the young are particularly oppressive to female individuality and freedom, and its negative effect is striking. Most of the female partici-pants in the May Fourth Movement were pioneers in resisting the patri-archal clan system, and bravely opposed the feudal ethical code. Women fought for freedom of marriage, and strove to become Chinese Noras by leaving their homes. Female writers today attempt to resist "maternal power" for the same reason, that is, they oppose the mother's complicity in the patriarchal system, and they denounce any form of control the mother imposes upon them. Although some male writers have reflected upon the negative influences of patriarchal culture, their sensitivity toward women's issues is somewhat inadequate and at times seriously distorted. The mother worship in the TV series *A Huge Family* (*Da zhai men*) and in the novel *White Deer Land* (*Bailu yuan*), which was awarded the Mao Dun Prize, are two examples. Bai Jingqi in *A Huge Family* is at first an arrogant person, but he later observes the rules of filial piety and obeys his mother, the junior Mrs. Bai and becomes a humble person with many accomplishments in life. However, Bai Jingqi's Oedipus complex finally results in the tragic death of two concubines. While revealing the contributing factors to the characters' tragic flaws and fates, the writer deliberately avoids mentioning filial piety and accentuates the myth of mother worship. In *White Deer Land*, Tian Xiao'e, who once opposed the traditional ethical code, is regarded in the patriarchal clan culture as a harlot and evil spirit. Her depravity leads her to a tragic end. Even after death, her corpse is dug up and burnt. By contrast, the writer allows the Confucian scholar Mr. Zhu to say to his wife on his deathbed, "I want to call you mama...." The Confucian scholar confesses that he feels so alone that all he wants is a mother. In the novel, Mrs. Zhu, the mother of Huairen and Huaiyi, becomes the emblem of Confucian culture. Mr. Zhu's desire for a mother is a desire shaped by patriarchal clan culture. Such works reveal the characteristics of mother worship in these Chinese male writers and the nature of the patriarchal clan system with great accuracy. In them, the Oedipus complex has become a collective cultural complex, for it directs its love towards a system. The Chinese male writers accept the patriarchal clan culture without any hesitation. This kind of mother love, which is imbued with filial values and Confucian ethics, is an important carrier of the will-power and latent desire of Chinese male writers.

The mother fetish in Mo Yan's novel *Big Breasts and Wide Hips* (*Fengru feitun*) has also aroused great interest. The book's title has been attacked by feminist critics such as Liu Huiying, who comments that "to display women's sexual characteristics before readers" is "sheer sexual seduction and rampant commercialism" (Liu, 2000, p. 5). Xu Kun (1999, pp. 171–185) also sees the novel as a narrative of the female body under the control of the meticulously designed patriarchal discourse. Shangguan Jintong's obsession with the female breast is directed toward not only his mother, but also other women, whose breasts become his victims once he catches sight of them. In his mind, the female breast is something he can grab and knead at will. Although the writer is dissatisfied with the good-for-nothing Shangguan Jintong, his obsession with women's sexual organs cannot be concealed. In comparison with the Oedipus complex which the novel emphasises strongly its idea of male supremacy seems less obviously presented. Mo Yan repeatedly proclaims "his special adoration for women." The goal of *Big Breasts and Wide Hips* is to mould the image of a great mother who endures all sorts of hardships (Li and Geng, 1999). However, a closer investigation would reveal the deeper meaning of the praise which the writer heaps on the mother. Firstly, the writer creates the goddess of reproduction and then he reveals his traditional views on reproduction. In order to improve her chance of survival in her household, a mother named Lu Xuan'er has to bear eight children with seven different men (her husband is impotent). The writer sympathizes with her humiliating history of procreation, but he approves the Chinese patriarchal concept that women are tools to extend the family line. Nowadays, marriage does not aim at reproduction, and the concept that reproduction is the sole purpose of a woman's existence is also criticized. In Betty Friedan's criticism of Freud, she points out that what a woman needs is "freedom as a person" and

"Freud's elevation of reproductive sex as the sole meaning and target of female existence must be reprimanded" (quoted in Tong, 1996, p. 252). While the writer creates the Gaea, the mother of the earth, he also uses a man's return to his infantile state as the main backdrop, and this shows that he is in effect retaliating against women. The mother Lu Xuan'er has suffered greatly in raising her children, but none of them torments her as incessantly as Shangguan Jintong does. He is always in the oral stage, and seeks pleasure from caressing and sucking his mother's breasts. This man wants to possess his mother forever and keep her bound to the toil of housework and childcare all her life. He blurs the boundary between his mother and himself and fails to realize and construct his own self. From the perspectives of Western feminism, the male fantasy of returning to his infantile state is linked to that of possessing his mother and an unconscious wish of taking revenge on women (Kaplan, 2000). There appears to be good reason for holding such a view.

It seems that the creation of myths about women to satisfy men's various needs is the enterprise of many male writers across national boundaries, and this reflects a universal feature of male discourse. Simone de Beauvoir's analysis of five male authors in *The Second Sex* explains this by pointing out that men always demand that women should make up for their own inadequacies and needs. Montherlant always looks for excitement in a female body, showing a form of pure bestiality. Lawrence expects a woman to be gentle and soft and demands that she "sacrifices herself to fulfil men's goals." How about Claudel? He expects women to be serving maids not only to God, but also to men. But Breton eagerly expects women to bring him "salvation," to help him escape from disasters. And Stendhal? He undoubtedly admires a woman who is noble and is willing to go through mishaps with her lover (quoted in Tong, 1996, p. 361). All of them expect women to "forget, disregard and deny themselves," and to devote themselves wholeheartedly to men. The Japanese feminist theorist Noriko Mizuta also notes that "all men in modern Japanese literature flee to women." They always want to reflect their inner worlds in the colourful looking-glass of a female body. They want to seek redemption of their "West European self" and "turbulent inner worlds" in the dreams of women. They want to find in feminine charms the vitality they have lost (Lippit, 2000, p. 244). Men hope to transcend themselves by integrating themselves into women's bodies, so that they can be women's masters (Lippit, 2000, p. 237). Many male writers consider such myths to be the best ways to control women. Compared with the foreign myths about women, are the Chinese ones inferior? Perhaps this is an issue the Chinese should consider. All myths about women were developed from the male perspective, and offer the male's answers to the same question "What is a woman?" They also represent male fantasy about women in the patriarchal world. Chinese myths about women are no exception.

## MALE FANTASIES ON SEX

Furthermore, it should be noted that when contemporary Chinese male writers are creating myths about women which turn women into men's servants, saviours and comforters, they are also glorifying the phallus, promoting the might and the prestige of men and masculinity and perpetuating patriarchy. Although the traditional Chinese belief in *yin-yang* (female-male) harmony has been instilled into male writers' minds, they still believe that the world belongs to men. They have detailed and developed the male chauvinist culture by either tracing its origin to ancient sex culture or deriving its characteristics from folk culture, so that the phallic symbol can be represented in a more complex way.

Su Tong's story *Wives and Concubines* (*Qiqie chengqun*) can be regarded as the most representative model of phallic worship in contemporary Chinese literature. It is said that Su Tong once heard a remark, "Every man has a fantasy—to have many wives and concubines." It was only after hearing this remark that Su's interest in deconstructing history was aroused and prompted him to write, in the late 1980s, his famous story about polygamy, which deals with the decline of China in history (Gan, 1993). Has he really deconstructed Chinese patriarchal history in which men are considered superior to women? Why does he invoke people's interest in polygamy? And why has his writing about polygamy become such a dominant theme on the literary scene? It is true that China, along with Turkey and India, was historically known for its polygamous culture. The magnificent spectacle of phallocentric rule is displayed by the imperial consorts and emperor's numerous concubines, the sexual indulgences of officials and rich men and the scholars' enjoyment in the boudoirs. Some men nowadays still yearn for this lustful tradition of the past so much that they indulge in erotic fantasies. The vogue of taking concubines resulted from the indulgent hedonism of the upper class, the royal family's wish for more descendants and the ordinary people's hope of continuing the family line. But women could not expect any happiness from such family life, for they were degraded by this practice and their lives can be described as painful. But Su Tong's so-called deconstruction in *Wives and Concubines* focuses mainly on the struggles between the wife and the concubines, and between the various concubines, and on the secret plots and murderous intentions of the women (including maids). He has not addressed the causes and impact of Chinese polygamy. What kind of deconstruction is this? This work provides glimpses of misogyny that surface in his later works with women as the subject—his habitual projection onto women of the dark side of human nature.

Jia Pingwa is always inclined to adopt the principle of harmony when dealing with the relationships between a wife and concubines. In *Abandoned Capital*, characters such as Niu Yueqing, Tang Wan'er and Liu Yue do not scramble to compete with each other for favour. The modern woman Xi Xia in *Gao Lao Village* (*Gao lao zhuang*) has no conflict with Gao Zilu's former wife Ju Wa. Furthermore, the writer even exaggerates Xi Xia's motherly affection for the descendant of the Gao family borne by Ju Wa, and imbues her with the ideas that "producing offspring is the top priority," and "maintaining harmony between the wife and concubines" is crucial. Jia Pingwa, who is knowledgeable about ancient Chinese culture, upholds the importance of producing "offspring as the top priority" and having "harmony between the concubines" in the patriarchal clan system. The wife and the concubines is a way to ensure the ly line. Jia also yearns for the age when there are s between a wife and concubines. That explains why ygamy, women usually live in harmony, without any n are thus spared family disputes while they enjoy sex. prise, the conservative writer Jiang Zilong also adopts an in his work *The Human Aura* (*Renqi*) that deals with This novel accentuates the male protagonist Jian Yexiu's d creates a web of phallic worship by women surrounding him. is is able to indulge himself in narcissism since women are so attracted to him. His admirers include his wife, who is a successful career woman, a female professor who taught him in the past, his childhood girlfriend, his secretary, an expatriate student who has just returned from the US for a vacation, and a female college student who works in a hotel as a hostess. They either offer him their bodies and ask for nothing in return, or respond to his "secret admiration" by giving him "wise ideas" about sex. His wife turns to religion after losing his love. There is a college student who tries her best to have sex with him.

He is obviously a womanizer, but is glorified as a great man who "cannot let women down."

Men's fantasies about rape are more startling. Zhang Yu's novel *Pain and Caress (Tengtong yu fumo)*, as both Liu Huiying (2000) and Xu Kun (1999) comment, is full of rape fantasy. The novel narrates the erotic stories of three women belonging to three generations of the Shui family. Their desire to be raped is delineated in great detail. It is even conceptualized in the portrayal of Shui Yue, alias Evil Flower, a woman of the third generation in the Shui family. In Zhang Yu's opinion, yearning for rape is Shui Yue's psychological secret and also her principle in choosing a partner. That is to say, she will marry the man who rapes her. The writer's descriptions of the erotic stories of the three generations of women, of their desires, moans and groans and sexual behaviour are reminiscent of lustful women in Ming and Qing dynasty novels—women with a burning desire to throw themselves before men's penises. Here, the writer exaggerates the women's unrestrained lust, while he celebrates the greatness of men's intelligence and power and of their phalluses, toward which women are drawn and to which they willingly submit themselves even when they are sexually abused. Shui Yue quickly changes after the branch leader Li Hong'en rapes her. She becomes submissive, and willingly commits adultery with him, thanking him for "ravishing her utterly" and for allowing her to go into "raptures ecstatically." To Xu Kun (1999), this is an unthinkable glorification of patriarchy. These women's sexual and psychological reactions have been screened, modified and distorted by patriarchal culture. Women's penis envy, as portrayed by the male writers, is charged with sadism and men's desire for possession. It is a manifestation of phallic rule.

Many women in Mo Yan's *Big Breasts and Wide Hips* also suffer from the symptom of phallus worship. The eldest sister, Shangguan Laidi, behaves coarsely and uses obscenities when she sees men. Wearing a flowery coat, she commits adultery with her younger sisters' husbands, and even lures them into a fight. The third sister, Lingdi, does not mind being raped by the mute monitor; she even runs to grab the monitor's penis and saves him when the army is about to execute him. The manageress of the chicken farm, Long Qingping, often fantasizes about a male fox sneaking into her bed, and even kneels naked before Shangguan Jintong, begging him to have sex with her. She shoots herself when she fails to have sex with him. When Long Qingping is lying on her deathbed, Jingtong's penis suddenly becomes erect. He finally grants her the favour she wanted and in so doing becomes a necrophiliac rapist. The fifth sister, Pan Di's daughter Lu Zaohua, inherits her mother's sensuous nature and invites her male cousin to take her virginal body. *Big Breasts and Wide Hips*, just like *Pain and Caress*, treats women's yearning for rape as an extension of the condition of life: it regards men's sexual violence as a sign of the power of life and women's eagerness for rape as rooted in female instinct. According to Freudianism, women are disturbed by penis envy throughout their lives, because of their primeval "castration." Their sensitive bodies instinctually crave masochism and violent penetration by men. The famous American feminist theorist, Kate Millett, criticizes this view as social Darwinism. She points out that Freud, in the field of psychoanalysis, ontologized the biological factors and extended the patriarchal cultural values to the field of anatomy in order to develop men's superego, transcendental morality, and cultural advantage. But all of these theories are assumptions caused by the threat of the women's rights movement (Millett, 1999, pp. 234–252). The fact that Chinese male writers also accentuate the power of the penis over women by means of male fantasy reflects the male desire for super sexual might and power, and their desire to conquer women.

The novel *A Sketch of the Dark Mountain Fort* (*Heishanbao gangjian*) is Ke Yunlu's recent work about power politics. The commander of the Black Mountain Fort, Liu Guanglong, is always engaged on two battle fronts: one is politics and the other, women. The protagonist's political and sexual ambitions are meticulously depicted in attempts to deconstruct them both. The writer cannot resist portraying phallus worship. Even while he is deconstructing absolute power and male power, he is pathologically obsessed with the depiction of phallus worship, which exposes his fascination for and infatuation with the phallus. When depicting Liu's sexual violence against women, the writer always makes use of the women's positive sexual response to show Liu's colossal "potency." Women in the fort compete for Liu's scratching, spanking, binding and pressing of their bodies. They are willing to be "stripped" and "devoured" by him. Women are proud of his sexual favours and some see having sex with him as a way to help their careers. Liu Guanglong's sadism seems to elicit sexual excitement in women. A look at the issue from another angle, however, shows that Liu's penis has become a tool to oppress and exploit women in a patriarchal culture.

Fear and avoidance of women is another facet of writers' treatment of phallic imagery in recent years. Women have been regarded as bad luck ever since ancient times. The *Huainan zi*, which was written in the Western Han dynasty says that if a woman does not avoid meeting a man on the street, the man must pray so as to avoid disaster and to bless himself. This was a rule adopted by the ancient emperor Zhuan Shuo. The idea of avoiding women out of fear has led to serious psychological and cultural "illnesses." It was believed in ancient times that avoiding women was a way to preserve a man's vitality and health. Imperial counsellors and doctors in the palace always tried to persuade the emperors to check their sexual desires in order to maintain their vigour. They offered the emperor advice on sexual skills which were ways to maintain their health (Liu, 1993, p. 182). Interestingly, the contemporary writer Li Peifu is well-versed in this kind of attitude towards sex. In his work *Sheep's Door* (*Yang de men*), Hu Tiancheng, the headman of a village named Hu Family Fort, practises *Tongzi gong*, the art of rejuvenation, in front of his beloved woman Xiu Ya's naked body. Li ingeniously propagates the ancient idea that it is possible for a man to succeed and stand out among others if he can resist women's charms, abstain from sex, and build a healthy body. Hu Tiancheng has saved Xiu Ya's life and is captivated by her beauty. She is willing to offer him her body out of gratitude. But Hu wants to achieve his political ambition and overcome himself as well as his opponents, so he trains himself according to the weird ideas given in a book called *Scriptures of Bodhi Dharma*. During his training, he lets Xiu Ya lie naked beside him. He gradually enters an ascetic state, while Xiu Ya burns with passion and desire for him. At the end, Hu succeeds in withholding his ejaculation, but his woman Xiu Ya's youthfulness and sexuality are mocked. In this novel, male sexual abstinence is just another form of sexual fantasy meant to satisfy men's curiosity in the victimization of women.

Penis worship is treated in another way in Jia Pingwa's novel *Missing the Wolf* (*Huainian lang*). The hunter Fu Shan never touches or looks at a woman because of his sexual impotence, but he does regularly masturbate to achieve an inner balance of his body. According to the ancient belief in the complementary relationship between *yin* and *yang*, the so-called theory of *yin-yang* harmony is actually the art of absorbing female essence without the discharge of semen. In such a process, men are only concerned about devouring women's yin elements to supplement their *yang* and thereby strengthen and invigorate their potency. Men should benefit from women's sexual desire and action. The patriarchal theory of *yin-yang* harmony does not aim at reaching psychological and mental balance or harmony between the sexes and shows very little concern about women's sexual rights. The writer also presents Fu Shan as someone who knows about geomancy, or *feng shui*. He believes that "the best tomb is located in any yard with the shape of the female genitals." He decides to find a tomb for himself in such a place, since he cannot extract yin from women when he is alive owing to his sexual impotence. He needs to find a tomb shaped like the female genitals to supplement his deficiency in *yang*. In this novel, Jia Pingwa mystifies sexual relations by turning them into a patriarchal discourse of *yin-yang* theory.

The recurrence of the imagery of phallus worship shows that ancient customs, habits and taboos remain unconscious forces in Chinese culture today. Such ideological trends reinforce patriarchal power. In recent years, it has become fashionable in literary writings to dwell on the old licentious social mores of polygamy, prostitution, gambling, and obsessions with virgin sex and foot-binding. Among such descriptions, the portrayal of prostitutes' desires and of men's malicious negligence of women exerts the worst influences in society. On the surface, male writers criticize such customs and defend themselves by saying that they are deconstructing them. Through such portrayal of women in sexual activities, male writers in fact play with their gaze on women. From women's viewpoint, these undesirable customs which are biased descriptions of women are essentially the perpetuation of male chauvinism and an advocacy of patriarchy.

Jia Pingwa often compares a woman to a zither, and he loves to say that the only way to know whether the zither produces music or just noise depends on how a man plays it. He particularly admires elegant women and thinks that only the famous prostitutes in ancient times are really elegant women. In *Yubai and Yelang*, Yelang is attracted to Yubai, unbeknown to the latter, and he can hardly sit still on catching sight of Yubai's zither-like back. Yubai admires ancient prostitutes who played the zither well and were good at chess, as well as painting and calligraphy. She thinks they lived as equals of men, and possessed the freest spirits of life, even though they were treated as men's personal belongings. Yelang wants to play the zither of women while Yubai takes pride in her cultivation and temperament. Together they stage a comic tragedy. Yubai's statement about ancient prostitutes as free women is patriarchal. In the Tang and Song dynasties, it was common practice for scholars to visit prostitutes. Such poets as Bai Juyi and Liu Yuxi never concealed their patronage of prostitutes, while stories of prostitution by Liu Yong and Su Shi were widely circulated as charming tales. But all of them should be seen as patriarchal propaganda, for they cannot show the desolate feelings of the prostitutes. The famous prostitute in the Song dynasty, Yan Rui, writes in a poem, "Never fond of the world of prostitution, / only driven astray by the former lover." But who can really depict the prostitutes' helplessness? Nobody can. Even Liu Yong, who was known to be a close friend of prostitutes, could not voice the prostitutes' grievances and vent their anger. It is utterly senseless to call ancient prostitutes the freest people! The modern writer Mo Yan, who always refers to prostitutes as whores and describes their lewdness, overemphasizes their ugliness and intensifies their power to excite. His short story "Super Patron of Brothels" (Shenpiao) is quite unusual. Ji Fan has a sex party at home and invites 28 prostitutes over. He asks them to undress in front of him, and lie on blankets. Then the impotent Ji Fan walks over their bellies. Afterwards, he asks his attendants to give one hundred dollars to each prostitute and to drive them home. Mo Yan builds up the atmosphere of prostitution by describing women's lecherous moans and groans and erotic behaviour. He presents men's authority through Ji Fan's extravagance, for even an impotent man can patronize prostitutes. From the narration of the story, one notices that the writer takes pride in his imagination of women's sexuality. However, it is this imagination that betrays his love of patriarchy.

Su Tong's famous work *Rouge* (*Hongfen*), as he himself has said, continues to describe women along the "Songlian" Complex he developed in *Wives and Concubines* (Su, 1995). In this novel, the prostitute Xiao E, just like the prostitute Songlian in the previous novel, is both pitiful and abominable, and is abusive both to herself and others. Xiao E is a "self-made" whore, and claims to have voluntarily become a prostitute and a "natural-born good-for-nothing." She falls in love with her good friend Qiuyi's boyfriend Lao Pu, and Qiuyi curses her as a born whore who cannot be corrected even by the threat of death. Lao Pu has also had enough of her, and hopes that his son will not become entangled in the webs of women, or else he will be in serious trouble. Whether writing about concubines or prostitutes, Su Tong is not interested in rethinking history and society. He uses women as the means to pursue form. He has said, "I like using the images of women to construct my novels" because "I feel that there are more novelistic elements in women." It is clear from his writing that he suffers from a misogynist complex in which women are demonized.

Another writer, Feng Jicai, presents maliciously humorous descriptions of women in his description of women's eroticism in the novel

*Three-Inch Golden Lotuses (Sancun jinlian)*, in which he pays excessive attention to foot-binding and the shapes of shoes. Li Peifu's shocking fascination with women's eyebrows and waistlines is revealed in the novel *Sheep's Door*. Temptation, tenderness, lewdness and loneliness are all displayed, along with a woman's sexual desire, in her eyebrows. The novel is full of descriptions which make out that most of a woman's charm is revealed in her waist, which is freely available for men to molest. In *Sheep's Door*, the deputy secretary of the provincial government has invented many different methods of sexual intercourse, which come from the practices in the repositories of folk culture and ancient sex culture, such as poses like "eating a delicious mouthful of sesame in the navel" and "dragon somersault," "tiger walk," and "gorilla wrestle." The presentation of such methods on so grand a scale in literary writings signifies the return of the lascivious ghost of the patriarchy, and exposes the compelling truth about the abuse of women in China. In "Five Hunks" (Wu kuai) and "Beautiful Cave Land" (Mei yu di), whose subject matters are the lives of bandits', Jia Pingwa depicts the marring of women's faces and the perverted sense of female beauty after the infliction of sexual violence on women (such as how fresh blood trickles down a snow-white abdomen, or how exciting it is to dye porcelain-white breasts with blood). If such cruel games are regarded as moderate, then Su Tong's portrayal of cruelty such as sadism and retaliation through sex is really brutal and unnerving. In *Rice (Mi)*, the male protagonist Wulong is accustomed to pouring rice into the female genitals prior to having sexual intercourse. In order to take revenge on the owner of a rice shop, the employee Wulong successively has sex with his employer's two daughters. When he stuffs a handful of rice into the elder daughter Zhiyun's genitals, he says, "Rice is cleaner than a man's penis. Why don't you want rice? You are so stupid and despicable that I must tell you how to be a woman" (Su, 1996, p. 90). After marrying the younger daughter Qiyun, he has sex in the same way, and proclaims that he plays with women to such a degree that they are frightened. He believes that the malicious sadistic trick has its violent nature masked and can pierce through women's bodies and minds. In the novel, women become floating pieces of flesh which men are free to toy with and damage.

Some Chinese male writers do not seem to be aware that when they write about women in such ways, they are actually treating women as an instrument for men to satisfy their desire for domination and power. Some male writers not only refrain from questioning the traditional patriarchy, they even pick up the debris of pornography and perversion from the ancient warehouse of sex culture, and use it openly to propagate phallic imagery, in a vain attempt to keep women as the material object of men's desires.

## REFERENCES

Chen Zhongshi (1993). *Bailu yuan* [White deer land]. Beijing: Renmin wenxue chubanshe.
Diao Dou (2000a). "Haishi xian ren ba" [Better be a human being first]. *Baihua zhou* [Continent of a hundred flowers], No. 4, 4–25.
Diao Dou (2000b). "Wo kan nüren" [How I see women]. *Baihua zhou* [Continent of a hundred flowers], No. 5, 92–97.
Feng Jicai (1987). *Sancun jilian* [Three-inch golden lotuses]. Hong Kong: Xiangjiang chuban youxian gongsi.
Gan Gan (1993). "Su Tong de meili" [Su Tong's charisma]. *Wenxue shijie* [The literary world], No. 2, 52–53.
Guo Baochang (2001). *Da zhai men* [A huge family] (Videorecording). Beijing: China Central Television. Distributed by Meiya leishe yingdie youxian gongsi (Hong Kong). Original novel published in Beijing by Renmin wenxue chubanshe in 2001.
Jia Pingwa (1992). *Renshen he guangshan* [Pregnancy and hiking]. Beijing: Zuojia chubanshe.
Jia Pingwa (1993a). "Du 'Deng xia xinyu'" [Reading "Words from the heart under the light"]. In *Jia Pingwa sanwen daxi* [A complete collection of essays by Jia Pingwa], Vol. 3, pp. 215–216. Guilin: Lijiang chubanshe.
Jia Pingwa (1993b). *Feidu* [Abandoned capital]. Beijing: Beijing chubanshe.
Jia Pingwa (1993c). "Qiuque ting" [Seeking-lack pavilion]. In *Jia Pingwa sanwen daxi* [A complete collection of essays by Jia Pingwa], Vol. 1, pp. 315–318. Guilin: Lijiang chubanshe.
Jia Pingwa (1994). "Xiezuo yu nüxing: Yu Mu Tao yixi tan" [Writing and the female: A talk with Mu Tao]. In *Zuofo* [Contemplation], pp. 284–304. Xi'an: Taibai wenyi chubanshe.
Jia Pingwa (1995a). *Baiye* [Yubai and Yelang]. Beijing: Huaxia chubanshe.
Jia Pingwa (1995b). "Mei yu di" [Beautiful cave land]. In *Jia Pingwa wenji* [Collected works by Jia Pingwa], Vol. 4, pp. 1–40. Beijing: Zhongguo wenlian chuban gongsi.
Jia Pingwa (1996). *Tu men* [Mud door]. Shenyang: Chunfeng wenyi chubanshe.
Jia Pingwa (1998). *Gao lao zhuang* [Gao lao village]. Xi'an: Taibai wenyi chubanshe.
Jia Pingwa (1999). "Wu kuai" [Five hunks]. In *Jia Pingwa wenji* [Collected works by Jia Pingwa], Vol. 4, pp. 94–144. Beijing: Zhongguo wenlian

chuban gongsi.

Jia Pingwa (2000a). "Guanyu nüren" [About women]. In *Pingwa sanwen* [Prose essays by Jia Pingwa], pp. 236–241. Hangzhou: Zhejiang wenyi chubanshe.

Jia Pingwa (2000b). *Huainian lang* [Missing the wolf]. Beijing: Zuojia chubanshe.

Jiang Zilong (2000). *Renqi* [The human aura]. Beijing: Zuojia chubanshe.

Kaplan, E. Ann (2000). "Ziyi huawenhua fenxi: Wanjin Zhongguo dianying zhong de funü ge'an yanjiu" (Questioning Cross-cultural Analysis: A Case Study of the Women in Recent Chinese Films). Trans. Huang Xianyang. *Wenhua yanjiu* [Cultural studies], No. 6, 255–267.

Ke Yunlu (2000). *Heishanbao gangjian* [A sketch of the dark mountain fort]. Guangzhou: Huacheng chubanshe.

Li Peifu (1999). *Yang de men* [Sheep's door]. Beijing: Huaxia chubanshe.

Li Zishun, and Geng Zongyin (1999). "Zai xiezuo zhong faxian jiantao ziwo: Mo Yan fangtan lu" [The discovery of the self in writing: An interview with Mo Yan]. *Renda fuyin ziliao* [Photocopy materials from People's University], No. 10, 204–209.

Lippit, Noriko Mizuta (2000). *Nüxing de ziwo yu biaoxian* (Hiroin kara hiro e/The female self and its manifestation). Ed. Ye Weiqu. Beijing: Zhongguo wenlian chubanshe.

Liu Dalin (1993). *Zhongguo gudai xing wenhua* [Sexual culture in ancient China]. Yinchuan: Ningxia renmin chubanshe.

Liu Huiying (2000). "Jiushi niandai wenxue huayu zhong de yuwang duixianghua" [The objectification of desire in 1990s literary discourse]. *Zhongguo nüxing wenhua* [Chinese female culture], No. 1 (October), 1–18.

Mao Zhicheng (1982). "Guanyu nüren shengshi de huati" [A theme about the age of woman]. *Wenxue shijie* [The literary world], No. 2, 47–49.

Millett, Kate (1999). *Xing zhengzhi* (Sexual Politics) (1969). Trans. Zhong Liangming. Beijing: Shehui kexue wenxian chubanshe.

Mo Yan (1996). *Fengru feitun* [Big breasts and wide hips]. Beijing: Zuojia chubanshe.

Mo Yan (2000). "Shenpiao" [Super patron of brothels]. In *Chulian · Shenpiao* [First love, Super patron of brothels], pp. 262–272. Shanghai: Shanghai wenyi chubanshe.

Su Tong (1992a). *Hongfen* [Rouge]. Hong Kong: Tiandi tushu youxian gongsi.

Su Tong (1992b). *Qiqie chengqun* [Wives and concubines]. Wuhan: Changjiang wenyi chubanshe.

Su Tong (1995). "Zenme hui shi" [What's the matter?]. In *Xunzhao dengsheng* [Looking for a lamp wick], pp. 128–130. Nanjing: Jiangsu wenyi chubanshe.

Su Tong (1996). *Mi* [Rice]. In *Su Tong wenji* [Collected works by Su Tong], Vol. 6. Nanjing: Jiangsu wenyi chubanshe.

Tong, Rosemarie (1996). *Nüxing zhuyi sichao* (Feminist Thought: A

Comprehensive Introduction) (1988). Trans. Diao Xiaohua. Taipei: Shibao wenhua chuban qiye gufen youxian gongsi.

Wang Hui, and Xu Kai (2000). "Haimingwei bixia de nüren" [Hemingway's women]. *Waiguo wenxue pinglun* [Review of foreign literature], No. 2, 33–43.

Wang Qingshu (1995). *Zhongguo chuantong xisu zhong de xingbie qishi* [Sexual discrimination in traditional Chinese customs]. Beijing: Beijing daxue chubanshe.

Xu Kun (1999). *Shuangdiao yexing chuan* [Night boat in double-tune]. Xi'an: Shanxi jiaoyu chubanshe.

Yan Lianke (2007). *Riguang liunian* [The day and the year]. Beijing: Renmin ribao chubanshe.

Zhang Xianliang (1999). *Qingchun qi* [Puberty]. Beijing: Jingji ribao chubanshe.

Zhang Xianliang (2002a). *Luhua shu* [Mimosa]. Beijing: Zuojia chubanshe.

Zhang Xianliang (2002b). *Nanren de yiban shi nüren* [Half of man is woman]. Beijing: Zuojia chubanshe.

Zhang Xianliang (2002c). *Xiguan siwang* [Getting used to dying]. Beijing: Zuojia chubanshe.

Zhou Guoping (1996a). "Nanren he nüren" [Man and woman]. In Chen Chaoying, ed., *Zhou Guoping zheli meiwen* [Essays on philosophy and aesthetics by Zhou Guoping], pp. 232–236. Guangzhou: Guangdong renmin chubanshe.

Zhou Guoping (1996b). "Nanren yanzhong de nüren" [Women in men's eyes]. In Chen Chaoying, ed., *Zhou Guoping zheli meiwen* [Essays on philosophy and aesthetics by Zhou Guoping], pp. 159–168. Guangzhou: Guangdong renmin chubanshe.

Zhou Guoping (1996c). "Nüren he zhexue" [Women and philosophy]. In Chen Chaoying, ed., *Zhou Guoping zheli meiwen* [Essays on philosophy and aesthetics by Zhou Guoping], pp. 156–158. Guangzhou: Guangdong renmin chubanshe.

Zhou Guoping (2003). "Wo suo xinxiang de nüren" [The women I admire]. In *Shouwang de juli* [Distance of watching], pp. 277–285. Taiyuan: Beiyue wenyi chubanshe.

## GLOSSARY

Ah-Can 阿燦

Bai Jingqi 白景琦

Bai Juyi 白居易

Bai Yanhua 白彥花

*Bailu yuan*《白鹿原》

*Baiye*《白夜》

Chen Zhongshi 陳忠實

*Da zhai men*《大宅門》

*Feidu*《廢都》

Feng Jicai 馮驥才

*Fengru feitun*《豐乳肥臀》

*Gao lao zhuang*《高老莊》

Gao Zilu 高子路

"Guanyu nüren"〈關於女人〉

*Heishanbao gangjian*《黑山堡綱鑒》

*Hongfen*《紅粉》

Hu Tiancheng 呼天成

*Huainan zi*《淮南子》

*Huainian lang*《懷念狼》

Huairen 懷仁

Huaiyi 懷義

Huang Xiangjiu 黃香久

Ji Fan 季範

Jia Pingwa 賈平凹

Jian Yexiu 簡業修

Jiang Zilong 蔣子龍

Ju Wa 菊娃

Ke Yunlu 柯雲路

Lan Sishi 藍四十

Lao Pu 老浦

Li Hong'en 李洪恩

Li Peifu 李佩甫

Lingdi 領弟

Liu Guanglong 劉廣龍

Liu Yong 柳永

Liu Yue 柳月

Liu Yuxi 劉禹錫

Long Qingping 龍青萍

Lu Xuan'er 魯璿兒

Lu Zaohua 魯棗花

*Luhua shu*《綠化樹》

Ma Yinghua 馬纓花

"Mei yu di" 〈美穴地〉

*Mi*《米》

Mo Yan 莫言

*Nanren de yiban shi nüren*《男人的一半是女人》

Niu Yueqing 牛月清

Pan Di 盼弟

*Qingchun qi*《青春期》

*Qiqie chengqun*《妻妾成群》

Qiuyi 秋儀

Qiyun 綺雲

*Renqi*《人氣》

*Riguang liunian*《日光流年》

*Sancun jinlian*《三寸金蓮》

Shangguan Jintong 上官金童

Shangguan Laidi 上官來弟

"Shenpiao" 〈神嫖〉

*Shouwang de juli*《守望的距離》

Shui Yue 水月

Sima Lan 司馬藍

Songlian 頌蓮

Su Shi 蘇軾

Su Tong 蘇童

Tang Wan'er 唐宛兒

*Tengtong yu fumo*《疼痛與撫摸》

Tian Xiao'e 田小娥

Tongzi gong 童子功

*Tu men*《土門》

"Wo suo xinxiang de nüren" 〈我所欣賞的女人〉

"Wu kuai" 〈五魁〉

Wulong 五龍

Xiao E 小萼

*Xiguan siwang*《習慣死亡》
Xiu Ya 秀丫
Xu Kun 徐坤
Yan Lianke 閻連科
Yan Ming 顏銘
Yan Rui 嚴蕊
*Yang de men*《羊的門》
yang 陽
Yelang 夜郎
yin 陰
Yubai 虞白
Zhang Xianliang 張賢亮
Zhang Yonglin 章永磷
Zhang Yu 張宇
Zhiyun 織雲
Zhou Guoping 周國平
Zhuan Shuo 顓碩
Zhuang Zhidie 莊之蝶

# 9 Three Chinese Women Writers and the City in the 1990s*

JIN YANYU

THE LAST DECADE OF THE twentieth century saw a close bonding between female writers and the city in China. The modes of expression of these writers are almost exclusively urban. The city not only provides a geographical background for the stories, but it also becomes a foil in female writers' works, paralleled and intertwined with the other major character: woman. While the city stages women's activities, women provide readers with new perspectives of the city. Representative works include Wang Anyi's *Song of Everlasting Sorrow* (*Changhen ge*, 1995), Shi Shuqing's "Bauhinia over the Mountain" (Bianshan yangzijing, 1995) and Zhu Tianxin's *The Old Capital: A Novel of Taipei* (*Gudu*, 1997). Set in three metropolises of the Chinese-speaking world, these works deal with the past and the present of the respective cities, as well as women's lives and personal histories. Shanghai, Hong Kong, and Taipei are also shown with their respective mannerisms, customs, and topographies. These novels also manifest the special features of female writing and reveal multi-lateral and multi-layered relationships between the urban and the feminine.

For women's lives, the city is a double-edged sword, with dual functions of construction and demolition. The city can make women's lives more dynamic, more colourful, and more poetic; it can also throw women into dark terrors when the female body becomes a commodity. To women, the city often denotes freedom, knowledge, education, career, and independence; but it also implies promiscuity, trading in flesh, and male dominance. In both positive and negative terms, the city influences women's lives in myriad ways. To understand the city, therefore, depends on individual perspectives and sensitivity, and the angle one takes to approach it.

---

* Translated from the Chinese by Terry Siu-han Yip.

## ANGLE ONE: WOMEN'S CLOTHING

In *The Song of Everlasting Sorrow*, Wang Anyi juxtaposes a picture of metropolitan Shanghai with her heroine Wang Qiyao, a common girl living in a dark meandering alley. The female protagonist's desire is intertwined with the desire of the city, so much so that Wang Qiyao's dramatic ups and downs from the 1940s to the 1950s seem to be plotted by the city. The first step of the city's plot is to differentiate girls based on their high or low births: "Although all were girls, they were forcibly divided into two types. Thinking of it, buds of hatred and desire began to grow in Wang Qiyao's heart. These two feelings were the roots of evil for the lives of women" (Wang, 1995, p. 12). It is precisely the feelings of hatred and desire that push Wang Qiyao onto the stage of a beauty pageant in Shanghai in the 1940s. The city provides the best environment for the further growth of Wang Qiyao's "roots of evil":

> Shanghai at the end of 1945 justified its nightly carousal amidst celebrations of Japan's surrender. Actually the dancing and singing had nothing to do with political affairs; they followed only the feeling of happiness. New fashions exhibited in shop windows, serialized novels in newspapers, neon lights, movie posters, the banners of big sales, flower baskets marking openings of businesses, all were singing aloud. This city was so happy that it almost lost control of itself. (Wang, 1995, p. 39)

In this city, which follows its own nature of happiness and perpetual celebration, Wang Qiyao becomes a beautiful "balloon," flying on the hot air of Shanghai's prosperity and vanity. She becomes the runner-up to Miss Shanghai and effects a move from her small attic in an alley house into a luxury apartment by becoming a government official's mistress. This is the first part of Wang Qiyao's trilogy. In the second part, the balloon deflates when Shanghai falls into the hands of the Communists. Wang Qiyao is forced to seek shelter in her mother's hometown, and then to retreat into the alleys again after returning to Shanghai. But her desires are never satisfied; she makes friends with old "capitalists" and dubious Russian-Chinese, until she gives birth to an illegitimate daughter. In presenting the various phases of Wang Qiyao's life in the thirty years from 1949 to 1979, Wang Anyi depicts a distinctive picture of Shanghai's petty urbanites:

> This was the winter of 1957. The outside world was turned upside-down, but it had nothing to do with this little world beside the stove. This little world was at a corner or in a hiatus of the big world; it was safe that the

two worlds forgot about each other. Snow was flying outside the window, the fire was crackling in the small room—what a beautiful scene at a beautiful time. (Wang, 1995, p. 174)

This scene depicts not only Wang Qiyao's life, but also that of the city. The desire of the city is hibernating, only to be quickly awakened in the 1980s, when both the city and Wang Qiyao have a brief moment of glamour. But the city is decaying as much as Wang Qiyao is aging. Wang Qiyao's violent death at the hands of a young man thus marks the end of an era for the city of Shanghai. One may very well say that part of the city also dies with Wang Qiyao: the Shanghai that is ridden with desires generated by friction between its inherent topological and social differences.

Every page of Wang Qiyao's life is therefore a page of the city's life. The signifiers for the desire of the city include fashions, the facades of boulevards, neon lights, and dancing halls; they all converge on women's hair-styles and clothing, which are best understood and interpreted by Wang Qiyao, the woman typical of all Shanghai women: "The vanity and glamour of Shanghai's streets yielded the true feeling of home. The dishes on Wang Qiyao's dinner table had the heart of the banquets in fancy restaurants; the clothes worn by Wang Qiyao had the heart of the dresses on display in shop windows; even Wang Qiyao's austerity had the heart of luxury" (Wang, 1995, p. 341). The word xin (heart) is used so frequently by Wang Anyi that it almost becomes excessive. Its usage is also ungrammatical. The standard sentence to describe someone possessing certain feelings should be the Chinese verb you (have), as in "Wang Qiyao you aimei de xin" (Wang Qiyao has a penchant for fashions). By using shi (be) to link Wang Qiyao's feelings with the city's material life, Wang Anyi directly equates the two, allowing women to achieve an intimate and ontological link with the city.

Clothing, for Wang Anyi, is thus the most overt manifestation of the ontological "being" on the level of representation. She depicts Wang Qiyao during the beauty pageant period in terms of clothes: "Clothes were embracing the future with Wang Qiyao. They were her companions when she was lonely; she and they shared the intimacy of naked skin. Clothes and Wang Qiyao, in short, were *heart touching heart*" (emphasis mine) (Wang, 1995, p. 76). One does not know exactly how Wang Qiyao dresses herself in a fashionable way except that we are told repeatedly by the author, in a definitive tone which is assertive about Wang Qiyao's intimate relationship with clothing rather than descriptive of it, that she does. But it is precisely this definitive tone that animates clothing, and, by extension, the city. The heart of the city still pumps rhythmically and strongly during the anaemic and plain 1950s, thanks to Wang Qiyao's fashionable touch of wearing a white *qipao* (a Manchu-style silk dress that emphasizes the curves of the female body). Wang Qiyao's heart for fashion further edifies her daughter Weiwei and Weiwei's friends, who, in the most colourless years of the Cultural Revolution keep the city from completely losing the glamour of its material life. Wang Anyi writes:

> In those lifeless and uninteresting years, they only needed a small amount of material and made life shining. They were not at all inferior to those "anti-trend" heroes. They spoke less; they were more hands-on, spreading no-nonsense life values and interests. From the end of the 1960s to the first half of the 1970s, a quick tour of Huaihai Road could easily put you in touch with an active heart hidden under the hypocritical and empty political life. (Wang, 1995, p. 261)

The life of the city is thus sustained by Wang Qiyao's fashion sensitivity. Again, one still does not know exactly what kinds of dress it is that beautify the city during the most fashion-less years. Instead of descriptive language, it is Wang Anyi's assertive tone that creates an urban aura, which can only be felt through a firm belief in the ontological link between woman and city. That the city's history is part and parcel of the history of women's fashions further contradicts the grand notion of history, which only views the city through a succession of "important" political events.

## ANGLE TWO: THE FEMALE BODY

The attention to women's clothing in Wang Anyi's writing is replaced by an attention to female sexuality in Shi Shuqing's "Bauhinia over the Mountain," which is part two of her *Hong Kong Trilogy*. These two female writers share a common goal and that is to re-interpret the history of their beloved city through female lenses. In tracing the origin of "1997," Shi Shuqing chooses to juxtapose the 100-year geo-political history of Hong Kong with the rise of a prostitute, Huang Deyun, from the lowest stratum of society to becoming a member of Hong Kong's elite. The first story line follows the territorial expansion of Hong Kong, while the second traces Huang Deyun's personal history, outlining how she was kidnapped and taken to Hong Kong from Dongguan in

Guangdong, how she became a popular prostitute, how she took a job in a pawn shop after a series of failed relationships with men, and how she eventually rises to the top of the pawn business.

Through this juxtaposition, Shi Shuqing highlights the parallel between Hong Kong's colonial territoriality and the female body. City and woman, once again, signify and symbolize each other. Territorial expansion allows Hong Kong to grow from a smallish "girl" to a full-figured woman, using her irresistible charms to earn maximal benefit for her colonizers. In a similar way, opportunities provided by urban economic structures allow Huang Deyun to "pawn" her body and later to redeem it, using the same strategies as in the city's expansion: long-term planning, negotiating, image-building, and exploitation. Similar to the city's glamorous facade, which disguises its exploitative nature, Huang Deyun puts on a mask of virtue to hide her humble past and her social ladder is built on layer after layer of her victims' bodies.

Huang Deyun eventually becomes the symbol of virtuous woman. She cleans up her act after the successful buyout of her body; she dresses plainly and only pays attention to work in order to become someone like the famous Aunt Eleven, who is the accepted leader of Hong Kong's pawn shops. Eventually she is able to slip onto Aunt Eleven's chair, a symbol of male power and masculinity. The price she pays is the complete loss of her female identity and sexuality:

> Rumours rose and fell continuously, but decreased were audiences who nodded their agreement. Huang Deyun unaffectedly came early to the pawn- shop everyday. Now her eyebrows were painted very thick and dark, her chin turned thinner, and her cheeks were tinted with rouge. Everyone in the pawn-shop agreed, behind her back, that her expression increasingly resembled Aunt Eleven, the righteous Aunt Eleven when she had tried desperately to save Li Quan, the old boss. (Shi, 1996, p. 52)

Huang Deyun's path to self-redemption denotes a path of gender reversion. But it is a forced choice. What she originally wanted was familial bliss and domestic serenity. She has a glimpse of such a simple everyday family life with Qu Yabing, a professional translator, after she is discarded by her British lover:

> Huang Deyun was stir-frying *jielan* vegetable, her child secured on her back. Next to her was a terra cotta jar in which Qu Yabing's favourite bitter-melon was simmering with spareribs. Stung by the sizzling oil splashed from the wok, the child started to wail. Without a word, Qu Yabing quickly untied the child, who soon stopped crying. With the child

in his arms, Qu Yabing stepped out of the kitchen. In the courtyard, he saw his clothes hanging on a bamboo pole; waving in the wind of dusk, they were already dry. On a bamboo stool, there was a half-finished shoe bottom with uneven stitches. Apparently coming out of a green hand, this was the shoe she was making for him. Qu Yabing held the child in one hand, freed the other hand to take out some rice grains and fed the speckled chicken. (Shi, 1996, p. 13)

This, for Huang Deyun, is the ideal life of an ordinary urbanite. But she again chooses a wrong partner and has to seek an alternative path.

Everyday life has a positive value in both "Bauhinia over the Mountain" and *The Song of Everlasting Sorrow*. Under Wang Anyi's lens, Wang Qiyao is also seen as a woman enjoying a peaceful family life:

Wang Qiyao's days were spent with meticulous care. All lives under Shanghai's roofs, in fact, had a careful and attentive nature. If someone was not this focused, or did not pay enough attention to these most concrete and trivial details, it would be very difficult to carry on with life. You cannot look at these days as a whole. Under the surface of carefulness, therefore, there was a strength of endurance. (Wang, 1995, p. 240).

Women enduring the vicissitudes of life in an everyday setting is a theme shared by both writers in their examination of the relationship between city and woman. Women's clothing or body has to succumb to the tyranny of natural time; only everyday life is the most powerful corner-stone for the city, be it Shanghai or Hong Kong.

The everyday experiences of Wang Qiyao and Huang Deyun have clear gender imprints. But the significance of the everyday in these two works transcends essentialized gender differences. As Wang Anyi remarks in her preface to *Among Female Friends* (*Nüyou jian*):

Under the floating sounds and colours, there is actually an eternal order, following the most basic of rationales. It is so plain that it appears to be simplistic. Falling into the gaps between revolutionary changes, it is too common to be seen. But it is the ultimate factor that steers the direction of movements. Within it, there is a kind of energy, accumulated through unyielding patience. This energy does not propel change; it is, in fact, the eternal force.... This should be the subject of artistic representations. (Wang, 2001, p. 1)

Neither revolutionary nor evolutionary, both macro and micro, this "eternal order" is a substance of the everyday. By focusing on the writings of this order, and by making female experience their integral part, Wang Anyi and Shi Shuqing each finds her own angle in writing about history, city, and woman. Their writings carry personal and cultural significance, and bring new aesthetic experiences to the representations of the city.

## ANGLE THREE: WOMEN'S TRAVEL

Zhu Tianxin's *The Old Capital: A Novel of Taipei* also addresses issues related to history and city. But her heroine, an independent and well-educated modern woman, has different personal traits from the characters of Wang Anyi and Shi Shuqing. Wang Qiyao and Huang Deyun are relics of history, holding tight to their memories of past glories and treasure boxes (Wang's wooden box full of golden bullion and Huang's leather jewellery case). In contrast, the heroine in *The Old Capital: A Novel of Taipei* has none of these "historical burdens." She travels with minimal luggage, shuttling between metropolises. She also lives on memories, but they are accumulations of her travelling experiences, not remnants of the past. This unique way of writing indicates new possibilities of representing the urban woman in an increasingly globalized world.

Readers do not know the name of the heroine in *The Old Capital: A Novel of Taipei*. She is addressed in the second-person pronoun— "you." By using this unusual narrative point of view, Zhu Tianxin brings an extraordinary intimacy to the relationship between the narrator and the heroine. The narrator's voice, too, possesses such intimate knowledge of the heroine that it is almost like a monologue. In this monologue, the protagonist, "you," goes through a series of travelling. The first part takes readers to Taipei, where the protagonist walks through the city as a young woman; the second part depicts Taipei in the protagonist's memory when she travels to Kyoto; and the third part recreates the protagonist's experience of Taipei, but this time the protagonist is walking through Taipei as a Japanese tourist. Taipei's past and present are intertwined in this series, forming a prism of the metropolis in different periods, with comparison and reference made to another city, Kyoto. From the age of seventeen, the heroine's life spans a period of twenty years, allowing readers to see and compare the city in different eras.

*The Old Capital: A Novel of Taipei* begins with reminiscences about the past. It, is full of nostalgia for the good old days and there are numerous poetic depictions of Taipei's idyllic beauty:

> Driving past Zhuwei, if it happened to be dusk, the setting sun would shine together with its reflection on the river. The sandbank was fully covered with trees and home to white herrings, ox-back herrings, and night herrings. Inevitably, one was reminded of the famous poem that reads, "Clear sky, river, vivid Hanyang trees; flowers, grasses, wild Yingwu sandbank." (Zhu, 1997, p. 153)

The protagonist's poetic recollection of these scenes is reinforced by the bodily sensations of a seventeen-year-old girl: "By then her body fluids and tears were as fresh as dew on flowers." The agile body of the seventeen-year-old girl wanders in old Taipei, a city blessed with natural beauties and cultural sophistication; everything is in a harmony. But the idyllic vision is not free of anxiety or melancholy. The street names and exotic trees bear colonial imprints, constantly reminding the reader of the heavy memories of the city's colonial past.

Some twenty years later, the protagonist is stunned by the damage done by commercialization, with its urban sprawl and political brawls, to Taipei's environment and beauty. The protagonist has reached middle-age, and the smell of her body and her body fluids are no longer fresh and fragrant:

> The smell that had lasted for more than twenty years was no longer existent. You never even realized it existed, until it disappeared after loyally following you around for more than twenty years. All you had left was a salty smell, which could easily congeal into salt. A dirty salt that must have had a different chemical structure from ocean salt. The continuous flow of body fluids and sweat was inevitable. Tears, however, refused to flow anymore. (Zhu, 1997, p. 168)

Her beloved city and beloved body have both aged, becoming ugly, unlovely, and full of foul smells. It is only natural for the protagonist to look for a place where both youth and ancient capital are preserved.

The second part of the trilogy begins with the question: "Is there such a place?" Kyoto seems to be the perfect answer. Mediated through Yasunari Kawabata's masterpiece *Ancient Capital*, the protagonist walks through Kyoto's streets in a trance-like state. Kyoto is as beautiful as always; but its beauty reminds her of Taipei in every minute detail. The journey in Kyoto thus becomes a journey through the memory and history of Taipei. Anxieties and depressions overwhelm the pure, well-preserved, and well-documented ancient Japanese capital. It is at this moment that the entire trip to Kyoto becomes meaningless. The protagonist comes to this Japanese city to meet with her old friend "A," but now she is questioning whether it is worth giving up her precious time together with her daughter.

The disappointing trip makes the protagonist's return to Taipei even more difficult. In the last part of the trilogy, she pretends to be a Japanese tourist, holding an old map from the colonial period so as to search for the "motherland," the "culture," and the green city of her memory. But all has been lost. In the end she finds "herself" lost on the banks of the Danshui River: "The river shore did not have rich farmlands, beautiful ponds, mulberry trees, or bamboo groves; nor did it have criss-cross paths or cocks crowing in the distance. This was apparently not Tao Yuanming's utopian peach-blossom spring. But what was this place? ... What was this place? You started to wail" (Zhu, 1997, pp. 231–232). The protagonist wails for the loss of the city in her memory. But interestingly, the lost city acquires new memories precisely because of her wailing. Female melancholy reconstructs the city's memory that is vital for its continuing survival. Through this melancholy, Zhu Tianxin displays a whole new relationship between woman and city. This relationship is different from either Wang Qiyao's symbiotic relationship with Shanghai, or Huang Deyun's metonymic representation of Hong Kong. This is a relationship of mutual gazing, woman toward city and vice versa. The protagonist in *The Old Capital: A Novel of Taipei* gazes at Taipei from the perspectives of the historical, the political, the cultural, the ecological and the aesthetic, comparing and contrasting in broad historical and geographical contexts. Conveyed through this gaze are a modern intellectual woman's strong feelings of anxiety, love, and hatred toward her home city. As Zhu Tianxin states in her preface to *The Old Capital: A Novel of Taipei*, "To face, to confront, and to acknowledge my various grudges and gratitude to this city," it is important to find a "willingness to naturally preserve traces of people's lives ... in a modern city that is proud of its civility and sophistication." Such idealistic yearning for a healthy city culture, which entails love of books and preservation of pieces of the idyllic past, is no doubt a cure for the diseases of modern cities.

City, in the meantime, also gazes at woman. The disturbance felt by Zhu Tianxin's heroine is not limited to anxieties about the aging of the female body. It also encompasses the psychic changes brought about by an unnameable, unconscious fear of uncertainties about her identity. The travelling urban woman thus resembles the female characters in Hitchcock's movies: fearful, neurotic, hysterical, helpless, yet brave enough to walk straight toward the thing that gazes at her. The profound sense of trauma is made possible by none other than the traveller herself, who brings changes of *mise-en-scène*, but is stuck with the uncanny similarities of women's urban lives.

It is not a coincidence that all three female writers seek to write about woman and city in the form of a trilogy, which is a powerful tool for telling history from an evolutionary and linear, muscular way. The three female writers' trilogies, however, all seek to go back from the third part to the first part so as to find faults in the seemingly truthful perceptions at the beginnings. They rewrite the history of city and woman through questioning their origin. Only by so doing can they eventually go beyond the limit of the trilogy and find possibilities of rewriting female subjectivity.

## REFERENCES

Shi Shuqing (1996). "Bianshan yangzijing" [Bauhinia over the mountain]. *Haixia* [Straits], No. 5 (May), 295–337.

Wang Anyi (1995). *Changhen ge* [The song of everlasting sorrow]. Beijing: Zuojia chubanshe.

Wang Anyi (2001). "Xu" [Preface]. In Wang Anyi, ed., *Nüyou jian* [Among female friends], pp. 1–18. Shanghai: Shanghai wenyi chubanshe.

Zhu Tianxin (1997). *Gudu* [The old capital: A novel of Taipei]. Taipei: Maitian.

## GLOSSARY

aimei 愛美

"Bianshan yangzijing" 〈遍山洋紫荊〉

*Changhen ge* 《長恨歌》

*Gudu* 《故都》

Huang Deyun 黃得雲

*Nüyou jian* 《女友間》

qipao 旗袍

Qu Yabing 屈亞炳

shi 是

Shi Shuqing 施叔青

Wang Anyi 王安憶

Wang Qiyao 王琦瑶
xin 心
you 有
Zhu Tianxin 朱天心

# 10 New Modes of Women's Writing in the Age of Materialism*

GUO SHUMEI

WOMEN'S WRITING IN CHINA HAS reached a new stage. It has departed from the conception of literature as an expression of grand social themes to take a new course towards the more affective and individualistic mode of writing. The flowering of women's writing since the establishment of the People's Republic of China has hinged on the ideological liberation of the 1980s. This was a movement on a large scale that reassessed a series of values and conceptions regarding human nature, self-esteem and independence. Every piece of creative work by female writers is a break from the old way of thinking that smothers humanity. The quest for such values as "freedom," "love" and "beauty" in literary works always invokes strong reactions. In many works, the female image focuses mostly on the elite class in mainstream society. Even the marginalized has the function of providing a critical perspective countering the mainstream view of women in society. A new image has emerged. It is that of women actively in pursuit of happiness and it presents an open challenge of established codes. Female writers have made daring and significant breakthroughs in terms of re-conceptualizing their roles, and this has given them the image of advocates of social change. A strong sense of social responsibility and a deep concern about national development pervade women's works. In the 1980s, female writers such as Dai Houying, Zhang Jie, Chen Rong and Zhang Kangkang all showed their concern about social issues in their writings and saw "social intervention" as their role. Such a trend is often labelled the "grand socialist representation" in women's literature in China.

---

\* Translated from the Chinese by Gerald W. Cheung, Yomei Shaw and Terry Siu-han Yip.

## THE AGE OF MATERIALISM IN THE 1990S

China entered the age of materialism in the 1990s. The new pluralism of China brought challenges to the elitist culture that had long cherished the grand themes in socialist representation. Controversy appeared when Chen Ran and Lin Bai emerged on the Chinese literary scene as deviants from the grand socialist representation. "Private writing" was at the epicentre of this controversy. In fact, "private writing" is only a convenient label for women's writings about the private parts of their bodies. The core issue lies in the liberation of the female writers from the constraints of the grand socialist representation to facilitate their engagement in writing of a more personal kind. They no longer focus on the narration of typical experience shared by most people or present their tales from a collective point of view. Their writings demonstrate a preoccupation with the unique life experience of an individual. Very often the experience depicted is unique to the character; it can be idiosyncratic, or devoid of any generalized meaning. The protagonist can be a rootless outcast, or she can be a solitary, unaccompanied wanderer. She might also be an unemployed person under pressure from the harsh realities of life, or a social deviant with unusual experiences, such as homosexuality. The female characters are no longer physical embodiments of abstract ideals, and the focus is no longer on the universal value of their lives. They become complex and ambiguous characters with independent understandings of the puzzles of life, and thus defy any reductive image. A question then arises about the value of such individualistic writings, with their emphasis on individual experience. Recognition of its value has met with setbacks. Is the grand socialist representation of a higher value and more profound meaning than the individualistic one? For writers who approximate reality and focus their work on the social themes in real life, writing about social problems is ultimately a bugle-blast that rouses the deaf and educates the masses. It has an easily identifiable value as a service to society. Literature with moral messages was once in vogue in China and the tradition that moral writing is comparable to running a nation or an immortal feat is rooted in the Chinese mind. Such a tradition has not been completely abandoned. With regard to readers' reception, the Chinese tend to have a higher regard for works written in a realistic style. There has been little appreciation for works that emphasize psychological growth, that explore and reveal dimensions of human thinking processes, that examine the general meaning of human existence, and that expose the secret stories of the human subconscious. The value of these works lies in their effect of revealing the inner selves of the characters, that is, their secret thoughts as well as the psychological aspects of their behaviour.

Furthermore, it is hard for many literary creations to shrug off traces of their age. In every age, trends and lifestyles peculiar to that age endow writers with unique visions that distinguish them from writers of other ages. The pluralistic cultural setting of the 1990s presented literature with multiple themes and perspectives. In the 1980s, when literature was thriving, it was possible for a novel to cause a stir in society. However, it is not realistic any more to demand that literature should serve the same purpose of propagating moral messages, for such a demand would not do justice to literature. Readers look on helplessly as writers' sense of mission in writing literature is gradually substituted by a desire to entertain and amuse. Literature now becomes a cultural product for relaxation amid the tensions of life. It is clear that what people expect from the experience of reading has changed tremendously in recent years. Readers are no longer interested in themes about the Cultural Revolution or about the education of youth. The collective and mainstream life experiences shared by so many no longer exist, and social groups which share collective and common experience are shrinking. People's mobility and relocation have caused the continuous split of different social groups into individuals, who are always on the move. Permanent settlement becomes an increasing rarity, and people on the road have diverse experiences. The pressure of living as an independent being, which comes with the increasing freedom of the individual, becomes magnified and more unbearable. Burdened by their different social titles and occupations, writers wander from public streets to bookstores, struggling to earn a living. In particular, the young writers have a profound sense of the enormous pressures of life. The great sense of having a duty to improve social life and the intention to fight to the last breath amid social turmoil have abated significantly. All of this has given rise to a much more diverse literature at the close of the twentieth century.

## THE SUDDEN RISE OF WOMEN'S WRITING

Since the new millennium, the writings of contemporary Chinese women have taken on a sudden and strong momentum. This has led many readers to question whether all women who write are qualified to be called writers. In China, the term "woman writer" has been a problematic expression. Twenty years ago, no one ever imagined a future with so many women in the field of writing. Then women started to write diligently and had published volumes of fiction, poetry, drama and essays. Any woman could then be regarded as a serious writer as long as she exerted some influence. She would then join the community of writers. Organizations such as "writers' associations" and "literary associations" would welcome her for her different experience and background, and she could make writing her profession. For a long time, writing was a respectable profession. True lovers of literature dared not even talk about literature openly at certain times, for fear of saying nonsense that would make themselves a laughing stock. Writers concentrated fully on creation and appreciation, playing gatekeepers to this sacred territory. Female writers who appeared in the 1980s pursued spiritual happiness that came with the creation of serious literature—happiness such as the free flight of the mind—and high social status as a literary writer. The literary fanaticism of that period produced a large group of literature lovers, who appreciated the thoughts, emotions, structures and perspectives in literature, and they craved for such intellectual and spiritual enrichment. They made themselves into literary fanatics who attached great importance to literature.

Now, in the age of materialism, the picture is totally different. Anyone can take part in literary creation. It is easy to publish a book. Anyone can write, as long as he or she is recognized by publishers. Publishing an article is even easier, as a large number of newspapers and magazines need contributions. Therefore, more women start to write and they write anything they wish. The field has become free, liberal and open. A woman does not need to have a strong sense of mission, so writing does not weary her. She can write something that is meant to entertain, and although such writing might be regarded as trivial women's literature, she will not mind. She can also write seriously, and such writing might be regarded as cultural critique. But she would not gloat over this. She can stop writing whenever she likes and take a job that earns her money; she can also settle down and write with all her energy in order to achieve some purpose. Women of this age can make their living by freelance writing. They can write for fashion magazines, for the leisure sections of newspapers, for variety shows, for the Internet or for advertising. They can also stay at home and write truly meaningful novels and dramas. Women of this age are at once professionals in their respective industries and amateur writers. "Writing" has become one of the myriad engagements in their lives, and one of the many circles they live in. Writing is no longer something sacred and serious that demands a person's full attention and total strength. Writers play other roles, and many people in other roles can also play the role of a writer.

All of this hinges on the new market demand. In response to this demand, publishers bring out new books and introduce new faces in order to create new cultural trends. Anyone from any occupation can write and publish a book. All of a sudden, the title "writer" does not bear as much weight as it used to. Some people who crave for reputation jump at the opportunity and casually adopt the title of writers, thus distorting the meaning of the term. Serious writers, on the other hand, have now lost the words to describe themselves, even though they continue to engage in serious literary creation. Under such circumstances, it is better to treat "women's writing" as a collective whole in understanding the direction of women's literature. It is certain that the situation is improving. Women writers would not have emerged in such great numbers and there would not have been such colourful stories from all walks of life told in so many different tones, had there not been the market demand, the active participation of women in writing, or the pluralistic values, psychologies and styles that now exist. There will eventually be women writers who stand out among this group.

## INCREASING USE OF PLOTLESS AND NON-SEQUENTIAL STYLE

The tendency toward the plotless and non-sequential style among female writers is related to these writers' predecessors. Such a tendency was already emerging in the previous generation of writers. Xiao Hong's *The Story of Hulan River* (*Hulanhe zhuan*) is an example. Works by writers of the new generation, such as Chi Zijian and Lin Bai, also exhibit such a style. The tendency for fiction to take on plotless and non-sequential features is an early sign that traditional boundaries between genres have become blurred. Take the novel as an example. Traditional Chinese novels place great emphasis on narrative structure, with chapter and section divisions, inner conflicts, character portrayal, atmosphere, setting, and the like. Most novels have developments in the plot and a unified story, and they provide a sense of completion. For mature writers such as Tie Ning and Wang Anyi, a novel is a self-contained artistic world. Through this world, readers understand the ideas the writer expresses, and the values the writer advocates in the novel, and are educated while being entertained. At the same time, the moral of the story lies in its plot, which follows a certain logic in development.

Recently there has been a strong tendency for novel writing to be plotless and non-sequential in style. Women writers have, either consciously or unconsciously, created an atmosphere, or a style, which has an affective influence on readers, who will not remember the plot after reading such novels, because they are plotless. Such writing breaks conventions, for it has no structure or fundamental conflict at its core. What counts in such a writing style is the general impression that readers get, which may be a strong mood of depression, distress or despair. The stories do not have a complete or comprehensible line of development, and narration becomes expressivistic. Some of the expressions and scenes may touch the reader's heart. For example, in Annbaby's stories, "Instant Blankness" (Xunjian kongbai) and "A Game" (Yige youxi), the images of the moving shapes of humans do not appear to be real, and they reveal the dream-like state of human beings and the nothingness of life. Such stories of nothingness are closely related to the nature of the Internet. In "Instant Blankness," "Jin Qing is a sudden shadow." When she wilfully tries to enter Ni Chen's life, the method she chooses is a virtual relationship in the cyber world. Ni Chen continuously receives e-mails from Jin Qing, and she relates her private stories in her e-mails, stories about her parents and her feelings when alone with a man in the dark: "A man and a woman who get along with each other, yet may not love each other." When Ni Chen gradually allows Jin Qing to enter his life, he starts to feel her distress and pain. In her last e-mail, sent from an Internet café at the airport, she says, "You are the sound of music that I hear when I stroll beside a river. It comes from the other side, but I don't have a boat to cross over." When the story reaches the point that Ni Chen clicks on "select all" and "delete" to deal with Jin Qing's e-mail messages and "in a second all the signs and words vanish," the writer's message is clear: everything has existed, yet no trace of its existence remains. The sudden appearance and disappearance of Joe, in "A Game," seem equally unrealistic. This uncertainty constitutes the fluidity of the work. Such melancholic writing, with a slight touch of philosophical incisiveness, brings to the readers the aesthetic experience of dark angst, which vortex- like, makes them sink deeper and deeper into its implicit meaning.

Wei Wei's collection of short stories, *A Kind of Emotion* (*Qinggan yizhong*), exhibits a non-traditional aesthetic element by depicting a passionate relationship that is dangerous and unstable. The author creates conflicts that are incomprehensible yet wonderful, ambiguous and unusual. Her characters are completely caught up in the human unconscious that explores the confused relationships of love between a man and a woman, such as that between father and daughter or an older sister and a younger brother. Conventional ethics are challenged when basic human relations deeply buried in the unconscious are uncovered and scrutinized. This forces the reader to look at tradition in a new way, leading him or her to wonder whether some ideas in our unconscious are more lasting and eternal than our real-life relationships. In some of her works that focus on the rethinking of accepted ideas, Wei Wei creates many "magnetic fields" that draw readers into the "other" relationships in life and into human feelings like fear, anxiety, eagerness, worry, impatience, perplexity and sorrow. Readers seem to be caught in a quagmire. The more pain they feel, the further they will sink into the mud. The sensation of sinking remains until every part of the body, except the two hands, is covered by mud.

Most of the novels by Zhao Bo, Dai Lai and Liu Yanyan also exhibit this inclination toward the plotless and non-sequential style. The plotless structure can be a sign of adequacy on the writer's part, but it can also be a sign of her creativity. The plotless and non-sequential style is more common among female writers, and is more often used in writing that focuses on psychological activities. These writers see life as plotless because it is made up of segments and is non-sequential. The use of different styles shows the writers' different viewpoints in life, and their unique ways of expressing their experiences and feelings. Presenting things with shape as shapeless is a choice these women writers have made.

## MARGINALIZED VOICES AND VALUES

Chinese women's literature which has emerged in recent years includes writings by women writers who were born after the Cultural Revolution. The works they have written, especially those that deal with their private feelings, have often been criticized as works of self-indulgence and anguish. People wonder what has gone wrong with these female writers, or with society. Such works of self-indulgence reflect a strong sense of anti-repression and subversion. Even in the portrayal of a tragic event, there is no discussion of the causes of the tragedy or description of the tragic character. Instead, the reader finds only a factual ending which is a display of indifference, with no distinction between the good and the bad, or the beautiful and the ugly. Life as such is presented with the writers' premature sense of being tired of life and their dissatisfaction with realistic styles in writing. These writers are premature in the sense that it is too early for them to feel weary of life before they experience disillusionment. They represent a generation with no ideals or illusions, and when they write about death they present it as a better choice than life. Their works are retaliations against the immense pressure of life, when material wealth does not necessarily provide a shelter to the wandering soul.

In an age of materialism, it must be recognized that a piece of literary writing is insignificant when compared with the ever-expanding quantity of material wealth. The experience of being a writer and the struggles involved in making a living by writing can only be felt by the writers themselves. Compared to the arrogant business elites who are now the cream of society, those who are engaged in writing are like roast chickens that are served on the table but ignored. The business people who are fully occupied with their business do not have time to write. Even if they do write, most of them often write about their successes, in a way which is hypocritical, and tends to mislead others. Only writers living outside the mainstream of society can attend to the inadequacies of human life from an observer's perspective. Their works often inspire others to think. Among the female writers who have just come onto the scene, some have been forced to move from place to place to try and find work. Time and again, they have looked for a job, only to be rejected. Works created out of such experiences, and with that kind of vision and standpoint deserve our attention.

The following characteristics are shared by many of these works. First is the vision of an unfriendly, loveless world. In many works, the male and female protagonists do not harbour any illusions about love. People live in a loveless world, and cohabitation is only a means of seeking comfort from each other. Emotional alienation is commonplace between man and woman. In Zhao Bo's "Dreaming Butterfly" (Xiaomeng hudie), for example, the narrator makes every effort to get away from her ongoing cohabitation with a man, who lacks promise and security. But the other man Ming, for whom she feels great passion, is also a reserved and grave person. Her expectation of the ultimate excitement is not realized. Characters finally come to the view that "love is like chewing gum; if it loses its favour, throw it away" (Zhao, 2000b, p. 58).

The second characteristic is that love is treated as a game. Several of Shu Shu's novellas depict a relationship between the narrator and a married man. Their relationship is basically physical, but one can also call it love. However, when the narrator in one of the novellas comes to the final showdown with Lao Mi, he hands the phone to his wife, and asks the narrator to "talk to her [his wife] first." This move marks the end of their relationship. The parting is so abrupt that the narrator becomes confused and wonders if it was really love. In other stories, indifference becomes the rule of the relationship game in the contemporary world. The loser in this game faces tremendous pressure, and can only feel sad for having no opponents. Indifference compels the characters to abandon any fantasy of love and put an end to all relationships.

The third characteristic which is common to contemporary women's fiction is the image of the materialistic woman. Many modern women love only when there is the promise of material comfort. In *The Goblin's Web* (*Xiaorao de wang*), by Zhou Jieru, Nian'er never knows how it feels to be loved by a young man. To her, fantasizing about being loved by a young man is silly, since young men cannot bring her material wealth. Du Yu looks for a boyfriend who can give her a villa and a BMW: "That's the sort of woman I am. This is me. That's my price." Another common feature is a tone of self-indulgence and gloominess. Many of Annbaby's novels manifest despair, a despair that occurs after looking closely at human nature. She writes about wanderers who live in meditation, and in a staunchly uncompromising manner. The wanderers' voice is that of solitude and loftiness. Dai Lai's collection of essays, *We Are All Sick People* (*Women doushi youbing de ren*), expresses a spiritless forbearance and acceptance of failure. All her titles convey a deep sense of helplessness. Examples are "Good, Yes, Good," "I'm Happy as Long as They Are," "Do You Feel Any Momentum?" and "In the Name of Writing." In addition, descriptions of human callousness are also common in many writers' works. For example, Zhou Jieru's novel, *I Know It's You* (*Wo zhidao shi ni*), expresses her disappointment with the callousness in life, especially in her exploration of childhood psychology. The education system is seen as problematic, for it inhibits psychological development, breaks down communication, and causes viciousness among children. Her portrayal of teenagers who have experienced trauma is particularly disturbing.

Women's writings in the materialistic age often show a tendency towards anti-heroism, which is perhaps a reflection of the fast-food culture that dominates contemporary life in China. The information explosion also makes it impossible for people to savour the flavour of life. People have no time to slow down and reflect on the meaning of what they have been doing. There is always a goal to achieve; there is always a reason behind every move that make people forget the process they have to go through. The transience of life is deeply felt in contemporary writing. Sensitivity allows these female writers to get at an underlying reality and to select concrete experiences from life to depict the fast-changing world. It seems inevitable that these writers experience early maturity or premature ageing as they write with their incredibly heavy pens—pens weighed down by the pressure of life, by the complexity of life, and by the unbearable indifference of society.

## REFERENCES

Anni Baobei (Annbaby) (2001a). "Xunjian kongbai" [Instant blankness]. In *Xunjian kongbai* [Instant blankness], pp. 75–96. Beijing: Zhishi chubanshe.

Anni Baobei (Annbaby) (2001b). "Yige youxi" [A game]. In *Xunjian kongbai* [Instant blankness], pp. 40–57. Beijing: Zhishi chubanshe.

Dai Lai (2000). *Women doushi youbing de ren* [We are all sick people]. Beijing: Kunlun chubanshe.

Liu Yanyan (2000). *Yinyou zhi hua* [Soft flowers]. Beijing: Zhongguo duiwai fanyi chuban gongsi.

Liu Yanyan (2003). *Niwo ruqi wanmei* [You and I are so perfect]. Wuhan: Changjiang wenyi chubanshe.

Wei Wei (1998). *Qinggan yizhong* [A kind of emotion]. Beijing: Zhongguo duiwai fanyi chuban gongsi.

Xiao Hong (1975). *Hulanhe zhuan* [The story of Hulan river]. Hong Kong: Xinwenxue yanjiushe.

Zhao Bo (2000a). "Dao Shanghai lai kan wo" [Come to see me in Shanghai]. In *Qingse wuyu* [Stories of sexuality], pp. 34–63. Beijing: Zhongguo duiwai fanyi chuban gongsi.

Zhao Bo (2000b). "Xiaomeng hudie" [Dreaming butterfly]. In *Qingse wuyu* [Stories of sexuality], pp. 64–113. Beijing: Zhongguo duiwai fanyi chuban gongsi.

Zhou Jieru (2000a). *Wo zhidao shi ni* [I know it's you]. Tianjin: Tianjin renmin chubanshe.

Zhou Jieru (2000b). *Xiaorao de wang* [The goblin's web]. Shenyang: Chunfeng wenyi chubanshe.

## GLOSSARY

Chen Ran 陳染

Chen Rong 諶容

Chi Zijian 遲子建

Dai Houying 戴厚英

Dai Lai 戴來

"Dao Shanghai lai kan wo" 〈到上海來看我〉

Du Yu 杜郁

*Hulanhe zhuan*《呼蘭河傳》

Jin Qing 靳輕

Lao Mi 老米

Lin Bai 林白

Liu Yanyan 劉燕燕

Ni Chen 倪辰

Nian'er 念兒

*Niwo ruqi wanmei*《你我如此完美》

*Qinggan yizhong*《情感一種》

Tie Ning 鐵凝

Wang Anyi 王安憶

Wei Wei 魏微

*Wo zhidao shi ni*《我知道是你》

*Women doushi youbing de ren*《我們都是有病的人》

Xiao Hong 蕭紅

*Xiaorao de wang*《小妖的網》

"Xiaomeng hudie" 〈曉夢蝴蝶〉

"Xunjian kongbai" 〈瞬間空白〉

"Yige youxi" 〈一個遊戲〉

Zhang Jie 張潔

Zhang Kangkang 張抗抗

Zhao Bo 趙波

Zhou Jieru 周潔茹

## 11 Writing Women's Literary History

*Gender Discourse and Women's Literature in Taiwan*

MEI-HWA SUNG

TWO ANTHOLOGIES OF WOMEN'S LITERATURE recently published in Taiwan—*From Red to Purple: Women Poets from Modern Taiwan* (*Hong de fa zi: Taiwan xiandai nüxing shi xuan*, 2000a) edited by Li Yuanzhen and *Women Novelists from Colonial to Contemporary Taiwan* (*Riju yilai Taiwan nüzuojia xiaoshuo xuandu*, 2001) edited by Qiu Guifen (Chiu Kuei-fen)—are landmark attempts at writing women's literary history and forming a canon of women's literature from Taiwan. Consciously subversive, they each aim at empowering a female poetics to counter the male-dominated historiography of Taiwan literature and, by implication, to construct a literary female subjectivity. The inadequate representation of literature produced by women in current, much acclaimed histories of Taiwan literature[1] is, they argue, symptomatic of the imbalance in power relations between male and female writers/critics in Taiwan.

Both Li Yuanzhen and Qiu Guifen try to arrive at a poetics by defining the features of poems/fiction by women and to respond to the thorny questions of "What constitutes a woman writer?" and "What do feminist critics want?" The familiar feminist agendas they bring to the fore in their selections and theories—female subjectivity, the female body and sexuality, self and other, sisterhood, etc.—are evidence of their academic training in Western feminist theories. Li Yuanzhen proposes to define women's literature as one born out of the particular experience and perspective possessed by women; Qiu Guifen, well-versed in postmodernist thought, identifies diversity, discontinuity, lacuna, and boundary-crossing as the key features of Taiwan women's literature and its historical trajectory. Faced with the tremendous task of selecting or excluding a vast number of texts written by women since Taiwan's colonial period, they try to give order to a hitherto amorphous (due to its marginalized status) body of literature. In doing so, they also raise a number of problematics regarding the gendering of literary historiography.

In this study, I will first delineate the formation of the two works as gender discourse: how each deploys a female/feminist poetics to construct a women's literary tradition for Taiwan. I will then examine the two anthologies as carrying on a debate between the competing claims of strategic essentialism and hybridity, or between poetics of solidarity and politics of difference. In conclusion, I wish to address the various problems incurred by such gender projects.

## WHAT CONSTITUTES A WOMAN WRITER?—WRITING WOMEN'S EXPERIENCE

The selections in *From Red to Purple: Women Poets from Modern Taiwan* cover a time span of almost fifty years, from 1921 to 1969. The writers are divided into four generations according to date of birth. In the introduction (or "Study Guide" as the author deliberately terms it to stress the anthology's epistemological nature), Li Yuanzhen emphatically appeals to gynocentric values and feminine sensibility. She defines the anthology as "a book of women's poetry which beckons to women to fulfil their dreams as readers" (Li, 2000a, p. 6).[2] She reminisces about her initial objective of "bringing to the fore female experience and perspective" (Li, 2000a, p. 7) in producing the anthology. She relates, in a moving sentimental touch, how she and her female friends[3] came to "name" the anthology. They agreed that red and purple were colours with distinctive feminine connotations—sensuality, menstruation, marriage ceremony, and procreation on the one hand, and melancholy, inferiority, animality, and the occult on the other. The consensus to use the two colours for the title of the anthology is a symbolic gesture of female solidarity which, as she explains, aspires to call forth "a vision of women's literature" (Li, 2000a, p. 8).

Femininity, with its cultural connotations, underlies the selective principle Li Yuanzhen adopts for the anthology. In her definition of the woman writer she privileges the exclusively female experience. What the woman writer thinks and feels—about love, marriage, society and nation, culture and language, and about herself—differentiate her from the male writer. This insistence on the woman writer as a cultural entity separate from the male writer provides the *raison d'être* for her anthology. In previously published collections of poetry, over 130 of them in total, poems by women are included for decorative purposes and are often dismissed as thematically shallow (Li, 2000a, p. 9). The texts of her anthology, however, do not necessarily all deal with women's experience in a strict sense. Some deal with "timeless," "universal" themes. Fully aware that women poets do not exclusively write about domestic life or romantic love, Li is convinced that women poets are capable of writing excellent poetry because of the particular "writing position and perspective" they assume (Li, 2000a, p. 9).

Almost concomitantly with *From Red to Purple*, Li Yuanzhen published *Female Poetics: A Collective Study of Women Poets from Modern Taiwan* (*Nüxing shixue: Taiwan xiandai nüshiren jiti yanjiu*), which can be read as the theoretical companion to her anthology of thirty-seven poets and a total of one hundred and ninety-four poems. In the Foreword and throughout the book, she dwells in more detail on the formation of her female/feminist poetics than in the "Study Guide" of the anthology. She relates this poetics to the Greek notion of "poesis," and thereby defines women's writing as "an open-ended feminist strategy with which women writers write/invent ... female identity or subjectivity, ... the "site" they occupy in a complex network of relationships (family, school, media, workplace).... [These are] the voices they utter under the multiple influence of culture and language.... 'Women' constitute a web-like site interwoven by obvious and real problems" (Li, 2000b, pp. 4–5). Li Yuanzhen is fully aware of the thematic limitations of women's writing. Women writers have internalized "femininity" in their self-images and produced oversimplified representations of female experience. However, she argues that this apparent weakness can be inverted to serve the cause of gender politics. Many women writers have been successful in employing femininity as a strategic location from which to subvert patriarchal hegemony.

The predominant use of feminine subject matter and themes by women writers, therefore, marks both their weaknesses and strengths. The overwhelming majority of women poets have dealt with love (romantic and maternal) in their poems, and very often their poems tend to be philosophical treatises on the female self and its emancipation. A small number of them, on the other hand, have moved beyond the private/domestic realm to write about public issues such as national identity and women's place in the national/post-capitalist context. The poems in the anthology have been selected to serve as examples of the practice of the female poetics mapped out by Li Yuanzhen.

The women poets anthologized in *From Red to Purple* are chronologically arranged, according to their dates of birth. The First Generation (1921–1940) is represented by eight writers: Chen Xiuxi, Hu Pinqing, Du Pan Fangge, Rongzi, Duo Si, Zhang Xianghua, Xiong

Hong, and Luo Ying. A predominant number of the selections deal variously with themes of romantic love, marriage, sisterhood, the mother-daughter relationship, and the quest for self and freedom. Women—in their roles as mother, daughter, and wife—are frequently associated with Nature. For example, botanic imagery recurs in Chen Xiuxi's poems to symbolize feminine resilience and nurturing beneath the surface of meekness: "[The leaves] have little concern for their own feebleness,/ Clinging tight to a tiny spot on a thin twig;/ They have become a verdant shelter against the scorching sun,/ And a roof that resists the winds and rains" (Li, 2000a, p. 18). In another poem, a woman wishes to "own a fertile garden in her nightly dreams" (Li, 2000a, p. 25). Taiwan is imaged as a land of "grasses/ banyan trees/ bananas/ magnolia flowers/ Which ceaselessly give forth milky fragrance" (Li, 2000a, p. 27). Hu Pinqing apotheosizes the Eternal Female as the transcendental signified of femininity: "There is this woman who is/ Beyond the realm of youth/ Beyond the realm of high noon/ Beyond the realm of old age/ No exact markings on her face/ Nor on her heart/ There is no place for her in the physical world/ And yet she is an absolute being/ An alter being" (Li, 2000a, pp. 40–41). She is a rose so pleasant to behold, even though enclosed in the blaze of war, a heart-rending sight (Li, 2000a, pp. 43–44). Rongzi departs from the romantic self-love of Hu Pinqing. In her elaborations of the quest motif, she visualizes the woman poet as the legendary bluebird taking wing to freedom (Li, 2000a, p. 64). In her other poems, she portrays herself using images of travel and flight: "Like in a miracle, [I] move forward/ Toward the distant horizon" (Li, 2000a, p. 73); or like the pair of golden birds who "in solitude/ … desire to swim the vast ocean of time/ … the immortal phoenixes" (Li, 2000a, p. 81). Zhang Xianghua imagines the mother-daughter relationship as a state of perfect harmony (Li, 2000a, p. 96). Another of her poems describes a chance meeting between two women writers, from two vastly different parts of the world (the culturally dichotomized East and West), one wondering how the other might respond to the existential question of self-choice (Li, 2000a, p. 106). Xiong Hong questions the permanence of romantic love (Li, 2000a, p. 112–115; p. 122) and in contrast reconfirms the true and never-ending love between her and her mother (Li, 2000a, p. 116). Luo Ying's poems are ultimately about the female self, imaged as a rose (Li, 2000a, p. 126), a silver jug filled with sorrow (Li, 2000a, p. 128), a book that defies the male gaze (Li, 2000a, p. 130) and a butterfly which "is the face of / Mother set in a picture frame" (Li, 2000a, p. 132).

The Second Generation (1941–1949) includes Dan Ying, Xi Murong, Zhong Ling (Chung Ling), Yin Ling, Li Yuanzhen, Hong Suli, Xiang Ling, Ye Xiang, and Su Baiyu. In their poems are found variations of the themes already dealt with by the First Generation women poets regarding patriarchal gender culture and autonomous womanhood: romantic love, the mother-daughter relationship, women's victimization and emancipation, their self-willed exile from cultural determinism, and so on. For example, Dan Ying opposes heroism (represented by warmongers such as Tsu Pa Wang) with a self-ironic indulgence in idleness—"I am a keeper of non-promises" (Li, 2000a, p. 138). Xi Murong, in strong contrast, validates her ties to her "fatherland"—Mongolia—in terms of marriage: "I should forever be the Bride from Luo Lan" (Li, 2000a, p. 164).[4] Zhong Ling bemoans the shattering of the Chang E myth as a result of the landing on the moon by Apollo 11 (Li, 2000a, p. 174). Wang Zhaojun is depicted as a tragic heroine seeking the pride and honour denied her by the Han monarch in an alien, backward land (Li, 2000a, p. 177). Yin Ling, an ethnic Chinese born in Vietnam, portrays Saigon and Taiwan as the mother-figure victimized by "man"-made war (Li, 2000a, p. 194). Li Yuanzhen meditates on the mother-daughter bond, reminding the daughter that "Outside the womb/ Beyond the fruit [begotten of heterosexual lust]/ There is yet the unbound female spirit" (Li, 2000a, p. 209). In another poem, she declares that "Women warriors have no fears" (Li, 2000a, p. 216). The motifs of gender confrontation and the imbalance in power relations between the sexes recur in the selections for the Second Generation, providing a link with the First Generation.

Many of the Second-Generation women poets, however, are able to move beyond their predecessors in their various treatments of gender issues. This has resulted from the contacts of these women poets with Western feminist thought.[5] They raise issues such as women's participation in the history and current "condition" of Taiwan. Enquiries into gender identity are tied to enquiries into national identity and social ills. Hong Suli writes about smog and acid rain which have long plagued an industrial southern city (Li, 2000a, p. 228), and about the dark side of the post-war history of Taiwan (coal-mine explosions and nuclear hazards) (Li, 2000a, p. 231). Ye Xiang exposes the stark reality of a woman worker's exploitation at the hands of multinational capitalism (Li, 2000a, p. 254). She goes even further to question female solidarity. "I"—the voice of an underprivileged woman speaking to another, better-off woman—"have never accepted the idea of totality/ Therefore, in a leisured manner/ I sit in a corner .../ A location I choose for myself .../ Your world is vastly different from mine" (Li, 2000a, p. 265).

Such hesitation to embrace any wholesale resolution regarding gender identity appears with greater emphasis in the Third Generation of women poets. They include Feng Qing, Si Ren, Li Yufang, Shen Huamo, Ye Hong, Cai Xiuju, Wang Lihua, Liu Yuxiu, Xiao Xiufang, Xiao Xiao, and Ling Yu. There is a greater attention given to the creative psyche of the woman poet, the conviction that women poets are individuals harbouring differences under the gender rubric of woman. The myth of a poetic alignment among women poets is challenged by Si Ren. She refuses the request of a male poet that she compose "feminine" poetry with a playful self-proclamation: "No, I am not Emily Dickinson, / nor was I meant to be" (Li, 2000a, p. 302). She possesses a song in the depths of her bosom, "my Song of Songs" (Li, 2000a, p. 303), which serves as a metaphor for the private/poetic covenant between her and her God. In another poem, she asks: "Who am I? Where do I come from? ... [I am] King Lear's daughter, the utterly forlorn one" (Li, 2000a, p. 318). This self-image of the woman poet as loner, cut off from sisterly ties, marks not only Si Ren's idiosyncratic poetry, but also an increasing trend to diversify/problematize self-definition among women poets of the Third Generation.

Cai Xiuju portrays the double discrimination suffered by Ami women and the environmental plight of the tribe (Li, 2000a, p. 367). Xiao Xiufang relates her wanderings among the Atayal tribe and expresses her outrage at the "mainlander" who prostitutes Atayal women (Li, 2000a, p. 420). Li Yufang and Ye Hong take up the familiar subject of a woman's ambivalent feelings toward her maternal role (Li, 2000a, p. 330; p. 356). Xiao Xiao asserts a daughter's unending love for her mother (Li, 2000a, p. 436; p. 440). Wang Lihua interrogates the prevalence in Taiwan of private interests rationalized as rightful pursuits of freedom (Li, 2000a, p. 380; p. 384). This diversity of themes, accompanied by a strong interest in public issues, evinces a growing trend of social and political involvement among women poets.

The Fourth Generation is represented by Jiang Wenyu, Zeng Shumei, Hong Shuling, Chen Feiwen, Luo Renling, Qiu Huan, Zhang Fangci, Yan Ailing, and Wu Ying. They show both change and continuity in subject and language in the development of poetry written by women. They continue to write about sisterhood and maternity (Hong Shuling, Wu Ying) (Li, 2000a, p. 512; p. 517; p. 615). However, they also depart from their predecessors by exhibiting a very significant degree of artistic self-consciousness. Jiang Wenyu experiments with the profane speech style of the Taiwanese dialect to advance her nativist political stance. She inverts the anti-feminism of the "three-letter words" (*sanzi jing*) in the local dialect to use/appropriate them as a feminist political weapon against the authoritarian patriarchal rule symbolized by the Chiang Kai-shek Memorial Hall (Li, 2000a, p. 474). Luo Renling ridicules the notion of chivalry by rewriting the fairy tale genre: "The princes and the princesses had long deceased in times undeterminable" (Li, 2000a, p. 554); the modern "feminist" Red Riding-Hood insists on venturing into the dark forest to verify for herself the extinction of the species called Fairy Tale (Li, 2000a, p. 552). Zeng Shumei revisits the motif of chivalric love but imbues it with strong lesbian overtones: The poetess/persona vows to shelter her (the addressee of the poem's) dreamland from decay because "you are my most cherished, never-ending love" (Li, 2000a, p. 497). In a similar vein, Chen Feiwen describes the bond between two women with the imagery of procreation, subverting the melodrama of heterosexual courtship. It is an/Other kind of procreation in which pregnancy never reaches full term, no abortion need be risked, and if the two should meet again after a long forced separation, they would listen to the song resounding loud in each of their wombs (Li, 2000a, p. 547). The womb is employed to symbolize the state of innocence; the song is a very fine tune sung by a child. In this manner, Chen Feiwen imparts a lesbian nuance to the familiar theme of sisterhood.

*From Red to Purple* concludes with two young women poets, who seek to (re)define the poetic/gender identity of women and thus gesture towards giving an answer to the question of "What constitutes a woman writer?" In the poem entitled "The Place We Are" by Zhang Fangci, the speaker craves to be at the starting station (*qizhan*) where freedom is unleashed/ Loaded with the past/ Where the heart passes through the tunnel/ The voice dimmed/ The face rocking/ The scenery colonized/ The memories tacked to the railroad sleepers/ .../ The starting station for discovering self-esteem/ .../ Where we move on toward true love/ Despite the dark that dogs/ The place we are now/ .../ Ought to be the beginning of our self-definition" (Li, 2000a, pp. 580–581). True love is prioritized in the feminist scheme of self-redemption. On the other hand, Wu Ying, in a self-ironic tone, imagines the woman poet as an urban loner who day in and day out munches on solitude (Li, 2000a, p. 610). An entire circus is placed on her shoulders and she must maintain her composure in order to move freely about among the jungle trails of life—in style (Li, 2000a, p. 618).

Li Yuanzhen's female poetics sets out to construct the female subject as a Woman of Feeling and a self-governing agent at the same time. It aims to empower femininity as a legitimate source of poetic inspiration, and justify the female creative psyche as autonomous, capable of self-representation. The poems selected for the anthology display diversity: they offer cacophonous variations on the themes of romantic love, marriage, selfhood, etc. Underlying this diversity, however, is Li Yuanzhen's insistence that women poets write differently from their male counterparts, that they write from their gendered experience. She is aware of the pitfalls of biological determinism. For her, an anthology of poetry by women and for women serves an epistemological and hence political function. *From Red to Purple* constructs a coherent narrative of the Other who resists othering and yet at the same time adopts an/Other's position as a feminist strategy.

## WHAT DO FEMINIST CRITICS WANT?——TOWARDS A POSTSTRUCTURALIST POETICS

Whereas Li Yuanzhen's selections are structured by an essentialist strategy, of viewing women poets as coming together to resist marginalization, Qiu Guifen is emphatically concerned with historiography, with establishing a poststructuralist frame of reference for women's literature. As enunciated in the titles of their works, both express an urge to historicize and localize their gender project: they are dealing with a literary phenomenon made by women as a gender species, produced in a place distinct from other places. In her attempt to "excavate" the hidden, silenced texts written by women since Taiwan's colonial period, Qiu Guifen defines Taiwan women's literature as displaying discontinuity, heteroglossia, and lacuna. In her introduction to the anthology, she claims to write Taiwan women's literary history from a void: "I shall start my narrative from a blank page.... On the threshold of the twenty-first century, it is high time that a history of Taiwan women's literature came into being" (Qiu, 2001, p. 3). This literary history is different from other, existing histories in terms of the historiographical method. It contrasts with monolithic traditional historiography in its attempt to construct "a multilateral dialogism" for representing women's literature. Writing women's literary history is manifestly proclaimed to be a discursive formation, intended to be a counter-discourse of "absence" and "heteroglossia" to simultaneously unsettle and supplement the grand narrative of traditional (literary) historiography. Qiu Guifen explicitly acknowledges her Foucauldian legacy, opposing notions such as progressiveness, structure, and unity with those of discontinuity, lack, and hybridity. Translating Foucault into literary/gender terms, she rejects also the notion of solidarity sanctified by radical feminists. Instead, she emphasizes lacuna, rupture, and difference as the "truths" about women's literature from Taiwan.

Male historiographers of Taiwan literature have come under attack from Qiu Guifen. She argues that Taiwan literature has not shown itself to be "a linear narrative," contrary to Ye Shitao's assertion that it "developed a strong desire for self-determination in the fluctuating course of history" (Ye, 1987, p. 2); nor has it "by way of literary creativity, meditated upon and searched for the experience of its national soul" (Peng, 1991, p. 17). In addition, Qiu disagrees with Chen Fangming, who divides Taiwan literature into "official" (*guanfang*) and "populist" (*minjian*) literature and locates its origins in the confrontation between the two. Refusing to dichotomize, she argues that (women's) literary history should be interpreted as a site, in which it reveals itself to be "a multi-layered structure, and in a state of alternating repetitions and clashes." In short, feminist historiography negates binarism, literary as well as gender-related. As an implicit reply to the question "What do feminist critics want?," she proposes a number of criteria: "the degree to which the text reflects the literary environment of the time, the text's aesthetic dimensions, and the artistry exhibited in the oeuvre of the writer" (Qiu, 2001, p. 10).

Accordingly, her anthology of Taiwan's women novelists lays little stress on periodization. Unlike *From Red to Purple*, *Women Novelists from Colonial to Contemporary Taiwan* does not group novelists according to the date of birth of the writer. The twenty selections are arranged in chronological order according to date of publication. Again, unlike in *From Red to Purple*, where Li Yuanzhen is the sole critic, the readers of *Women Novelists from Colonial to Contemporary Taiwan* are provided with a "study guide" for each of the selections. All the guides/critics are literature professors, of whom the majority (fifteen) are female. While most of the female critics elaborate on gender issues, two of the male critics and a couple of the female ones tend to either downplay gender issues or disapprove of a gendered reading strategy. There is, hence, no clear biological line of demarcation between the critics. Rather, the difference between gendered and non-gendered readings grows out of each individual critic's explicit or implicit commitment to "identity politics." The lack of unity in gender identity among the critics is in apparent keeping with the poststructuralist non-dichotomy upheld by Qiu Guifen.

The selections in the anthology span a period of sixty-five years (1935–1999). The two texts from the colonial period, by Ye Tao and Yang Qianhe, deal with the themes of marriage and maternity, and their impact on women's lives. In the first selection of the anthology, a short story entitled "Love's Fruit" (Aide jiejing), two women chat about childbearing. For them, the meaning of a woman's life rests on her prospects of and success in producing offspring (love's fruit). Both meet with frustration—one is infertile while the other's only son goes blind as a result of malnutrition. At the end of the story the two women aspire to a brighter tomorrow when the fertile one shall give birth to a healthy child. The study guide focuses on the imbalance in power relations between the sexes, lamenting women's victimization (their sense of guilt for failing in the maternal role). The commentator hails Ye Tao for her realistic portrayal of such victimization: "'Love's Fruit' depicts realistically the experience and condition of Taiwanese women living in the thirties" (Qiu, 2001, p. 62). Ye Tao, a socialist activist of her time, was defiant enough to fight colonial oppression. And yet, her story seems to celebrate women's assigned gender role as nurturer. The commentator points to this obvious gap between Ye Tao and her literary creation, but at the same time argues for a favourable reading of this gap as an indication of Ye Tao as a complex woman and novelist. The grand metaphor of the story, "the womb," can be read paradoxically as both an incarcerating and a life-giving/liberating force.

Like Ye Tao, Yang Qianhe wrote in Japanese. "Season of Flowers" (Huakai shijie) discusses a set of gender issues—women's education, feminine virtues, women's marital and maternal roles, and their self-images. The story involves an intimate trio of girls on the eve of their graduation from high school. They wonder about the various fates that await them beyond this point. Their conversations evolve around the topic of marriage: their desire for and fear of married life, who will get married off first, and who will produce a male child first. Before the story ends happily with the birth of a male child to one of the girls, Yang Qianhe questions the solidarity of female friendship among the girls, which threatens to turn sour because getting married means social accomplishment for the bride-to-be, but loss and betrayal for the others. The author tries to find a reason for this fragile sisterhood: "Perhaps it is because unmarried girls lead an aimless life; it's only natural they pity themselves" (Qiu, 2001, p. 90). For its commentator, "Season of

Flowers" reflects a time still in the grip of patriarchal culture. Though aware of the plight in which women are placed, Yang Qianhe has little intention of challenging the cultural givens of her time. Critiquing from her vantage point in time and a drastically different culture, the commentator finds the text unsatisfactory in its treatment of gender issues.

In their feminist readings of "Love's Fruit" and "Season of Flowers," the commentators appropriate the texts for feminist ends. With a sudden shift of tone and terminology, the "study guide" of the third selection, "Cousin Lianyi" (Lianyi biaomei) by Pan Renmu, lauds the author for her artistry (a successful manoeuvring of narrative points of view and characterization). For the commentator, the achievement of the novel lies in the writer's epic, panoramic depiction of the nation's history during a time of crisis and turbulence. The fate of the female protagonist Lianyi is closely bound up with the fate of the nation during the Sino-Japanese war and on the eve of the 1949 KMT (Kuomintang) debacle. The female commentator leaves gender issues untouched. In the selection that follows, "The Last Night Performance" (Zuihou yexi), by Chen Ruoxi, the male commentator ignores its apparent woman-as-victim theme. He surveys Chen Ruoxi's literary career, and commends her various successes where she "tells stories," instead of resorting to "heavy touches" (Qiu, 2001, p. 142), as in this piece, in depicting the wretched life of the female protagonist Aunt Jinsui. He regards this short story as an artistic failure.

If Qiu Guifen had claimed to be forming the canon of women's literature for Taiwan with her anthology, the negative commentary on "The Last Night Performance" as we have just seen, would have ended the project. In the Introduction, she places "The Last Night Performance" in the "Nativist Literature" category, in an attempt to enhance Chen Ruoxi's image as a writer. In the early sixties, the literary winds of change in Taiwan were obviously blowing against the Modernist trend. One of the items on the poststructuralist agenda of Qiu Guifen's literary historiography is to argue for women writers' participation in the writing of Nativist Literature, a term made synonymous with social/socialist commitment. By retrieving women's voices in the Nativist discourse, Qiu Guifen also tries to unsettle the familiar binarity between nationalism and internationalism in Taiwan literature. For her, "The Last Night Performance" deserves a place in the anthology because it exemplifies the hybrid nature of a woman writer's creative psyche.

Throughout the anthology, there is a sustained debate between writer and commentator, or between commentator and Qiu Guifen, the commentator-in-chief. There are a number of instances where a commentator either disapproves of a text or deviates from the strategic layout of the Introduction. While this "heteroglossia" may be a fascinating invention/discovery in theory/poetics, one wonders if it would serve as a practical "study guide" for the reader. In "Two Women on the Back Porch at Dusk" (Huangfen, langli de nüren) by Yu Lihua, the commentator takes issue with the writer's "overemphasis on the insinuation and jealousy between the women. Although by doing this, the writer gives an added tension to the story; she oversimplifies the rich dimensions of the female psyche and the reciprocal rapport between women" (Qiu, 2001, p. 163). The next selection, "Candle Rush" (Zhu xin) by Lin Haiyin, tells the story of a woman deserted by her husband, who flees to Sichuan and then Taiwan during the war. Her husband remarries without her knowledge. She rejoins him later, and tolerates his betrayal for twenty years until the day she awakens to a sense of self. She asks for a divorce, leaves him, and is happily remarried. In the study guide, the commentator lauds the writer for her ability "to cross ethnic and generic boundaries ... blending a variety of often conflicting discourses.... Her works are distinguished by an attempt to mediate an equilibrium among opposing forces and locate a position for female subjectivity" (Qiu, 2001, p. 192). The commentator affirms the effectiveness of the text in subverting the myth of "boudoir literature" as dealing exclusively with the private sentiments of women and hence being limited in scope. "Candle Rush" proves the contrary: it inverts the narrative mode of traditional political fiction by inserting into the public sphere a female/private position. It succeeds, therefore, in questioning the legitimacy of the male/female (public/private) binary opposition.

Several selections in the anthology are interpreted from a poststructuralist perspective. The commentators stress the motifs of the exiled self, diaspora, and cultural dislocation. "Sangqing and Taohong" (Sangqing yu Taohong) by Nie Hualing and "A Day in Aunt Changman's Life" (Changmanyi de yiri) by Shi Shuqing provide apt material for such readings. Both writers have a migratory (self-)identity: Nie relocates to America while Shi migrates between Taiwan, New York, and Hong Kong. The change of location/identity recurs as a prominent motif in their works. For its commentator, "Sangqing and Taohong" "occupies a multi-layered discursive sphere which accommodates feminist, minority, and migratory literature," and has rightfully been considered a canonical text of Chinese-American literature (Qiu, 2001, p. 219). The narrative is strung together by a series of periods of exile experienced by Sangqing—from her home in wartime Chongqing, from Beijing (on the eve of the communist takeover), and from Taipei (during the White Terror of the fifties) to America (the turbulent sixties of the Vietnam War). The metamorphosis of virginal Sangqing into nymphomaniac Taohung is meant to be a gender/political allegory: Sangqing's quest for freedom is paralleled with Taohong's erotic emancipation. Female sexuality is capable of resisting patriarchal formations of violence—warfare and white terror; it also promises redemption. On a smaller, more mundane scale, "A Day in Aunt Changman's Life" adopts the same motif of diaspora. Jilted by her good-for-nothing husband, Changman earns a living working as an amah for expatriate American families in Taipei. Cunning by nature, she finds her way to New York on the coat-tails of her American employers. The narrative focuses on a typical weekend day she spends in an alien and alienating metropolis visiting a young man she fancies. She does housekeeping for him, harbouring a secret lust for his youthful body. Taiwan is no home for her; she hardly wishes to look back on the miserable times she has spent there. In New York, she never feels at home. She is harassed by a black man, and when she has finally got rid of him, she thinks to herself, "[I] have no place else to go" (Qiu, 2001, p. 317). That is why she clings to the young Taiwanese artist, who walks out on her, putting an end to her unrequited love, and her long day's wandering in New York. The commentator remarks that this short story, with its theme of frustrated female sexuality, marks a new phase in its author's writing career. In other words, Shi Shuqing succeeds in placing female sexuality in a cosmopolitan/metropolitan context.

The last selection of the first volume, "The Incarcerated Heart" (Xin suo) is presented to the reader in the form of an absence. Qiu Guifen explains her initial hesitation to include "The Incarcerated Heart" in the anthology: that it borders on popular writing, showing inadequate artistry. She finally decided to include it in order to highlight the conflict between erotic writing and state censorship. Guo Lianghui, however, declined to have her novel abridged for inclusion in the anthology. In the absence of the text, the critics (Qiu and the commentator) collaborate in guiding the reader. Qiu Guifen takes this as a fine illustration of lacuna (both as a victim of censorship and as a physical absence from the anthology) argued by her to be an important feature of women's literary history. Two years after its publication in 1961, "The

Incarcerated Heart" was banned and its author expelled by the Writers' Association. The charge was a grave one: the novel deals with the incestuous relationship between a man and his sister-in-law and is shot through with pornographic innuendoes. In the study guide, the commentator urges the reader to enquire into the gender politics involved in banning "pornographic" literature, which generally highlights the female body and female sexuality. The absence of a controversial and yet highly saleable text like "The Incarcerated Heart" from mainstream literary histories reflects the collective fear and oppression of the female body in the early sixties.

Li Ang has two short stories selected for inclusion in the anthology, an exception among the writers. The earlier work, "Curvaceous Dolls" (You quxian de wawa) (1970), probes into the unconscious of a young woman for the answer to her obsession with dolls that have prominent nipples. In a narrative style that borders on the grotesque, Li Ang describes how in her fantasy the young woman sees the nipples on her husband's chest growing larger and larger. Frustrated in her married life because of her husband's indifferent and even contemptuous attitude toward her many such dreams, she decides to continue her quest for the slimy snake she meets in her dreams. The sperm-like liquid oozing out of the snake's mouth spreads all over her body, causing her stifling pain and yet at the same time entrancing pleasure. According to the commentator, this short fiction testifies to Li Ang's artistic flair for Modernist writing, and her superb mastery of writing-as-feminist. A rare case during her time, Li Ang was experimenting with the notion of female writing as auto-eroticism, when realism was still the dominant narrative mode. In the later work, "The Masquerade for a Blood Sacrifice" (Caizhuang xueji) (1997), Li Ang blends the personal with the political, treating the motif of the February 28th Incident of 1947 from a gender perspective. The story tells of a woman who, having lost her husband to the political crackdowns of the fifties, now again loses her only son to AIDS. She finally comes to terms with the "truth" of her son's "anomalous" sexuality. In parallel to this, the narrative itself succeeds in stripping the February 28 Incident of its long sanctified political veneer. Writing-as-feminist in the manner of Li Ang is invested with a power capable of subverting patriarchal hegemony in the gender sphere as well as the political sphere. It is, the commentator notes, "a feminist counter-discourse to the nationalist discourse" (Qiu, 2001, p. 265).

The second volume of the anthology covers two decades, from 1980 to 1999. In the Introduction, Qiu Guifen elaborates on the need for feminist critics to problematize the traditional distinction between high literature and popular literature. "A Place of One's Own" (Ziji de tiankong) by Yuan Qiongqiong is a case in point. The author, the commentator observes, has been able to freely cross the divide between the two kinds of literature throughout the 20-some years of her writing career. Her fiction is "wonderfully readable" (Qiu, 2001, p. 73). "A Place of One's Own" is a feminist textbook story of a woman betrayed by her husband, who divorces her because she cannot bear him any (male) children. During the years after her divorce, she gradually becomes an independent, "strong" businesswoman and is also involved in an affair with a married man. When she meets her ex-husband again, he is with his family (wife and two daughters) and she is holding in her arms her friend's son. The story ends with this chance "reunion" where the victory clearly belongs to the wronged ex-wife. This story is generally interpreted as the feminist manifesto of self-reliance with a vengeance. However, there is a touch of ambivalence in Yuan Qiongqiong's depiction of the female protagonist: a victim of extra-marital love, she nevertheless has no qualms of conscience about being the "third party" herself. It is this hesitation to pass moral judgment, together with a will to tell a story with rich and complex implications, that saves this feminist story from becoming banal propaganda.

The eighties witnessed a major trend among women novelists toward writing about women's urban space. This trend can fairly be said to have begun with Yuan Qiongqiong, and is carried on in "Fin-de-Siècle Splendour" (Shiji mo de huali) (1990) by Zhu Tianwen, and "Hungary Water" (Xiongyali zhi shui) (1995) by Zhu Tianxin. "Fin-de-Siècle Splendour," says its commentator, "opens up a new field for Taiwan literature of the nineties ... cleared out for the theme of gender difference/sexuality in the postmodern urban context" (Qiu, 2001, p. 96). This story about "vanity"—about sensual pleasures as fleeting phantoms—is paradoxically told with dazzling linguistic density and virtuosity. For the commentator, the minute detailed depictions of fashion and perfume create an aura of verbal decadence. In "the absence of truth," the author tries to deliver her apocalyptic message of the metropolis as the Great Equalizer that erases any and all binary distinctions—moral/immoral, man/woman, heterosexuality/homosexuality, and so on. In "Hungary Water," the title referring to the first perfume made in fourteenth-century Europe, the imaginary urban high society associated with perfume is implicitly opposed to the semi-rural "military dependants' village" (juancun) of Zhu Tianxin's memory. The commentator points to the possibility of reading the complex, multi-layered story as an attempt to unsettle the private/public duality. The personal/physical/sensual is indeed the political.

On the other hand, the debate between Nativism and cosmo/metropolitanism continues into the nineties. The former, however, gains added strength from an emerging generation of Aboriginal women writers. "Vu Vu with the Red Mouth" (Hong zuiba de Vu Vu) by the Paiwan writer Ah Nü Wu embodies tribal history in the arch-matriarch Vu Vu. The linguistic gap between her and her grandchildren (Vu Vu's daughter is married to a veteran soldier from mainland China) is symptomatic of the decay of Paiwan culture. In the eyes of the young "mixed bloods," Grandma Vu Vu, whose mouth is constantly stained by red juice from betel nuts, is more than a frightening stranger; she is "the witch with the red mouth." The legal practice of naming children after their father, with strong implications that children are the rightful property of the male parent, wreaks havoc on the matriarchal culture of the Aborigines. In this rare piece of female writing that critiques the double colonization of Aboriginal women, the Nativist literature that emerged in the sixties has evolved into a postcolonial discourse. The story is a protest not only against the political hegemony of the government in "civilizing the mountains," but also the Han cultural hegemony which crushes the matriarchy of the tribe by taking away its right to name its progeny.

*Children of the Salt Pans* (*Yantian ernü*) by Cai Sufen depicts the life of poor people in southern Taiwan. As the commentator observes, this novel proffers a link in the Nativist tradition despite its author's disavowal of this apparent legacy (Qiu, 2001, p. 141). Different from its "progenitors," "Children of the Salt Pans" problematizes the romantic notion of "love of the native land." The salt pans are not imaged solely as a last-resort sanctuary to which the female protagonist returns for psychic rejuvenation and renewal. They are also a land of harsh reality from which Mingyue and Dafang have fled. If nothing else, this ambivalence toward the native land adds an artistic nuance to the Nativist narrative of Taiwan literature. The commentator regards this novel highly, calling it "a rare achievement which displays yet another facet of Taiwanese fiction by women" (Qiu, 2001, p. 140).

In addition to diversity in subject and theme, fiction written by women in the nineties boldly experiment with language. In line with the Modernist writers of the sixties, the younger generation of metropolitan writers manifest a keen sensitivity to international postmodernism. Qiu Miaojin, author of "Notes from an Alligator" (Eyu shouji) studied in

France; Ping Lu, author of "Letters from Madame Chiang upon Her Hundredth Birthday" (Bailing jian), lived a number of years in the United States. From an academic background, they each try a free hand with the theme of sexuality and the narrative mode of anti-structure. Qiu Miaojin shocked readers with her short story about lesbian love and with her suicide in Paris. "Notes from an Alligator" deals with the schizophrenic psychic underworld of two women in love with each other and yet torn by guilt. The narrator images this lesbian relationship as a two-headed monster tearing at her body, where desire and fear battle to cancel each other out. At the end of the narrative, fear wins over desire. The "I" retreats and seeks shelter on the safe ground of normality. "Notes from an Alligator" is included in the anthology to represent "the lesbian voice which has emerged as a force among the women writers of the 1990s (Qiu, 2001, p. 41).[6] Since the publication of this short story, the term "alligator" has been widely used as a nickname for a lesbian woman in Taiwan. Calling attention to the grotesque/fantastic in the narrative, the commentator at the same time reads the story as an allegory, relevant to the lesbian as well as the male homosexual situation in Taiwan (Qiu, 2001, p. 122).

"Letters from Madame Chiang upon Her Hundredth Birthday" attempts to write a "grand narrative" of female sexuality, blending the former First Lady's private life with the history/life of Republican China. Madame Chiang writes letters to the orphans in the orphanage she has long patronized and to President Clinton of America. She reminisces on her past glories and defeats and comments on international and domestic politics. Even though she was the paragon of the "liberated woman" of her time, Madame Chiang is shown to be most concerned with her married life and her strained relationship with her husband, the strongman of Republican China for many years. She is shown to be highly dexterous in amorous intrigues, not to mention in political manoeuvrings. Writing letters becomes for her a narcissistic obsession: she places herself at the centre of many historical events that were to have grave consequences for the future of the country (for example, her role in the Xi'an Incident). For the feminist commentator, "Letters from Madame Chiang upon Her Hundredth Birthday" is intended to expose the "complicity between Madame Chiang and patriarchy, and the ambiguous nature of her feminist consciousness" (Qiu, 2001, p. 310).

The anthology concludes with "The Story Above ..." (Yishang qingjie ...) by Su Weizhen, which probes into the meaning of being a feminist, or being the daughter of a not-so-successful feminist, and hence provides a very apt coda for the anthology, unsettling the euphoric calm of the feminist discourse. The narrative method and theme of the story converge upon the idea of negativity. The main character, Baosheng, does not have a father in the social and legal sense because her mother wanted a child but not a husband. A parody of the feminist mother-daughter solidarity, the relationship between Baosheng and her feminist professor mother is deliberately shown to be non-existent. Her mother is "a woman incapable of love—as a woman and as a mother" (Qiu, 2001, p. 342). She seeks her father but finds him equally uncaring. Baosheng turns herself into a writer and escapes to the virtual world created by the film industry only to find it void of meaning. At the end of the story, she is sure about only one thing—that her mother lives the life of a misfit, inverting the "Way" of the world ("male subjectivity"), and therefore she is summarily disavowed by her daughter. The narrator tells us: Baosheng never comes out of the movie theatre again. The moral of the story might be phrased as follows: All is vanity in the life of a feminist, and in that of her daughter. With this self-reflexive enquiry, Qiu Guifen rounds out the poststructuralist poetics she constructs for writing women's literary history. Gender identity, after all, exists ultimately as a construct, in the Imaginary as an existential fiction.

For both Li Yuanzhen and Qiu Guifen, writing women's literary history is a political act as well as a poetic one. This essay has tried to delineate the discursive formation of writing-as-women in each of the anthologies. It has concentrated on re-presenting the "order" constructed in the selections/selecting of texts by Li and Qiu, but not the exclusions (the "lost pearls").[7] To anthologize Taiwan women's poetry is to inscribe order on the voices of the other. The different strategies (essentialism/heteroglossia) they adopt can be viewed as complementing, not contradicting, each other. In his review of *Women Novelists from Colonial to Contemporary Taiwan*, David Der-wei Wang states, "Female/feminist discourse has entered a new phase of paradigm-formation, moving beyond the past phase of land-clearing" (Wang, 2001, p. 15). This observation is also applicable to *From Red to Purple: Women Poets from Modern Taiwan*. Together, the two anthologies have succeeded in writing a dialectical history of women's literature from Taiwan. The debate they carry on enables feminist/postfeminist discourse to be a viable and interesting literary as well as political strategy in the formation of the women's literary canon of Taiwan.

## NOTES

1. Ye Shitao, for example, names about thirty poets to represent the sixties. Rongzi appears on the list, the only female poet writing about feminist themes (Ye, 1987, p. 125). Qiu Guifen (Chiu Kuei-fen), on the other hand, takes Ye Shitao, Peng Ruijing, and Chen Fangmin to be typical writers of "linear narrative," who insist on structure and dichotomy (Qiu, 2001, p. 6).

2. "This is a collection of poetry that appeals to women's reading of dreams." With this statement, Li Yuanzhen tries to conjure up a gynocentric utopian vision where writer and reader collaborate in an epistemological/empowering project.

3. Jiang Wenyu, Liu Yuxiu, and Liu's daughter.

4. Xi Murong identifies herself with the mummy bride excavated from the archaeological site Lop Nur.

5. Western feminism was systematically brought to the attention of Taiwan's reading public and university campuses in the mid-1980s. *Chung-Wai Literary Monthly, Unitas: A Literary Magazine,* and the "Literary Supplement" sections of the major newspapers were the key factors during the early period of the dissemination of Western feminism.

6. Besides Qiu Miaojin, Qiu Guifeng also mentions Chen Xue and Hong Ling. All college graduates, they represent the small number of lesbian writers.

7. David Der-wei Wang, in his review of Qiu Guifen's anthology, jokingly (perhaps) proposes the idea of an anthology of "lost pearls," another of "mothers and mother-in-laws," etc. for pedagogic purposes. For details, see Wang, 2001.

## REFERENCES

Chang, Sung-sheng Yvonne (1993). *Modernism and the Nativist Resistance: Contemporary Chinese Fiction from Taiwan.* Durham, NC: Duke University Press.

Chen Fangming (1999). "Taiwan xinwenxueshi de jian'gou yu fenqi" [The construction and periodization of Taiwan new literary history]. *Lianhe wenxue* [Unitas: A literary magazine], Vol. 15, No. 10 (August), 162–173.

Li Yuanzhen (2000a). *Hong de fa zi: Taiwan xiandai nüxing shi xuan* [From red to purple: Women poets from modern Taiwan]. Taipei: Nüshu wenhua shiye youxian gongsi.

Li Yuanzhen (2000b). *Nüxing shixue: Taiwan xiandai nüshiren jiti yanjiu* [Female poetics: A collective study of women poets from modern Taiwan]. Taipei: Nüshu wenhua shiye youxian gongsi.

Mei Jialing et al., eds. (2000). *Xingbie lunshu yu Taiwan xiaoshuo* [Gender discourse and Taiwan fiction]. Taipei: Maitian.

Peng Ruijin (1991). *Taiwan xinwenxue yundong sishi nian* [Forty years of the Taiwan new literature movement]. Taipei: Zhili.

Qiu Guifen (Chiu Kuei-fen), ed. (2001). *Riju yilai Taiwan nüzuojia xiaoshuo xuandu* [Women novelists from colonial to contemporary Taiwan]. Taipei: Nüshu wenhua shiye youxian gongsi.

Wang Dewei (David Der-wei Wang) (2001). "Taiwan nüzuojia zouchu yitiao lu" [The path of Taiwan women writers]. *Zhongguo shibao* [China Times] (September 23), p. 15.

Ye Shitao (1987). *Taiwan wenxue shigang* [An outline history of Taiwan literature]. Kaohsiung: Wenxuejie zazhishe.

## GLOSSARY

Ah Nü Wu 阿女烏

"Aide jiejing" 〈愛的結晶〉

"Bailing jian" 〈百齡箋〉

Cai Sufen 蔡素芬

Cai Xiuju 蔡秀菊

"Caizhuang xueji" 〈彩妝血祭〉

"Changmanyi de yiri" 〈常滿姨的一日〉

Chen Feiwen 陳斐雯

Chen Ruoxi 陳若曦

Chen Xiuxi 陳秀喜

Chen Xue 陳雪

Dan Ying 淡瑩

Du Pan Fangge 杜潘方格

Duo Si 朵思

"Eyu shouji" 〈鱷魚手記〉

Feng Qing 馮青

guanfang 官方

Guo Lianghui 郭良蕙

Hong Ling 洪凌

Hong Shuling 洪淑苓

Hong Suli 洪素麗

"Hong zuiba de Vu Vu" 〈紅嘴巴的Vu Vu〉

Hu Pinqing 胡品清

"Huakai shijie" 〈花開時節〉

"Huangfen, langli de nüren" 〈黃昏‧廊裡的女人〉

Jiang Wenyu 江文瑜

juancun 眷村

Li Ang 李昂

Li Yuanzhen 李元貞

Li Yufang 利玉芳

"Lianyi biaomei" 〈蓮漪表妹〉

Lin Haiyin 林海音

Ling Yu 零雨

Liu Yuxiu 劉毓秀

Luo Renling 羅任玲

Luo Ying 羅英

minjian 民間

Nie Hualing 聶華苓

Pan Renmu 潘人木

Ping Lu 平路

Qiu Huan 丘緩

Qiu Miaojin 邱妙津

Rongzi 蓉子

*Sangqing yu Taohong* 《桑青與桃紅》

Shen Huamo 沈花末

Shi Shuqing 施叔青

"Shiji mo de huali" 〈世紀末的華麗〉

Si Ren 斯人

Su Baiyu 蘇白宇

Su Weizhen 蘇偉貞

Wang Lihua 王麗華

Wu Ying 吳瑩

Xiang Ling 翔翎

Xiao Xiao 筱曉

Xiao Xiufang 蕭秀芳

"Xin suo" 〈心鎖〉

Xiong Hong 敻虹

"Xiongyali zhi shui" 〈匈牙利之水〉

## 12 The Subaltern Woman's Voice and the (Film-)making of Modern Taiwan

KUEI-FEN CHIU

... It is through the re-appearance of this knowledge, of these local popular knowledges, these disqualified knowledges, that criticism performs its work.

—Michel Foucault, *Power/Knowledge*

Differences do not only exist between outsider and insider—two entities— they are also at work within the outsider and the insider—a single entity.

—Minh-ha T. Trinh, *Woman, Native, Other*

AS THE CALL FOR HISTORIOGRAPHY from below has gradually gained currency, oral history and documentary film-making begin to attract attention for their concern with the representation of the voices/views of subaltern people. In these two genres, the monopoly of the literary word is disrupted and the power of the spoken word is reconfirmed. The subaltern subjects talk; and what they say carries weight. *Fengming: A Chinese Memoir* by the Chinese film-maker Wang Bing, which won the Grand Award at the 2007 Yamagata film festival—one of the most important documentary film festivals in Asia—is an illustrative example. The documentary presents the story of a Chinese woman who suffered repeated persecution under two reform campaigns in China from the 1950s through her rehabilitation in 1974. What is striking about this documentary film is that the film has the interviewee talk in front of the camera for several hours with very few changes of shot. There is no docudrama, no archival footage, no old photographs, and no staging of other interviews to "balance" the interviewee's point of view. In other words, with the noteworthy exception of the "talking head," all other devices commonly found in documentary films are missing in this remarkable film. The film relies almost exclusively on the interviewee's voice in its attempt to resurrect the historical past. Thus, as a historiographical endeavour, *Fengming: A Chinese Memoir* deliberately employs image minimalism in order to underscore the importance of the spoken word in constituting historical truth. The voice of the subaltern interviewee is all that matters in this award-winning film. As a filmic representation of oral history, this film demonstrates very well how oral history and documentary film-making can open up a space of self-representation for people without the power of literary production. It is in these two genres that we constantly come across the voice of the traditionally voiceless subaltern woman. The rise of these two genres not only signifies the democratization of history writing but also brings into relief the problem of subaltern representation in cultural practice.

## DOCUMENTARY PRACTICE AND THE VISION OF TAIWANESE NEW LITERATURE

In Taiwan, this interest in the representation of people from lower social strata can be regarded as a legacy of the so-called "Nativist" (*xiangtu*) literature in the 1970s which placed the issue of "grass-roots vision" at the top of its agenda. It can be traced even further back to the 1920s, when the so-called Taiwanese new literature emerged as a response to Taiwan's shocked discovery of its "tardiness" vis-à-vis Japan (and the West) in the so-called "project of modernity." Central to the vision of modern Taiwan was the question of "the voice of the oppressed class." Because of the insurmountable difficulty of exploiting what Rey Chow calls "technologized visuality" (Chow, 1995, p. 9), which required advanced technology and finance beyond the reach of colonial intellectuals at that time, the literary word took upon itself the responsibility of representing the subaltern vision and voice. The question of the voice of the subaltern was displaced by the question of representing—in the sense of "speaking for"—the subaltern in intellectual literary production. As a result, the problematic of re-presenting the voice of the subaltern was not fully addressed. It was not until the mid-1980s that the question of how to re-present the voice of people from the lower strata of society began to appear again as an urgent issue on the cultural agenda in Taiwan. The divorce of documentary film-making from the traditional reliance on the power of the written word in literary/cultural practice marks a sea-change in tackling the representation of the subaltern voice. The meaning of the term "representation" is no longer restricted to the sense of "speaking for." Re-presentation, or *Darstellung* as analysed by G. C. Spivak, is resuscitated for the agenda of literary and cultural studies as a critical issue. This paper analyses two contemporary Taiwanese documentary films to show how documentary practice, at its best, creates a space of heteroglossia that brings subaltern voices into play and shows both the strengths and limitations of the subaltern vision. In these two documentary films that seek to re-envision the history and world of Taiwanese opera, the voice of the female subaltern subject comes to the fore and speaks with a kind of authority seldom realized in literary writings. I argue that documentary, as a genre, provides special recourse to the vision of modern, democratized Taiwan that the literary word has been struggling unsuccessfully to embody.

## MEMORY TALKS

In an essay published some years ago, Andreas Huyssen remarks that "memory has become a cultural obsession of monumental proportions across the globe" (Huyssen, 2000, p. 26). The drastic political changes in former Communist Eastern Europe, the reunification of Germany, and the overthrow of apartheid in South Africa all contributed to this interest in memory writing. In addition, the increasing importance of multiculturalism in shaping contemporary democratic societies makes ethnic identity a dominant theme in political and cultural discourse, which further boosts the trend of resurrecting suppressed memories and personal histories. Understood in this context, the compulsive (re)production and almost obsessive fascination with memory discourse are inseparable from the attempt to intervene in contemporary struggles for memory in the (re)construction of national as well as personal identities (Grossmann, 1995; Esbenshade, 1995). Memory is turned into a site of resistance and struggles. Memories can be deployed to produce counter-narratives that subvert official historical discourse, as in the practice of the so-called "historiography of everyday" (Yip, 2004, p. 70). They work to empower minority subjects in their search for ethnic and gender identities (hooks, 1989; Smith, 1987). Finally, they can also operate in such a way as to conjure up visions of an alternative life-world resistant to the encroachment of globalization (Wang, 2002, pp. 13–18).

Taiwan in the late twentieth century also witnessed the proliferation of memory discourse. With the lifting of martial law in 1987, the project of reconstructing Taiwan's history was set in motion. Essential to this project was the reclaiming of suppressed (popular) memories which were deliberately erased in the official history discourse (Yang, 1995, pp. 3–4). The memory of the February 28 Incident is a case in point. Just as the Holocaust signifies devastating trauma in the West, the February 28 Incident has become for people in Taiwan a trope for traumatic memory and continues to invite representation through re-membering (Hillenbrand, 2005). The attempts to rescue memories of the Incident from oblivion and thereby to address the wounds of the past have yielded a considerable corpus of creative works, among which Hou Hsiao-hsien's awards-winning film *City of Sadness* (*Beiqing chengshi*, 1989) is the most celebrated example. Apart from the drive to address taboo political subjects from non-official perspectives, the surfacing of ethnic identities in post-martial law Taiwan also accelerated the production of memory discourse. The re-collection of cultural memory has become a common practice in writings that seek to foreground the writers' ethnicities. This is particularly noteworthy in contemporary aboriginal literature in Taiwan. As aboriginal languages exist mainly in oral forms and have no standard transcription systems, the continuation of aboriginal cultures depends largely on oral histories and older generations' memories. Thus, to emphasize the aboriginal identity of his/her writing, the writer often highlights the importance of memory and incorporates acts of story-telling into his/her writings (Sun, 2003).

Memory is also accorded a prominent place in Taiwan women's writings of the past decade. Quite a few established women writers have experimented with the theme of memory in their works, which have attracted much critical attention and discussion. Li Ang's *The Labyrinthine Garden* (*Miyuan*), Zhu Tianxin's *Remembering My Childhood Friends in the Days of the Military Village* (*Xiang wo juancun de xiongdimen*), Ping Lu's *Wandering* (*Xingdao tianya*), Shi Shuqing's *Passing by the Small Town of Lojin* (*Xingguo Lojin*), and Chen Ye's *The Muddy River* (*Ni he*) readily come to mind. Through skilful strategic exploitation of their female protagonists' personal memories, all the writers named above have made a critical intervention in the ongoing reconstruction of the Taiwanese historical imaginary. The concern with suppressed popular memory and gender voice in the realm of women's writing, however, inevitably led to the concern with the issue of representing the voice of the subaltern as the call for "history from below" gradually gained currency in the post-martial law period. In a way, this can be seen as a legacy of the so-called Nativist Literature Movement in the 1970s. Although the heated Nativist literature debate was abruptly brought to an end with the arrest of several writers from the Nativist camp, the urge for committed engagement with "the voice of the people" which marked Nativist discourse continues to resonate today (Chen, 2004; Peng, 2004). In the realm of women's cultural production, it spurred the development of two particular genres—oral history and documentary film-making. Both genres take the representation of the voices of the oppressed as their central task. Since subaltern women are often those without literacy, oral history as a genre comes to be seen as particularly effective in re-presenting suppressed women's voices (Jiang, 1995, p. 13). *Disappearing Taiwan Grandmas (Xiaoshizhong de Taiwan A-ma)* (1995), a collection of oral histories based on interviews with seven "grandmas" from different backgrounds, is representative of such efforts. Another noteworthy piece of gendered oral history is *High Is the Mountain, Long is the Road (Shanshen qingyao)* (1997), an autobiographical account by an Atayal woman about her complicated relationship with a Japanese spy after Japan was forced to turn Taiwan over to the Chinese KMT party (Kuomintang) in 1945. Although, as we learn from a note provided by the editors, the period covered in the autobiographical account coincides with the aftermath of the "February 28 Incident," which made the spying job particularly difficult for the Japanese man, the interviewee-narrator makes no reference to the Incident as she traces her memories of those years (Chiu, 2003, pp. 198–201). The gap between the subaltern woman's memory and (suppressed) "collective" memories brings into sharp focus the strengths and limitations of written oral history as recourse to "historical truth." Oral history, when presented as an autobiographical account by a subaltern subject, often diverges from historical representation constructed from an elitist perspective and thus sheds light on aspects outside the vision of official history. It is thus arguable that oral history may produce alternative historical narratives that challenge dominant historical views. But "alternative historical representation" should not be conflated with "better historical representation." To do so is to romanticize the subaltern as a privileged historical subject possessing exclusive access to the so-called "historical truth." The limitation of the vision of the aboriginal subaltern narrator in *High Is the Mountain, Long Is the Road* points to the fallacy of such a simplistic view.

If the emergence of oral history as an important genre of representation in women's writing signifies the turn to the subaltern voice in contemporary cultural discourse, documentary film-making is another genre which concerns itself with the voices and views of those who cannot be properly represented in written literature. Documentary films often make full use of interviews which also constitute the core of oral histories. Insofar as both genres place the representation of voices from lower social strata as the central issue, documentary seems to outdo written oral history in performing the task. It is widely acknowledged that oral history as a genre is one of the few historiographical practices that take seriously into account the views of common people in historical discourse. In a way, the rise of oral history signifies the increasing democratization of historiography (Hobsbawm, 1988, p. 13; Thompson, 1998, p. 26). However, oral history in written form involves the transcription of what is spoken into written words, which often fails to convey unspoken messages in the interview. Subtle signs carrying significant unspoken or unspeakable messages from the interviewee— such as changes of tone, facial expressions, and body language in the process of interview—are often lost in written oral history (Sipe, 1998, pp. 382–383). Moreover, the less articulate the subaltern interviewee, the wider the gap between what s/he means and what is transcribed. Indeed, it is important to note with Pierre Bourdieu that the most deprived are often those with poor linguistic competence (Bourdieu, 1991, pp. 98–99). Challenging the monopoly of the written word, the dynamics of multimedia in documentary representation documents not only what is said by the subaltern subject but also his/her non-verbal responses and interaction with the interviewer/director during the interview process, which are crucial dimensions of the politics of representation (Sipe, 1998, p. 382).

In the following, I will analyse two contemporary Taiwanese documentary films to demonstrate the potential of documentary film as a powerful genre for representing subaltern women. Both documentaries, *Gongleshe: The Lost Kingdom* (*Gongleshe: Xiaoshi de wangguo*, 1998) and *Liao Qiongzhi: The Taiwanese Opera Singer of Pathos* (*Taiwan gezaixi kudan Liao Qiongzhi*, 2003), are historical documentaries based on interviews with Taiwanese opera singers. Both films focus on the life story of a specific person who promoted Taiwanese opera and shaped the development of this particular form of popular entertainment in post-war Taiwan. The memories of the interviewees help redeem an important part of Taiwan's history muted in traditional historical narratives. It is noteworthy that, as various scholars interviewed in the documentary *Liao Qiongzhi* point out, Taiwanese opera is basically a form of popular entertainment closely associated with women. Female singers constitute the main body of a Taiwanese opera troupe; and the majority of the audiences are also women, who tend to project their dreams and frustrated desires onto the stage as the singers act out the pathetic stories of women in traditional Taiwanese society. Taiwanese opera is thus seen as excelling in rendering women's usually inaudible voices. Paradoxically, while the singers spoke to and spoke for their female audience, they seldom had a chance to voice their views as real persons. Most of the singers came from the lowest social stratum and had little access to self-representation in real life. Documentary film-making, because of its heavy reliance on interviews in constructing its filmic discourse, creates a space for these subaltern women singers to speak for themselves as real persons in real life situations rather than in their onstage dramatic personae. However, this does not mean that in documentaries these subaltern women's voices and views are presented as embodying the historical truth. Voices and perspectives other than those of the opera singers are brought into play to create a Bakhtinian space for heteroglossia where various voices and perspectives intersect with, supplement, and even contradict one another. The result is a rather complicated, layered documentary vision in which the memories of these subaltern women appear to be simultaneously valid and limited.

## THE SUBVERSION OF A HISTORICAL LEGEND

*Gongleshe: The Lost Kingdom* took six years to finish. Filmed between 1993 and 1998, the film situated itself in the expanding network of memory discourse in the 1990s that aimed to forge the Taiwanese identity. This is made quite clear in the inter-titles through which the film-maker speaks directly to the audience. At the very beginning of the film, the film-maker Li Xiangxiu, posing herself as a narrator in the film, states through an inter-title that she was alerted to the now forgotten history of *Gongleshe* in 1992. Surprised that she knew nothing about this "kingdom of popular entertainment," Li then embarked on a journey of archeological research which not only produced the documentary film but also helped her come to terms with her Taiwanese identity, which she had rejected because of its stigmatization in post-war Taiwan. The intermittent inter-titles therefore create a narrative parallel to the main narrative in the film, which portrays the rise and fall of the private enterprise of the legendary entrepreneur Chen Chengsan. This personal, autobiographical touch positions the film as a historical-project of counter-memory rescuing history from state-sanctioned memories.

The counter-memory the woman film-maker sets out to redeem is the memory of Chen Chengsan—a Taiwanese entrepreneur from a well-to-do family in a provincial town. The film shows how Chen revived the Taiwanese opera suppressed by the Japanese colonial government and then by the succeeding KMT government. He was also the film producer who created the golden age of Taiwanese-language films at the time when the government propagated the Mandarin-only policy and suppressed local languages and cultures. It is not difficult to understand why in the film Chen is made to stand for Taiwanese popular cultural tradition. Both Taiwanese opera and Taiwanese-language films were extremely popular in the 1950s and 1960s. The fact that memories of Chen and his private entertainment culture industry have fallen into oblivion points to the historical suppression of the Taiwanese identity. As Natalie Zemon Davis and Randolph Starn remark, if memory is often endowed with identity-defining functions (Davis and Starn, 1989, p. 4), to reclaim these memories means to reclaim the Taiwanese cultural tradition and identity.

It is noteworthy that the significant historical past portrayed in the film is reconstructed mainly through the memories of selected women interviewees who were formerly singers in Taiwanese opera troupes owned by Chen. Chen was already dead when Li Xiangxiu began to make the documentary. In order to paint the picture of her Taiwanese hero, Li interviewed former Taiwanese opera singers who worked for Chen. The film begins with the voice of a woman who recalls how she was sold into the opera troupe at the age of five or six. As the narrative unfolds, we learn that the woman's experience was not exceptional at that time. In traditional Taiwanese society, trafficking of young girls was a common practice. Chen's troupes were extremely popular, for stage performances by these young girls he recruited easily impressed the audience. In spite of all their praise for Chen and their portrayal of him as a hero, these women interviewees, perhaps unconsciously, reveal in their casual recollections the oppressive dimension of the cultural tradition that the film appears to endorse. A curious tension begins to surface in the film. On the one hand, we have memories which stress the talents and clever tactics of the private entrepreneur who worked against all odds to open up a space for the survival of Taiwanese culture; on the other hand, the same memories unwittingly problematize the heroic status of the man by exposing the gender oppression and child labour exploitation that made the heroism possible. It is in these unintended and unexpected fissures that the voice of the subaltern woman comes to the fore.

The interviewees' unexpected subversion of what the documentary film-maker originally intends is one of the most fascinating features of the documentary as a genre of representation. It has been by now well acknowledged that documentary films are not objective representations of reality but, in the words of Bill Nichols, "a discourse of sobriety" which tries to make a case with referential evidences (Nichols, 1991, p. 3). Documentary film-making involves subjective practices of shooting (such as the positioning, angling, settings and movement of the cameras) and the process of editing, which inevitably transforms the pro-filmic material (Corner, 1996, p. 21). Thus one of the crucial themes in documentary studies is the degree of control on the part of the film-maker in producing the meaning of the filmic text. Having said this, it is necessary to note that good documentary films are collaborative works by the film-makers and their filmed subjects. The film-maker alone does not determine the meaning of the film, for, as has been pointed out by David MacDougall, it often so happens that the interviewee's performance in front of the camera runs out of the film-maker's control and totally unsettles his/or original plan (MacDougall, 1994, p. 32). Produced through the negotiation between the film-maker and the filmed subjects, the final product of the film seldom comes out in complete compliance with the film-maker's preconceived purpose. The filmed subjects arc not completely powerless in front of the camera, subject to the manipulation of the film-maker's camera and interpretation (Trinh, 1992, p. 194).

The necessity to take into consideration the participatory role of the interviewees in producing the meaning of the film is born out in the documentary *Gongleshe*. If we take the inter-titles intermittently inserted into the film discourse as representing the voice of the film-maker, what the inter-titles show is the film-maker's coming to terms with her Taiwanese identity through the resurrection of the memories of a legendary Taiwanese hero. However, if the film-maker sets out with the intention of portraying Chen as the hero of Taiwanese culture, the contradiction of the interviewees' memories drastically unsettles such a script. On the one hand, we have these subaltern women remembering Chen Chengsan as an admirable, heroic Taiwanese entrepreneur who revived Taiwanese cultural tradition; on the other hand, these women's memories also throw the whole project of hero-building and hero-worship into question as they reveal how heroism was built on gender oppression and child labour exploitation. One should note here an interesting split between the film-maker as a narrator in the filmic discourse and the film-maker as the composer of the film. While the former is shown to be re-constructing her identity through the resurrection of the story of a Taiwanese hero, the latter skilfully weaves the story of the subaltern women into the story of the hero so as to come up with a more nuanced version of the forgotten history. In contrast to the former's attempt to direct her intended audience's attention to the hero and his kingdom-building project, the latter highlights the voices of subaltern women interviewees, which gradually reveal another narrative beyond what is intended by the narrator. The final output of the historiographical project appears to be far more complex and sophisticated than the original script pre-formulated before the act of filming.

As a historiographical practice, *Gongleshe* calls our attention to the documentary as a specific form of historical representation. First of all, it registers the importance of the subaltern voice in shaping a historical narrative. With the exception of the expository mode, I would argue, documentary modes of representation seldom structure different voices and views into a hierarchy with the narrator's voice occupying the position of "the voice of God." According to Bill Nichols (1991), there is more than one mode of documentary representation. The expository mode often employs an authoritative voice-over to present an argument. It tends to de-emphasize the give-and-take between the film-maker-cum-interviewer and the filmed subjects/interviewees (Nichols, 1991, p. 37). This mode of documentary representation dominates the films shown on TV channels like Discovery or National Geographic. The observational mode, often adopted for ethnographical purposes, stresses the non-intervention of the film-maker and cedes the authority of the narrative to what occurs in front of the camera (Nichols, 1991, p. 38). The reflexive mode is a self-conscious mode of representation that draws attention to the process of film-making and reflects on documentary conventions (Nichols, 1991, p. 57). The interactive mode revolves around interviews, implying a shift from narrator-centred voice of authority to witness-centred voice of testimony (Nichols, 1991, p. 47). This is the mode of representation we find in *Gongleshe*. Although Bill Nichols points out that "interviews are a form of hierarchical discourse deriving from the unequal distribution of power, as in the confessional and the interrogation" (Nichols, 1991, p. 47), we should nevertheless avoid over-emphasizing the controlling power of the film-maker at the cost of the interviewee's agency. People who confess are not totally deprived of power. Rather, in many situations, they act with unexpected cunningness, exploiting the power of words to their advantage. Unlike written history or the expository mode of documentary representation, the interactive documentary mode exemplified by *Gongleshe* does not have the narrator-historian's voice dominating its narrative. Instead, the interviews in the documentary open up a space for subaltern people to participate in the representation of the historical past. What the subaltern subjects remember simultaneously supports and unsettles the historiographical project originally intended by the film-maker. Thus, the documentary film-maker no longer claims the unquestionable authority of the narrator-historian in traditional historical discourse. The documentary space is a space of heteroglossia, where different voices and views are brought into play.

## FROM SUBALTERN PERFORMER TO ARTIST

*Liao Qiongzhi: The Taiwanese Opera Singer of Pathos*, like *Gongleshe*, takes the world of the Taiwanese opera as its central subject. If *Gongleshe* aims to redeem the memories of a male hero who thrived on Taiwanese popular culture, *Liao Qiongzhi* is built on the memories of a female singer Liao Qiongzhi who survived on Taiwanese opera. The film begins with cuts from several Taiwanese opera scenes with Liao as the main performer. These Taiwanese operas all portray suffering women betrayed by love. A voice-over then appears to define Liao as "a singer of pathos" who speaks for suffering women. As the film unfolds, we have Liao constantly appearing in front of the camera, tracing memories of her childhood and youth. She was sold into a Taiwanese opera troupe at a very young age by her step-mother. As a Taiwanese opera singer, she occupied an extremely low social status at that time, which prevented her from marrying the man she was in love with. Later, she was forced to become the mistress of the troupe owner. According to an interviewee in the film, this was what commonly happened to Taiwanese opera singers at that time. The subsequent recollection reveals a difficult struggle for survival as Liao tried to raise her children at a time when the popularity of the Taiwanese opera was on the decline, owing to the introduction of other popular entertainment forms in an increasingly modernized Taiwanese society.

Liao's life story as represented in the documentary is in fact an epitome of the lot of subaltern women, constantly plagued by disappointments and hardship. What makes her story different is that, as a scholar in the film points out, she feeds all her life sufferings into her stage performances and finds in the Taiwanese opera form an outlet for and expression of her frustrated hopes. The interweaving of interviews with Liao and other experts on Taiwanese opera is crucial to the layered vision of the documentary. In contrast to *Gongleshe*, in which the interviewee's memories almost usurp the authority of the film-maker/narrator's voice and disrupt the script pre-formulated by the film-maker, the voices in *Liao Qiongzhi* supplement each other and reveal dimensions that transcend the vision of any single interviewee. For example, while Liao's memories present a personal account of her life as a Taiwanese opera singer, it is through the comments of other interviewees that we learn how the roles of the characters she played on the stage infiltrated her life. Liao's unconscious conflation of stage performance with real life is what gives "life" to her performance and elevates her Taiwanese opera singing to the status of "art," but it also traps her in the roles of suffering women and thereby forecloses many possibilities of life for her. Moreover, the interplay of these interviews and Liao's memories builds up a historical vision of the rise and fall of the Taiwanese opera in the post-war era. The comments of the scholars interviewed in the film place Liao's rather personal account in a broader historical context and turn the personal into the political. Finally, as the Taiwanese opera used to be regarded as a form of popular entertainment rather than a serious art form, the comments by various scholars on the artistry of Liao's performance implicitly lend it a kind of "cultural capital" that her interview alone cannot possibly secure. The ultimate validation of these scholars' high regard of Liao's performance, however, comes from the filmic re-presentation of Liao's stage performances. The film's multimedia function bears witness to the scholars' comments on Liao's artistry. The visual and acoustic effects of documentary filmic representation obviously far surpass the words of written history in testifying to the beauty of Liao's art.

It is worth pointing out that the documentary film has a more ambitious plan than tracing the life story of a Taiwanese opera singer. Among other things, what it offers is a re-visioning of Taiwanese opera as an artistic form. Taiwanese opera, as a popular entertainment, used to occupy a very low status in the hierarchy of art forms and was accorded no esteem. The singers, likewise, were relegated to the lowest of the social strata, comparable to that occupied by prostitutes and beggars. With the rise of Taiwanese consciousness in the 1970s, Taiwanese opera gradually came to stand for the oppressed Taiwanese cultural tradition because of its popularity among the Taiwanese people. Like *Gongleshe*, the documentary film *Liao Qiongzhi* embodies a historiographical attempt to forge the Taiwanese identity through the redemption of a popular cultural tradition. At the same time, it also elevates a subaltern woman singer from a low social status to the respected position of artistic performer. The film's emphasis on Liao's life-long devotion to the perfection of her performance underscores her professional integrity and achievement as an artist. Individual memories are deployed in the film to redeem not only a subaltern woman's life through art but also a whole cultural tradition.

## THE DOCUMENTARY AND THE SUBALTERN SUBJECT

The documentary representation of subaltern women in the two films may help us reconsider several important questions raised by G. C. Spivak in her celebrated essay "Can the Subaltern Speak?" Although this essay was published some decades ago, the issues it brings up are still relevant for contemporary cultural critiques and help us avoid glossing over some theoretical short-sightedness in discussing the politics of representation. Spivak begins her famous essay with a critique of what she perceives to be a lacuna in the exchange between Michel Foucault and Gilles Deleuze and Félix Guattari; that is, their unwitting introduction of the undivided subject into their discourse due to their resistance to ideological critique (1988, pp. 273–274). Spivak criticizes these three philosophers for "an unquestioned valorization of the oppressed as subject" and their abandonment of the historical role of the intellectual by insisting that the masses know themselves very well and that they will speak if conditions are established for them to speak (1988, pp. 274–275). Spivak then delineates two nuanced layers of meaning in the term "representation"—representation as "re-represent" ("placing there" or "portraying") and representation as "speaking for." Attention to the two different meanings of "representation" necessitates not only "a critique of the subject as an *individual* agent" but also "a critique even of the subjectivity of a collective agency" (Spivak, 1988, p. 277). Ultimately, Spivak refuses to answer the question "Can the subaltern speak?", but demonstrates how the figure of the subaltern disappears into dominant discourses constructed by the British colonizers and the Indian nativist elites.

Spivak's insistence on the notion of "divided subject" where interest and desire fail to coincide is important in addressing the question of the subaltern voice. It is important to consider, as Spivak points out in citing Louis Althusser, that the subaltern subject does not live outside ideology but is constituted by ideological interpellation that (re)produces the subject's submission to the ruling ideology (Spivak, 1988, p. 273). Subject formation necessarily involves the process of subjection (Althusser, 1971, pp. 172–174). The vision of the subaltern therefore does not automatically guarantee subversive progressiveness. In the documentary *Liao Qiongzhi*, Liao's conflation of stage performance and real life testifies to the disjuncture between interest and desire. Taiwanese operas, as an interviewee in the film points out, are saturated with Confucian doctrine which allows subjects to move only in circumscribed space and discourages any transgression of conventional moral teachings. Liao's total immersion in the world of Taiwanese opera, which makes her a virtuoso of this specific form of performance, implies her unquestioned subjection to the conventional ideal of woman. It is not without reason that Spivak cautions against an "unquestioned valorization of the oppressed subject" and alerts us to the importance of ideological critique in tackling the problem of subaltern representation.

This issue of the subaltern voice as resistance is further complicated when one takes into consideration the common practice of the so-called "outcast's aristocratism" analysed by Pierre Bourdieu in his discussion of the linguistic performances of the socially dominated. Bourdieu demonstrates how a stigmatized group may deliberately flaunt the stigma in defiance of social norms so as to assert its identity (Bourdieu, 1991, p. 95). The poses of bravado by social outcasts, often intended as acts of resistance to authority and rejection of social regulations, imply "a deep-seated conformism regarding everything concerning hierarchies, and not only between the sexes; and the ostentatious toughness which human self-respect imposes in no way excludes a nostalgic yearning for the solidarity, indeed the affection, which, simultaneously gratified and repressed by the highly censored exchanges of the gang, expresses or betrays itself in moments of unself-conscious reflection" (Bourdieu, 1991, p. 96). In addressing the issue of subaltern (self-)representation, the ideological ambiguity of the subaltern's speech performance should be examined critically.

But the rejection of unquestioned valorization of the oppressed subject does not entail the view of the intellectual(-film-maker) as capable of offering a better historical vision. It is necessary to realize that intellectuals are not outside the structure of ideology, either. Aside from the ideological limitation of intellectuals' vision, we cannot overlook the fact that their interpretations of the utterances of the subaltern are likely to be constrained by the social and cultural scripts they are familiar with. If speaking is defined as "a transaction between the speaker and the listener" (Spivak, 1996, p. 289), how to "unlearn" in order to enter that transaction is a most challenging task. Thus, there always remains the question as to whether one has really heard and understood the utterance by Liao or the subaltern women-singers in *Gongleshe*. In both documentaries, conditions seem to be established to allow the subaltern to speak. But does that speaking really take place? This is a question that continues to haunt both the film-maker and the audience.

As the same question is also raised in the realm of ethnography, which is more than anything else a discipline concerned with the representation of the other and increasingly involved with documentary practice, we may benefit from the insights of ethnographical reflection on the possibility of representing the other. While Spivak speaks of the disappearance of what the subaltern tries to say into the discourses constructed by elites, critics of ethnography point out that ethnographic writing is often dictated by dominant figurative modes of narrative drawn from the ethnographer's own culture, which may cast the gathered ethnographic data in ways divorced from the indigenous understanding of the meaning of these data (Crapanzano, 1986, p. 76). The problem, in the words of the critic Vincent Crapanzano, is that "there is never an I-you relationship, a dialogue, two people next to each other reading the same text and discussing it face-to-face, but only an I-they relationship" (Crapanzano, 1986, p. 74). Crapanzano is referring to ethnography in the written form, but what he says can also be applied to conventional ethnographic documentary film which employs authoritative voice-over commentary to represent cultures other than the ethnographer's own (Nichols, 1994, p. 68). It is worth pointing out here that Crapanzano is calling for the creation of dialogues in ethnographic discourse rather than a complete surrender of ethnographic authority to the native's perspective. In other words, he is not advocating a mode of ethnographic discourse that privileges the native's point of view. Self-representation by the oppressed, important as it is, should also be subject to close analysis, not simply because what the subjects say about themselves and their cultures should not be taken at face value but also because no one can claim the privilege of providing the ultimate insight into one's own history or culture (Trinh, 1992, p. 145; Ginsburg, 1999, p. 164; Ruby, 2000, p. 207). The point, then, is not simply to create conditions where the subaltern/native can speak, but to create a space of dialogues that allow different views and voices to come into play, a space that makes it possible "to know difference differently" (Nichols, 1994, p. 80). This is, in other words, a space shaped by the practice of "shared authority" (Ruby, 2000, p. 207).

The notion of "shared authority" is exactly what informs the two documentary films discussed in this essay. The two films offer a historical vision that arises out of the dialogical tension of different voices and perspectives. In *Gongleshe*, interviews with subaltern Taiwanese opera singers dominate the film, but it is framed within the narrative structured by the inter-titles which voice unequivocally the film-maker/narrator's pursuit of the forgotten story of a legendary hero. What the subaltern women say in the interviews simultaneously supports and undercuts her intention. By foregrounding what the Taiwanese opera singers remember about the past in its reconstruction of Taiwanese history, the film deliberately performs an archaeological resurrection of what Michel Foucault calls "subjugated knowledge" from women relegated to the lowest stratum of society. The subjugated knowledge in *Gongleshe* is deployed against state-sanctioned forgetting to rebuild the legend of a master of Taiwanese popular entertainment. But, as subjugated knowledge is "far from being a general commonsense knowledge, but is on the contrary a particular, local, regional knowledge, a differential knowledge *incapable of unanimity* and which owes its force only to the harshness with which it is opposed by everything surrounding it" (Foucault, 1980, p. 82; italics mine), it unexpectedly resurrects the history of subaltern women often marginalized or muted in histories of heroic men. The redemption of a hero's history accidentally leads to the redemption of subaltern women's history. Ultimately, the meaning of the documentary is not determined solely by the intention of the film-maker. Equally important is the implicit message imbedded in the words of the filmed subjects.

In *Liao Qiongzhi*, the dialogical tension of different voices is not created by the ambiguous interstices between what the filmed subjects say and what the film-maker intends to say. Rather, the voices supplement each other in conjuring up a historical vision that transcends the limited vision of each interviewee. Unlike *Gongleshe*, which calls upon the memories of subaltern women to bring into being the life story of a male hero, *Liao Qiongzhi* places a subaltern woman at the very heart of its filming project and seeks to turn her into a heroine. While Liao speaks about her personal sufferings and frustrations, the comments of other interviewees shed new light on what she says. Liao's story is no longer the unfortunate story of a woman, but is turned into an epitome of the common story of women betrayed by life. Represented in the film as "the number one singer of pathos," Liao is shown to act out the lot of women onstage and speak for the muted hopes and disappointments of women in her age. With its emphasis on the gender dimension of the Taiwanese opera as a genre, the film orchestrates the comments of selected scholars who are interviewed in such a way that turns this stigmatized popular entertainment into a serious subject for critical study. At the same time, Liao is also elevated to the status of a virtuosic professional artist. She is no longer regarded as a mere street performer. However, it is important to note that, important as the opinions of these interviewees are in shedding new light on Liao and Taiwanese opera, they are not presented as superior to the vision of Liao, for it is she who is *the* mistress of the Taiwanese opera. It is she who holds the key to the beauty of this performing art. Whatever she says carries exclusive weight.

## DOCUMENTARY AND THE VISION OF MODERN TAIWAN

Discussing the emergence of China's modernity, Rey Chow offers an interesting re-interpretation of the well-known episode of Lu Xun's shocked discovery of China's "belatedness" in a visual experience and his consequent determined pursuit of the project of modernizing the Chinese through the transformation of the literary word (Chow, 1995, p. 49). In his visual encounter with modernity embodied by the overwhelming, powerful "technologized visuality," Lu Xun saw projected on screen the violent scene of a Chinese spy being beheaded while surrounded by a "completely apathetic" crowd of his fellow countrymen. What is so violent about this visual experience, in Rey Chow's interpretation, is Lu Xun's shocked experience of the power of the visual medium, which jolted him into an acute consciousness of how China was visualized by the modern West. In other words, the "modern" Chinese consciousness is deeply implicated in a heightened consciousness of visuality as the violence of modernity and as the new representational medium in the modern age. However, instead of responding directly to the challenge of the power of visuality, Lu Xun (re)turned to literary culture as the way of salvation for China (Chow, 1995, p. 17). The whole project of modernizing China was launched in association with a literary reform directed at the transformation of "the people." Thus, in addition to the challenge of the visual image, the question of China's modernity is always tied up with the question of "the people."

In the words of Rey Chow:

> If the centrality of the literary sign is (re)moved by the increasing omnipresence of the visual sign, and reading and writing decentered by the coming of the film medium, the literary sign is also (re)moved democratically, from being the agent of record of life among the elite classes to being the agent of record of life among the masses. Reflection on "China" would increasingly mean coming to terms with China's people, in particular the oppressed classes. (Chow, 1995, p. 19)

Like their Chinese counterparts, Taiwanese intellectuals in the early twentieth century also sought to transform Taiwan into a modern society through a literary reform that placed the question of "the Taiwanese people" at the top of its agenda (Xiang, 2004). But unlike Rey Chow, who seems to stress the Chinese intellectual's role as an enlightener vis-à-vis "the people," Taiwanese intellectuals were more ambivalent apropos the issue of the people. While the people are often represented as the masses waiting for enlightenment, there are also moments in the writings of intellectuals that show the people as guardians of a certain kind of wisdom, beyond the limited vision of the intellectuals. The story "Homecoming" (Guijia) by the writer Lai Ho, reputedly the father of the Taiwanese new literature, is a case in point. The two vendors' remarks provide a counter-vision to the intellectual narrator's (over-)optimistic view of modernization. Their insightful observation is deliberately set in sharp contrast to the naivety of the narrator. The bifurcated vision of the people as the unenlightened masses and as enlightening teachers betrays the hesitating uncertainty on the part of the intellectual vis-à-vis "the people." "The people," indeed, is as much a question as a problem.

On the other hand, the intellectuals' turn to the literary word in their attempt to transform Taiwan into a modernized society does not mean that they were blind to the power of images as a useful medium of reform. In fact, as early as 1925, the Association of Taiwanese Culture, a dissident organization opposing the Japanese colonial rule, had already began to exploit films as a medium of consciousness-awakening by showing throughout Taiwan educational films imported from abroad (Ye, 1997, p. 185). This attempt to bring modern Taiwan into being through visual communication was soon aborted, not simply because of strict colonial censorship but, more importantly, because of the absence of a sustainable film industry to continuously supply films for the reformers' intended purposes (Lü, 1961, p. 6). If film is a form of what

Rey Chow calls "techologized visuality," securing the finance and the technology needed for film production appeared to be an insurmountably difficult task for colonial intellectuals. The written word therefore took upon itself the responsibility of writing a modernized Taiwan into being. But the problem of representing the people, which is inseparable from the representation of modern, democratized Taiwan, remained unresolved. The gap between the literary word and the illiterate people was not easy to overcome, for the representation endeavour by the literary word could do no more than performing representation as "speaking for," often at the sacrifice of "re-presentation."

It was the emergence of new documentary filming practice in the mid-1980s that provided a possible solution to this long-standing problem. Thanks to the invention of lightweight and less costly shooting equipment, independent documentary film-making became possible and quickly became involved in the production of counter-representation that resisted the monopoly of state-controlled media (Dai and Wei, 1992, p. 47). Documentary filming emphasized "grass-roots" vision and insisted on the rights of common people to historical representation. It was deliberately and self-consciously practised as "historiography from below," bearing witness to the voice of the people in shaping the history of Taiwan under transformation. As such, it proves especially helpful in cracking open a space for the play of the subaltern's voice which is seldom articulated in conventional discourses of the "people." Documentary film-makers at that time were extremely conscious that, together with their filmed subaltern subjects, they were *making* history, calling into being a modern, democratized Taiwan while rendering a vision of it from the perspective of subaltern subjects traditionally muted in official documents. With the literary word no longer occupying the centre of discursive formation, historiography is finally able to take into account what the subaltern tries to speak. And, as I have tried to show in my analysis of the two documentaries above, this is done without too much romanticization of the subaltern subject. It is dialogical tension, rather than monological domination, that characterizes documentary representation as the modern mode of re-envisioning Taiwan.

### REFERENCES

Althusser, Louis (1971). *Lenin and Philosophy, and Other Essays*. Trans. Ben Brewster. New York: Monthly Review Press.

Bourdieu, Pierre (1991). "Did You Say 'Popular'?", trans. by Gino Raymond and Matthew Adamson. In John B. Thompson, ed., *Language and Symbolic Power*, pp. 90–102. Cambridge: Polity Press.

Chen Xin-yuan (2004). "Yijiuqiling niandai Taiwan de xiangtu wenxue lunzhan" [The nativist literary debates in Taiwan in the 1970s]. In *Taiwan xinwenxue fazhan zhongda shijian lunwenji* [Essays on key issues in the development of Taiwan new literature], pp. 21–47. Tainan: Guoli Taiwan wenxue bowuguan.

Chiu Kuei-fen (2003). "Tumo dangdai Er'erba tuxiang" [The February 28th incident images]. In Chiu Kuei-fen, *Houzhimin ji qiwai* [Re-conceptualizing post-colonial literary theories in Taiwan], pp. 183–208. Taipei: Maitian.

Chow, Rey (1995). *Primitive Passions: Visuality, Sexuality, Ethnography and Contemporary Chinese Cinema*. New York: Columbia University Press.

Clifford, James (1986). "On Ethnographic Allegory." In James Clifford and George E. Marcus, eds., *Writing Culture: The Poetics and Politics of Ethnography*, pp. 98–121. Berkeley and Los Angeles: University of California Press.

Corner, John (1996). "Documentary Theory." In *The Art of Record: A Critical Introduction to Documentary*, pp. 9–30. Manchester: Manchester University Press.

Crapanzano, Vincent (1986). "Hermes' Dilemma: The Masking of Subversion in Ethnographic Description." In James Clifford and George E. Marcus, eds., *Writing Culture: The Poetics and Politics of Ethnography*, pp. 51–76. Berkeley and Los Angeles: University of California Press.

Dai Bofen, and Wei Yinbing (1992). "Taiwan fanzhuliu yingxiang meiti de lishi guancha" [A historical note on anti-mainstream media in Taiwan]. *Dianying xinshang* [Film appreciation journal], Vol. 10, No. 3, 45–51.

Davis, Natalie Zemon, and Randolph Starn (1989). "Introduction." *Representations*, No. 26 (Spring), 1–6.

Esbenshade, Richard S. (1995). "Remembering to Forget: Memory, History, National Identity in Postwar East-Central Europe." *Representations*, No. 49 (Winter), 72–96.

Foucault, Michel (1980). *Power/Knowledge: Selected Interviews and Other Writings, 1972–1977*. Trans. Colin Gordon, Leo Marshall, John Mepham and Kate Soper. New York: Pantheon Books.

Ginsburg, Faye (1999). "The Parallax Effect: The Impact of Indigenous Media on Ethnographic Film." In Jane M. Gaines and Michael Renov, eds., *Collecting Visible Evidence*, pp. 156–175. Minneapolis: University of Minnesota Press.

Grossmann, Atina (1995). "A Question of Silence: The Rape of German Women by Occupation Soldiers." *October*, Vol. 22 (Spring), 43–63.

Hillenbrand, Margaret (2005). "Trauma and the Politics of Identity: Form and Function in Fictional Narratives of the February 28th Incident." *Modern Chinese Literature and Culture*, Vol. 17, No. 2 (Fall), 49–89.

Hobsbawm, E. J. (1988). "History from Below—Some Reflections." In Frederick Krantz, ed., *History from Below: Studies in Popular Protest and Popular Ideology*, pp. 13–27. New York: Basil Blackwell.

hooks, bell (1989). "Writing Autobiography." In bell hooks, ed., *Talking Back: Thinking Feminist, Thinking Black*, pp. 155–166. Boston, MA: South End Press.

Huyssen, Andreas (2000). "Present Pasts: Media, Politics, Amnesia." *Public Culture*, Vol. 12, No. 1, 21–38.

Jiang Wenyu (1995). "Yi *A-ma de gushi* jian'gou Taiwan nüxing shenghuoshi" [Constructing life histories of Taiwan women through *The Stories of Grandmas*]. In Yang Zhao, *Xiaoshizhong de Taiwan A-ma* [Disappearing Taiwan grandmas], pp. 11–20. Taipei: Yushanshe.

Lü Su-shang (1961). *Taiwan dianying xiju shi* [A history of cinema and drama in Taiwan]. Taipei: Yin-hua chubanbu.

MacDougall, David (1994). "Whose Story Is It?" In Lucien Taylor, ed., *Visualizing Theory: Selected Essays from V.A.R., 1990–1994*, pp. 27–36. New York: Routledge.

Nakamura Nasaru, and Hung Jin-chu, eds. (1997). *Shanshen qingyao: Taiyazu nüxing Chuwas Lawa de yisheng* [High is the mountain, long is the road: The life story of an Atayal woman—Chuwas Lawa]. Taipei: Shibao wenhua chuban qiye gufen youxian gongsi.

Nichols, Bill (1991). *Representing Reality: Issues and Concepts in Documentary*. Bloomington: Indiana University Press.

Nichols, Bill (1994). "The Ethnographers' Tale." In Bill Nichols, *Blurred Boundaries: Questions of Meaning in Contemporary Culture*, pp. 63–91. Bloomington: Indiana University Press.

Peng Ruijin (2004). "Cong Huang Shihui dao Ye Shitao: Taiwan wenxue bentu lunzheng de faduan he zhongduan" [From Huang Shihui to Ye Shitao: The beginning and end of nativist debates on Taiwan literature]. In *Taiwan xinwenxue fazhan zhongda shijian lunwenji* [Essays on key issues in the development of Taiwan new literature], pp. 156–174. Tainan: Guoli Taiwan wenxue bowuguan.

Ruby, Jay (2000). "Speaking For, Speaking About, Speaking With, or Speaking Alongside." In *Picturing Culture: Explorations of Film and Anthropology*, pp. 195–220. Chicago: University of Chicago Press.

Sipe, Dan (1998). "The Future of Oral History and Moving Images." In Robert Perks and Alistair Thomson, eds., *The Oral History Reader*, pp. 379–388. London: Routledge.

Smith, Sidonie (1987). "'Maxine Hong Kingston's *Woman Warrior*: Filiality and Women's Autobiographical Storytelling' from *A Poetics of Women's Autobiography*." In Robyn R. Warhol and Diane Price Herndl, eds., *Feminisms: An Anthology of Literary Theory and Criticism*, pp. 1117–1137. Basingstoke: Macmillan.

Spivak, Gayatri Chakravorty (1988). "Can the Subaltern Speak?" In Cary

Nelson and Lawrence Grossberg, eds., *Marxism and the Interpretation of Culture*, pp. 271–313. Urbana: University of Illinois Press.

Spivak, Gayatri Chakravorty (1996). "Subaltern Talk: Interview with the Editors (1993–1994)." In Donna Landry and Gerald MacLean, eds., *The Spivak Reader: Selected Works of Gayatri Chakravorty Spivak*, pp. 287–308. New York: Routledge.

Sun Da-Chuan (2003). "Yuanzhumin wenhua lishi yu xinling shijie de moxie" [A portrayal of aboriginal culture, history, and their life-world]. In *Taiwan yuanzhumin Hanyu wenxue xuanji pinglun, juan shang* [Essays on Taiwan aboriginal literature in Chinese, vol. I], pp. 17–47. Taipei: Ink.

Thompson, Paul (1998). "The Voice of the Past: Oral History." In Robert Perks and Alistair Thomson, eds., *The Oral History Reader*, pp. 21–28. London: Routledge.

Trinh, Minh-ha T. (1989). *Woman, Native, Other: Writing Postcoloniality and Feminism*. Bloomington: Indiana University Press.

Trinh, Minh-ha T. (1992). *Framer Framed: Film Scripts and Interviews*. New York: Routledge.

Wang Xiao-ming (2002). "Cong Huaihai lu dao Meijia qiao: Cong Wang Anyi xiaoshuo chuangzuo de zhuanbian tanqi" [From Huaihai Road to the Bridge Mei: On the re-orientation of Wang Anyi's creative works]. *Wenxue pinglun* [Literary criticism], Vol. 3, 20.

Xiang Yang (2004). "Minzu xiangxiang yu dazhong luxian de jiaogui: Yijiu-sanling niandai Taiwan huawen lunzheng yu Taiyu wenxue yundong" [Intersection between the national imaginary and the mass movement: The debate on Taiwanese language in the 1930s and the Taiwan literature movement]. In *Taiwan xinwenxue fazhan zhongda shijian lunwenji* [Essays on key issues in the development of Taiwan new literature], pp. 21–47. Tainan: Guoli Taiwan wenxue bowuguan.

Yang Zhao (1995). "Suozai chufang li de lishi" [Histories locked up in the kitchen]. In Yang Zhao, *Xiaoshizhong de Taiwan A-ma* [Disappearing Taiwan grandmas], pp. 2–10. Taipei: Yushanshe.

Ye Longyan (1997). "Taiwan de dianying bianshi" [Movie interpreters in Taiwan]. *Taibei wenxian zhizi* [Taipei literature (vertical layout version)], Vol. 121 (September), 173–200.

Yip, June (2004). *Envisioning Taiwan: Fiction, Cinema, and the Nation in the Cultural Imaginary*. Durham, NC: Duke University Press.

## GLOSSARY

*Beiqing chengshi*《悲情城市》

Chen Ye 陳燁

*Gongleshe: Xiaoshi de wangguo*《拱樂社：消失的王國》

"Guijia"〈歸家〉

Hou Hsiao-hsien 侯孝賢

Jiang Wenyu 江文瑜

Lai Ho 賴和

Li Ang 李昂

Li Xiangxiu 李香秀

*Miyuan*《迷園》

*Ni he*《泥河》

Ping Lu 平路

*Shanshen qingyao*《山深情遙》

Shi Shuqing 施叔青

"Suozai chufang li de lishi"〈鎖在廚房裡的歷史〉

xiangtu 鄉土

*Xiang wo juancun de xiongdimen*《想我眷村的兄弟們》

*Xiaoshizhong de Taiwan A-ma*《消失中的台灣阿嬤》

*Xingdao tianya*《行道天涯》

*Xingguo Lojin*《行過洛津》

Zhu Tianxin 朱天心

# 13  Desire, Fear and Gender in Dong Qizhang's Novel *Dual Body*

KWOK-KAN TAM

THE DOUBLE IS AN INTRIGUING psychological phenomenon, as well as a recurrent philosophical theme in Western culture. In ancient Greece, there was already the observation that human beings are by nature incomplete and need to seek out partners to make up for their incompleteness. In Plato's *Symposium*, Aristophanes has the following comment on the split between the male and the female among human beings:

> First of all, you must learn the constitution of man and the modifications which it has undergone, for originally it was different from what it is now. In the first place, there were three sexes, not, as with us, two, male and female; the third partook of the nature of both the others and has vanished, though its name survives. The hermaphrodite was a distinct sex in form as well as in name, with characteristics of both male and female, but now the name alone remains, and that solely as a term of abuse. (Plato, 1952, pp. 60–61)

Aristophanes' story offers the view that it is the physical incompleteness of the human body that causes the psychological incompleteness of desire. He relates the origin of desire to a myth about how the Greek gods decided to punish the rebellious human race. Aristophanes imagines a conversation among the gods, in which there is the suggestion to cut human beings in half so that they become weak and will not be able to cause trouble:

> Zeus had an idea. "I think," he said, "that I have found a way by which we can allow the human race to continue to exist and also put an end to their wickedness by making them weaker. I will cut each of them in two; in this way they will be weaker, and at the same time more profitable to us by being more numerous. They shall walk upright upon two legs. If there is any sign of wantonness in them after that, and they will not keep quiet, I will bisect them again, and they shall hop on one leg."

Man's original body having been thus cut in two, each half yearned for the half from which it had been severed. When they met they threw their arms around one another and embraced, in their longing to grow together again, and they perished of hunger and general neglect of their concerns, because they would not do anything apart. When one member of a pair died and the other was left, the latter sought after and embraced another partner, which might be the half of either a female whole (what is now called a woman) or a male. (Plato, 1952, pp. 60–61)

## PSYCHOANALYSIS OF PERSONALITY INCOMPLETENESS

The passages quoted above are the earliest reference in Western culture to the idea that individual human bodies are actually incomplete split halves, rather than self-sufficient wholes. In philosophical enquiry, what is of interest is the insight that the fundamental incompleteness of the human body causes us to yearn for what we lack; in psychological terms, this lack becomes an incompleteness in the human personality. This dualism points to not just a difference between the two sexes, but also a politics of gender, for implied in it is a love-hate relationship that has become an age-old theme in psychology. Thus human beings, male or female, are all split halves of an incomplete self.

This myth from Plato's *Symposium* further marks the beginning of a philosophical consideration of the constitution of the self in two paradigms: the body and the psyche, which are seen to complement each other. However, in the Renaissance, Descartes' "mind-body dualism" turns this philosophical enquiry around by arguing that it is the mind that informs one's identity and thus the existence of one's body. Descartes' interest lies in an "archaeology of the mind," to twist Foucault's terminology slightly. Descartes seeks to prove the existence of himself by way of logic, that is, it is the mind's process of rational thinking that makes one know one exists. In other words, it is through consciousness that one knows about oneself. This assertion of the importance of consciousness in Descartes' methodology establishes the Western approach to the concept of self, which emphasizes rational thinking as a distinction between the sane and the insane. While the Cartesian approach lays the foundation of cognitive philosophy, it fails to account for the role the body plays in the constitution of self. It is not until Freud's theory of the unconscious at the beginning of the twentieth century that the human mind began to be seen as a complex function of the body. Despite the fact that Freudianism has been attacked as biased against women in its theorization, which is based on a male model, the theory of the unconscious and the role the body plays in the constitution of self are of paramount significance in modern philosophical consideration of the subject. Freud's notion of the unconscious brings a new dimension to re-conceiving of the self as a complex subject of repression. Personality incompleteness, first discussed in Greek mythology, is now given a new explanation in Freudian psychoanalysis as dissociation of personality in the form of a conflict between the "ego" and the "alter ego," which in severe cases may lead to schizophrenia. As informed by psychiatry, schizophrenia makes a person lose touch with reality and enter a state of the unconscious that will cause dissociation of personality. In such a state of mind, known as "fugue," the multiple selves of the same person project onto one another their psychical lacks and anxieties in an effort to deny one another. This is a central thesis in Otto Rank's theory of "Der Doppelgänger." The double is seen as a projection, or mirror, of the ego. Rank points out that the double is a self-defence mechanism against castration anxiety and the fear of death, which threaten a person's self-love. At the same time, the ego hates the double and wishes to kill it. By killing the double, the ego also kills itself. This is a psychoanalytic explanation of suicide. On the basis of Rank's theory, Freud expands the notion of the double by pointing out that in the psyche there is the "principle of repetition compulsion." Freud's concept of "the uncanny" is developed from psychoanalysis of the double.

While Freudian psychoanalysis offers an explanation of schizophrenia as a psychical disorder, there have been various efforts to re-conceptualize this psychical disorder as a cultural formation over the past thirty years. Deleuze's notion of the "anti-Oedipus" points at a new theoretical orientation, in which schizophrenia is seen from a Marxist point of view as a psychical dissociation caused by sociocultural disorder. The dissociation of personality is thus theorized as political and cultural dislocations of the self in temporal and spatial dimensions. This new orientation in the conceptualization of schizophrenia implies that we should bring in temporal and spatial dimensions in reconsidering the formation of the self and personal identity.

## LOCATION/DISLOCATION IN *DUAL BODY*

Theories about the psychological double, or multiple personalities, have now become useful not only as methods for psychiatry, but also as interpretive tools for reading literary characters. *Shuangshen* (*Dual body*,

1997), by the Hong Kong writer Dong Qizhang, is an award-winning novel. It is a story about a man, Lin Shanyuan, who loses his memory and wakes up to discover that he has a female body. The novel is set in both Tokyo and Hong Kong, and the narrative alternates between the two places. Lin Shanyuan attempts to define his identity, both physical and psychological, in relation to the cultural spaces that the two locations provide. By alternating between the space and time of Hong Kong and Tokyo, Lin Shanyuan is depicted as dislocated in his attempt to find his identity and redefine himself. Hence, the physical disjunction between two locations is related to the psychological dislocation of the protagonist.

Tokyo is a place where Lin Shanyuan, now in his new female body, finds himself culturally feminized and inferiorized. It is also a place that rejects his previous masculine self. The question of "Who am I?" has appeared numerous times in the mind of Lin Shanyuan, who cannot reconcile his new identity as a female and his old identity as a male. This confusion occurs not only because Lin Shanyuan has lost his male body and acquired a female body, but more importantly because both his new and old selves are culturally dislocated in a society in which the female does not have a voice. As a person who does not speak Japanese, Lin Shanyuan finds himself dumb and powerless in all attempts to reposition his self (Dong, 1997, p. 7). Among the many people whom Lin Shanyuan meets in Tokyo, only two are willing to listen to him and care about his story. Unfortunately, these two people are not much better off than Lin Shanyuan, since they are both leading alienated lives in Tokyo. Ah Che, the man who provides temporary shelter for Lin Shanyuan, is half Chinese and half Japanese, and is himself a cultural outcast in Japanese society. Xiumei, a Chinese woman working in a Japanese bar, lives a life of diasporic dislocation in Tokyo.

Wandering through Tokyo, Lin Shanyuan finds that he has lost all sense of direction in the big city, where he sees nothing but neatly dressed people rushing home after a day's work (Dong, 1997, p. 6). No one cares about anyone's real identity, and in the vast space of the city, people are addressed and treated simply according to their outward appearance. Spatially and psychologically disoriented, Lin Shanyuan is alienated from others and finds it impossible to explain his true identity to people. As the protagonist says, "You simply can't imagine, can't admit that this male-dressed person with a female body is you yourself" (Dong, 1997, p. 6).

The cultural dislocation Lin Shanyuan experiences in Tokyo is due partly to the new temporal space that he is given in his new identity as a female. Tokyo at its best is a place that opens up desire and futuristic imagination, but at the same time forces the visitor to have a keen sense of the present, accompanied by a fear of uncertainty and unpredictability (Dong, 1997, p. 7). For the protagonist, however, returning to Hong Kong does not bring back his sense of belonging. To the new female self of Lin Shanyuan, everything in his old male identity belongs only to the past, which is firmly located in a geographical space: "Returning from Japan to Hong Kong is like returning from a world of fairytales, where anything can happen, to a world of reality, where nothing happens" (Dong, 1997, p. 19). Back in Hong Kong, Lin Shanyuan finds that, as a female, he is forever cut off from his male past. His mother and his friends no longer recognize him as Lin Shanyuan. The only way he can be accepted is to give up his original identity as a male and assume a new identity as Lin Shanyuan's sister. To the new, feminized Lin Shanyuan, who acquired a female body in Osaka and a new female identity in Tokyo, Hong Kong is an unfamiliar place of enclosure, in which he has to struggle to relocate himself.

## BODY SELF AND GENDER SELF

The alternating narrative space in the novel provides another dimension of psychological dislocation. Lin Shanyuan, in his female embodiment, who is confused about his gender and wanders about Tokyo in search of his true sexual identity, is the double of the former male-bodied Lin Shanyuan, who lived in Hong Kong lamenting his incompleteness as a male. Yet, in his present female body, he finds that he is far from being a complete woman. His gender is determined not just by the body he has, but also by the history of a traceable past in his life:

> I am not a normal woman. In bearing the burden of my past, which means only harm to me, where is my position among people?

> My life has come to an end.
> Thus, I will not wake up from sleep. (Dong, 1997, p. 19)

The narrative alternates not only between two geographical locations, Tokyo and Hong Kong, but also between the temporal spaces of the past and the present. Lin Shanyuan has two present selves: one is the female identity accepted in Tokyo and the other is the newly assumed female identity in Hong Kong, both of which are "alter egos" that emerge out of his hidden psychical desire to be female. These two present "alter egos" contrast with his past self as a male, whose "ego" has been hurt since his teenage years.

In his attempts to reassert his original identity as a male, Lin Shanyuan searches through everything he can find in his private experience, as well as in the collective memory of his friends and family members. In re-establishing his connections with the past, he finds that the circumcision that he had as a young boy has left an indelible mark in his sense of himself as a castrated male, which is a psychological trauma that has shamed him and given him an incomplete masculine identity and fear of women. In the operating theatre, he heard mocking voices:

> His face is so red! He has a handsome face.
> Right! He is handsome, because when he grows up he will be a bridegroom.
> Why not be a bridegroom today!
> Don't make any mistake, otherwise he cannot be a bridegroom!
> Then he can still be a bride!
> A beautiful bride, with a red, red face!
> Don't make any jokes, he is a real male!
> A bride with beautiful eyes!   (Dong, 1997, pp. 52–53)

As a child, his interest in women was also repressed when he was overpowered by a big, muscular classmate, who bullied weaker boys into playing sexual games and assumed the role of a patriarchal figure in school.

In trying to look back at his childhood self, Lin Shanyuan searches for any means to help recover his memory. The photos that he finds in his photo album remind him that he had once admired the female body when he was a little boy. His earliest experience of masturbation, as he remembers, was a little boy's test of his own maleness and is an imagination of masculinity. The young Lin Shanyuan was a boy with a male body but a castrated masculine identity. Yet, in his present female-bodied self, the memory of his former masculine self leads him to detest his own body, for it causes not only gender confusion in him, but also rejection by his friends. His body contradicts his psychologically masculine identity, and so Lin Shanyuan hates his body, because it does not gain him social recognition and acceptance.

## DESIRE, FEAR AND GENDER DISCOURSE

The split between body identity and gender identity in Lin Shanyuan results in the dissociation of personality. His present female body informs him of a feminine self, which is in conflict with his former male body that reminds him of a masculine self. However, neither his present female form nor his former male body is what he desires. While his present female body is thrust upon him without his consent, his past male body is an incomplete one through no choice of his own. The circumcision signifies not just an incompleteness in Lin Shanyuan's masculinity, but also a repressed desire resulting from the psychological feeling of lack in the body. With his present female body, Lin Shanyuan is also incomplete, as he is no more than a "hollow woman" without any sense of femininity.

While Lin Shanyuan is still puzzling about his gender identity in Tokyo, one day he has a dream, in which all images of the past and the present, Tokyo and Hong Kong, are mixed up in the form of the uncanny that Freud has theorized as a projection of repressed fear and anxiety:

> What beautiful eyes!
> The sound of fierce winds outside the windows, but everything indoors is frozen.
> Look at this pair of girl's eyes!
> In Xiumei's big eyes is my shadow.
> A girl holding a knife.
> Lying on a bed, I feel dizzy in my head. I am being pushed along the hallway, and then enter a room with lamps that are hung from the ceiling and arranged in a circle.
> My classmates are flickering in front of me. I can't tell which face is whose.
> The nurse in white lifts up my clothes, and my lower part feels cool.
> What a crimson red face! A beautiful bride indeed.
> The sound of laughter from the nurse in white.
> We see our distorted selves in the distortion.
> A girl holding a penis full of blood.
> The display of love in the extreme.
> This is just a small operation!
> The sound of laughter among classmates. (Dong, 1997, p. 165)

*Dual Body* can thus be read as a novel about the protagonist's fluid identity, as well as identity stereotyping in society. In a conversation among the split selves of Lin Shanyuan, one of them says: "Because I am made from sand, I cannot be held in the hand. I don't have a fixed form. I am solid, but I can also flow" (Dong, 1997, p. 137). A fluid identity is seen as "queer" in society, which tends to simplify people by stereotyping them. In both Tokyo and Hong Kong, Lin Shanyuan encounters various gender stereotypes . Since Lin Shanyuan's transformation has left him with no strong sense of his own gendered identity, the only way for him to recreate a new identity for himself is to rely solely on the impression he can create in other people's eyes. Again he finds that society is full of biased gender discourses, which serve only to trap people in the hollowness of stereotyped language. The conversation with his three male friends in an attempt to explain to them his "bi-sexual/bi-gendered identity" only renews his frustration in constructing his identity. Lin Shanyuan finally gives up all hope of reasserting his contradictory double self, which is neither male nor female, as he is convinced that the more he explains the "uniqueness" of his self, the more he will feel drowned in the hollowness of language.

The lack of an identity that can be categorized and can fit into people's stereotypes implies Hong Kong people's lack of a cultural identity that can be categorized as either Western or Chinese. In another sense too, the novel can be read as a symbol of Hong Kong people's lack of a definable identity. Hong Kong people are bilingual, bicultural, and now also bi-sexual and bi-gendered. This bi-sexual and bi-gendered identity and the trouble of misrecognition that it brings is perhaps the unique gender politics that Hong Kong has.

## REFERENCES

Deleuze, Gilles, and Félix Guattari (1977). *Anti-Oedipus: Capitalism and Schizophrenia*. Trans. Robert Hurley, Mark Seem and Helen R. Lane. Minneapolis: University of Minnesota Press.

Dong Qizhang (Dung Kai Cheung) (1997). *Shuangshen* [Dual body]. Taipei: Lianjing.

Plato (1952). *The Symposium*. Trans. W. Hamilton. London: Penguin.

## GLOSSARY

Dong Qizhang (Dung Kai Cheung) 董啓章

Lin Shanyuan 林山原

*Shuangshen* 《雙身》

Xiumei 秀美

# 14 Men Aren't Men

*Feminization of the Masculine Subject*
*in the Works of Some Hong Kong Male Writers*

KWAI-CHEUNG LO

THE REASON WHY MASCULINITY HAS become an interesting topic for gender studies today is probably because of its collapse or near demise. There has been much discussion about a "crisis" of masculinity (Gardiner, 2002). The so-called crisis is not due to the onslaughts and advances of feminism, nor is it the growing impotence of men or "boys"[1] that leads to the falling apart of traditional masculinity. On the contrary, masculinity has always been a disjointed, fragmented and self-contradictory concept that could never live up to the unified image of power to which it aspires. The distinctive demarcation of pure masculinity in opposition to pure femininity is never to be found in any psychological or biological sense. Perhaps it is the process of modernity that not only turns humans into subjects and the world into an object, but also polarizes the two sexes into opposing categories of pure masculinity and pure femininity.

Undoubtedly, the recent search for a new image of the modern man in contemporary China is closely linked to the country's quest for modernization and economic reforms (Zhong, 2000). Although Chinese society, like many other patriarchal cultures, is predominantly male-oriented, Chinese men have been figured in the gaze of the West as being in some sense feminized, dependent and passive (Chan, 2001). The Western perception of the oriental male is undoubtedly a product of the self-representation of Western man that relies on an inferior other to constitute his identity in a dualistic fashion and to justify the hegemonic assumption of masculinity as pure strength and mastery. Not totally unaware of the orientalist motives behind the Western view, the Chinese male subjectivity still inscribes such bias (which we can also call, the desire for the other) in its own self-conception and generates some phantasmatic longing for a more macho self-image that could match the one in the West. Indeed, the preoccupation with the new ideal masculinity in contemporary Chinese society also coincides with the emerging celebrations and essentializations of gender binarism in the nation's fast-developing market economy and consumer culture. In the market economy of mainland China, images of straightforward gender difference rather than those marked by gender ambiguity can better facilitate the sales of commodities to less sophisticated consumers.[2]

The historical construction of the Chinese male in Hong Kong may shed light on this issue. Masculinity in Hong Kong is not only related to the reconstruction of Chineseness (or Chinese cultural identity in particular), but is also related to the fact that the colonial modernity of the port city over the last several decades has been displacing traditional concepts of what a Chinese male is supposed to be.[3] As a cultural critic argues, "icons of the Hong Kong male were transformed from the weaklings of earlier Cantonese comedies and given new identities as stylish playboys or muscular heroes. A unique combination of Western body-building and Chinese Kung Fu (with an admixture of James Bond karate and Mainland flying action) were brought together in the figure of Bruce Lee and the characters of Wong Yuk Long's early comics" (Turner and Ngan, 1995, p. 38). Hence, Hong Kong has gone through a process of erecting new and Western-looking idealized masculine figures, accompanying the city's capitalist development.[4] But the westernized masculine image in Hong Kong, which is supposed to deviate from the ideal in traditional Chinese culture, is still relatively low-key in comparison to that of the West.

Hong Kong cinema, especially its action movies, has successfully developed a different mode of male heroism in contrast to the archetypes of male identity and masculinity seen in Hollywood films.[5] Although Hong Kong cinema has been exporting, through the masculine and muscular body of its action stars, a generic Chinese national identity to diasporic Chinese communities, the push toward effeminacy, or feminization, still occupies a significant place in many other discourses of Hong Kong. The term "feminization" here is not intended to follow Ann Douglas's understanding that the engulfing influence of mass culture and the widespread consumption habits of American society since the nineteenth century have weakened, emasculated or "feminized" the previously tougher and more manly cultural condition (Douglas, 1977).[6] Neither does it intend to suggest that the effect of the changing environment on male hormones leads to a decreased sperm count in men, thus indicating unmanliness and a loss of virility. On the other hand, there has been a gender-specific impression invested in the popular consciousness that literature or writing with literary elements is endowed with a gender, that is to say, embodied as "female" (Danahy, 1991). But the "feminized" image of Chinese men in the post-colonial city has become more a matter of choice or conscious commitment than a derogatory stereotype externally imposed by others. The femininity of men, especially fathers, in Hong Kong in the 1990s is evident in the fact that many male celebrities have reconstructed a public image of themselves; they are no longer the traditional Chinese patriarchs only concerned with external, serious, public, socio-political and national interests. Rather, they have become more family-oriented, compassionate, tender and kind to their offspring. In a way, these men are undergoing a process of "becoming female." Deleuze and Guattari have provocatively argued that any social, political or cultural movement should be understood as a mobile and active challenge of becoming. Any assertion of woman as a subject in feminism should not simply oppose man, but must affirm itself as an event in the process of becoming. Hence, becoming-female should go beyond binary opposition so that man and woman can be seen as variables on a continuum. But in the context of contemporary Hong Kong Chinese society, is this strategy of becoming-female just a masculine cannibalization used only to shore up a new male identity?

In the following I shall discuss three different discourses (religious, liberal and literary-imaginary) written by Hong Kong Chinese males in order to understand the ways in which masculine sexuality reconstructs itself in relation to the notion of femininity in the sexual confusion and sexual paradoxes of our modern society. I shall also point out how the changed male images are related to the different meanings of Chineseness construed in the post-colonial community.

## THE LACK IN THE HEAVENLY FATHER AND THE EARTHLY ONE

For quite some time, the feminist movement has challenged men to reconsider the character of fathering and their involvement with children. That is to say, men have been encouraged to develop more compassionate, involved and personal relationships with their children, to do what was traditionally done by mothers, and to redefine the nature of fathering. Men are urged to liberate themselves from the rigidity of rational thinking and admit that men also have emotions, feelings, and emotional needs. Like women, they have the right to cry in front of others. Traditionally, fathers of the older generation were distant and respected figures. Paternal authority and discipline blocked the emotional link between fathers and sons. A father was only regarded as a symbol of authority, not of love, and thus many young males have grown up without the emotional support of their fathers. To put it symbolically, the father is "not always at home." Some local leaders of Christian groups in Hong Kong have started a campaign encouraging men to remake themselves as caring and compassionate fathers in the 1990s, through reading popular books like *Father in the Making* (*Congwei yushang de fuqin*), *Proverbs for Good Daddies of the 21st Century* (*Wo gai dui haizi shuo shenme: Ershiyi shiji hao baba zhenyan*), *Men Behind the Masks* and others.[7]

The traditional images of a father as an authoritative, strict and insensitive figure and of a man as a strong, emotionally distant person are debunked in these books, and a new meaning of manhood or fatherhood is advocated. Always written in a confessional, autobiographical mode, these self-help books with a strongly religious tone tell the traumatic experiences of the male authors' relations with their conservative fathers from childhood to manhood. They assert that there is always a significant male in every man's life, and that is his father. The relationship with one's father always plays a determining role in one's life. However, fathers in Hong Kong, according to a social survey conducted by the Christian groups, are always absent in parenting, and are spending very little time with their children. Incompetent at expressing themselves, fathers remain emotionally detached from their children; and, in the Chinese tradition, they always discipline their young children too severely and tend to remain silent at home, even though they can be easygoing and talkative with their friends. Fathers are also the ones who easily lose their temper and take out their anger on their children, especially when they suffer stress from life in the metropolitan city. The failure of traditional fatherhood, for these religious writers, may have a traumatic impact on children. For instance, they claim that some children become homosexual due to a lack of heterosexual male guidance. Adult males do not have a sense of security and confidence, and girls make wrong choices in marriage because they cannot find a role model in their own fathers. Bad memories of the unhappy past with their fathers always impair the younger generation's relationships with their own children, and they often unconsciously repeat the same behaviour patterns in dealing with them. But it is only when these men are placed in the position of a father, according to these religious writers, that they begin to understand more about their own fathers and desperately seek new ways of fathering in order to regain their confidence and to teach their own kids in different ways. Furthermore, it is through the Christian God that these men find a new path to becoming ideal fathers.

In these religious writings on fatherhood and manhood, God is always referred to as the Heavenly Father. As the evangelist counsellor Philemon Choi states, "The Bible says: God created man according to His own image. But we create the image of the Heavenly Father according to the images of our own fathers" (Choi, 2002, p. 12). Indeed, when many Christians are asked to describe how they picture God, the features they give are surprisingly similar to those of their biological fathers. Choi has encountered some Christians who have difficulties in communicating with the Heavenly Father precisely because of their conflicts and tension with their biological fathers. In their eyes, the Heavenly Father, somewhat like their biological fathers, is "distant, compassionless, stern and even violent." Hence, Choi's mission is, through recounting his own experience, to teach his readers, especially male Christians, how to learn more about their fathers, about the trauma left by their fathers in their lives and about fatherhood in general by knowing the other father, the Heavenly Father. The images of the earthly father and the Heavenly Father were at first separated by a huge gap. Choi had to rely on the love of the Heavenly Father to compensate for his lack of love from his earthly father.

The first major conflict with his biological father was Choi's conversion and devotion to Christianity. From the beginning, his father was against his decision to be baptized as a Christian because he wanted Choi to fulfil his promise to Choi's grandfather to continue worshipping at the shrine of their ancestors. Choi made another controversial choice that damaged his relationship with his father. His father had financially supported him through medical school in Canada out of his meagre income as a sailor. But when he returned to Hong Kong, Choi gave up his respectable career as a doctor—the dream profession of many Chinese fathers. Instead, Choi made up his mind to become a full-time evangelist. In other words, Choi not only preferred the Heavenly Father to his earthly father, he also took on a Western religion in preference to traditional Chinese beliefs characterized by filial piety and ancestry worship.

The pain is perhaps mutual to both son and father, though the son may always feel that he is the only victim in the dispute and is shocked by the father who, in the eyes of the son, turns from being a protector into an oppressor. If the relationship between the Heavenly Father and the son has alienated the son from his earthly father, it is also the Heavenly Father who enjoins the son to love his earthly father and care for him again. The Chinese title of Choi's *Father in the Making* is *Congwei yushang de fuqin* (The father whom no one has ever encountered). It suggests that everyone must demystify their father, unmasking him and discovering his other side. That is, to discover his wounds, weaknesses, vulnerability or so-called "femininity," in order to understand him, and through him to discover a masculine role model in order to understand oneself. The "invisible or missing father" also implicitly refers to the fact that the Heavenly Father is also a father who could never be literally met on earth. Choi implies that it is only through the making of the earthly father that God Himself can be fully realized, and only through improving the tie with the earthly father that He can become an approachable living God. The paternalization of the almighty God does not necessarily lead to the deification of the earthly father. It may not be a male conspiracy to elevate men once again to a position of dominance, if masculinity is already in crisis. The phantasmatic identification of God with the father image is a possible way to come to terms with the impenetrable and enigmatic kernel of religious belief itself. It could also be a way out for the Chinese Christian evangelist, to ease the trauma of choosing a foreign religion over the traditional cultural heritage. The Christian love is, in a sense, reconfigured into the son's renewed filial piety with a Confucian flavour. However, this should not be simply understood as a strategy of domestication. Rather, it is the realization of Christian faith in a particular Chinese context that could make up for the imperfection of traditional Chinese fatherhood. This Chinese Christian evangelist, who was previously torn between the two different cultures and values, can now find comfort in the reconciliation between them.

For Choi, the crisis of the "fatherless generation" is actually the crisis of the generation without beliefs. People of modern times have no belief because they cannot find God on earth. But if they were to rediscover a new relationship with their fathers, the most significant men in their lives, they would encounter God in this world. The images of the earthly father on the Chinese side and the Heavenly Father imported from the West ultimately have to come together in a complementary relationship, even though they appear to be far apart at the beginning of Choi's narration. Despite their mutual lacks (the lack of religious belief and the lack of fathering), the earthly father and the Heavenly Father may supplement each other and generate a meaningful life for Hong Kong men who embrace the new sense of masculinity.

## THE FEMINIZATION OF PATERNAL POWER

The awareness of changing or reconstructing meanings of fatherhood and hence manhood is not confined to those men with religious beliefs. Liberal middle-class men are the other group that pays much attention to parenting and they do not mind turning themselves into family men in order to develop stronger emotional ties with their children. The trend for professional middle-class Chinese males in Hong Kong to rediscover themselves and the meaning of life through the process of fathering is growing, but the writing that records such awakening remains rare. Although there is an increasing number of parenting columns published in Chinese-language newspapers, the writers are mostly women who share with the readers their experience of mother-hood. The anthology *Twelve Papas* (*Shi'er baba*), edited by Lenny Kwok (Guo Danian), a self-claimed anarchist musician in the local under-ground rock band Blackbird, is one collection of such essays by men. The twelve contributors include a professional storyteller, a musician, a film director, a photojournalist, a secondary school teacher, two univer-sity professors, and others working either for newspapers or electronic media as editors, producers, directors, or TV programme hosts. They have all received a western education, have admirable careers, belong to the elite intellectual and professional class, and would probably be cate-gorized as the privileged of society. But like many liberal bourgeois intellectuals who are relatively pro-feminist and who seek gender equality,[8] they consciously attempt to place their subject positions outside the boundaries of a purely patriarchal and capitalist order, that is to say, outside the bounds of the phallic signifier.

To varying degrees, these intellectuals all dis-identify with and ques-tion the mainstream ideology of the patriarchal-capitalist world, though they are fully aware that they also benefit from such a system. Working in or studying the mass media, they are aware that children or youths are now manipulated into an unthinking conformity by the engulfing media power and dominant values of global capitalism. In their eyes, the new paternal authority is a possible foundation for the development of a critical consciousness among children. This new generation wants to become fathers with emotional ties with their children, and taking up shared parenting with their wives so as to serve as role models for their young. Some of them even see themselves as marginalized rebels who lead a bohemian lifestyle in order to subvert mainstream values. According to what they write, these men spend no less time than their wives involved in their children's daily lives, including bathing their new-born babies, changing diapers, cleaning, cooking, feeding the children, taking them to school, playing with them, looking at their homework and reading bedtime stories. Owing to some special circumstances in their lives (either having been unemployed or living abroad while their wives are working or at university), a few contributors have even taken up these household chores as a full-time job for some years (Kwok, 2001, p. 31; p. 51). One of them even playfully gives himself the new title *"zhǔfū"* (househusband) vis-à-vis the conventional and slightly derogatory term *"zhǔfù"* for housewife. Indeed, these young middle-class fathers are far more ready than the older paternal generation to place themselves in a domestic position usually occupied by the wife in the household. No longer the sole bread-winner in the double-income nuclear family, these bourgeois men from the Hong Kong Chinese community can always make themselves more flexible and adopt a feminine role when needed. No longer using his professional career to define his subjectivity, the film director Herman Yau (Yau Lai To) writes in the anthology that he even turned down an offer from an American film producer when asked to leave his daughter for a year to make a movie in the US: "An American independent film-maker came to invite me to go to the States to make a movie. If I had accepted the offer, I would have been away for almost a year. They told me, 'You can see it as a sacrifice for the sake of art.' I said, 'Sorry! The name of my daughter is not "art." Her name is Enya.'" (Yau, 2001, pp. 70–71). Between career opportunities and family, new middle-class fathers choose the latter.

The way these men define themselves is not unlike what Jacques Lacan means by the definition of "woman": not all of a woman is defined by the phallic function, but she is nevertheless situated within the symbolic order of her psychic development. For these liberal men, they may see themselves as "women" in the Lacanian sense; though they are at least in part determined by the phallic-patriarchal function, they believe they do not totally fall under such an order. Some militant feminists may consider these phenomena to be men's conspiracy against women, because men's transformation does not address the consequences of their social privileges. That is to say, they still retain their privileges in a patriarchal society, even though they are adjusting their traditionally defined positions in changing circumstances. Such a "new male order" may threaten to infringe on the conventional territory and dignity of women; when men occupy the position of femininity, they will become even more privileged than ever.

These men's self-assumption of the "female" position of being loving, sensitive, nurturing, family-oriented and sometimes even self-effacing is connected with their general dis-identification with the traditional patriarchal values. They not only distance themselves from the rigidity, sternness and authoritarianism of the paternal images of the previous generation, they also see themselves as different from other fathers of the same age in their style of fulfilling the duties of parenthood. These middle-class fathers belonging to the cultural elite group who love to talk about parenthood in a democratic, liberal discourse, which is still not very popular among Chinese bourgeois families in westernized Hong Kong. One of the contributors has had the experience of living in the West, and guiltily admits that he and his wife could not help but fall into the stereotype of typical "Asian parents," who pamper and treat their kids with excessive indulgence (Kwok, 2001, p. 54). As believers in liberalism and disciples of equality and autonomy, these fathers always struggle not to intervene too much in the upbringing of their children, although they do keep a very close eye on them. One of the contributors, Lui Tai Lok, uses the example of teaching children how to ride a bike as a metaphor to indicate how the new liberal father's role should be played:

[Fathering or parenting is] just like watching the children learn how to ride a bike. If the parents protect the children all the way, it will be very difficult for them to learn how to balance their bikes from their own experience. If the parents do not allow the children to speed up and go beyond their reach, the children will find it difficult to learn how to manoeuvre their bicycles. The children can learn how to control their bikes only when the parents let go of their hands... From watching the children learn how to ride a bike, I understand that parents have to learn to release their grip on their children. (Lui, 2001, pp. 33–34)

Lui is proud of himself having grown up in a public housing estate during childhood and remains thankful to his working-class parents for giving him enough space and freedom. He observes that parents of his generation are always over-anxious about their children and worry so much about bringing them up that they tend to be over-protective and try to provide them with the richest material conditions they can offer. Lui believes that more autonomy, more space and more trust should be given to children in order to let them explore freely and develop their potential. But surprisingly, what Lui, a well-known sociologist, fails to point out in his essay is that social status or class background has largely determined the different ways of parenting. Many fathers in the anthology may share Lui's ideal of liberal parenting (although this does not mean that, in reality, they can let go of their children) since they belong to the same middle-class. Their relatively high social position offers these "new good fathers" a significant amount of time to become compassionate and caring fathers when their own less wealthy parents could never afford it.

Giving up the authoritarian attitude toward their children and open-mindedly treating their children as friends, these men are never shy to apologize or "say sorry" to their young ones, for they emphasize equal status. The phrase "I'm sorry" would hardly ever have been uttered by Chinese fathers of the older generation to their children, even though they might know in their hearts that they had made mistakes. However, these liberal fathers can take off the mask of an authoritarian face and apologize to their children on many occasions. One of the fathers in the collection writes, "If I have promised my son to be home at seven but have to be half an hour late because of work, I will definitely call him before seven, and the first word I'll say would be 'Sorry.' Then I will explain to him why I have to go home half an hour late" (Kwok, 2001, p. 100). Another father also shares his experience of teaching his child to follow the traffic lights when crossing the street. It turns out that it is his son who has become the teacher: "It happened once that when the light was red and there was no traffic, I thoughtlessly stepped out from the pavement to cross the street. My son made a great effort to pull me back. I immediately felt ashamed of myself and said to him at once, 'You are really smart. Daddy is wrong. Sorry'" (Kwok, 2001, p. 118). What the new father can do is not to impose or instruct but to let the young ones make their own decisions and discover their own potential. The editor of the anthology shares Lui's experience in teaching children how to ride a bike so much that he supports the liberal approach with another example of teaching his children how to swim. His idea is that babies are all born swimmers and it is often the adults who make them afraid of water and prevent children's true nature from its full manifestation. Children who enjoy liberal fathering or parenting are told to make decisions according to their inner nature.

If authoritarianism has been the principle used by fathers of the older generation to teach their children either because they could not afford the time or did not have the patience, these fathers of the new generation who have moved up the social ladder adopt liberalism in parenting in order to legitimize the exercise of their paternal authority. To believe that they will totally let go of their children is merely an illusion, if not a self-deception. The exercise of paternal power over children has not been lessened. The only difference may be that liberalism, together with the new compassionate and feminized images of these middle-class fathers, "naturalizes" the power imposed on the subjected group and makes its exercise of power more humanized and acceptable not only to the children but also to the fathers themselves. The so-called freedom and space given to the children have to be within the boundaries of the existing paternal power relations. Any intervention to undermine the framework itself would not be allowed. The strictly defined freedom of choice provided by the liberal fathers to their children is probably only a covering-up of the mechanism of paternal power.

We have to admit that the liberal or "feminized" mode of rationalizing power is not only applied to the way that children are parented but is also bestowed upon the personal journey towards manhood among these middle-class fathers. Perhaps power is not only exerted on the subordinated group but also upon the exerciser. These liberal men believe that by fathering their children, they also discover their own inner growth and become aware of new and better dimensions of their personalities. When one contributor shares his experience of fathering with his male friends, all the men come to these similar conclusive remarks: "I understood what life means once I had children!" "If life is a book, kids give you another totally unexpected, brand-new chapter." "I understand more about women now I have children." "The growth of my child has made me grow." "It would be the most miserable thing in life if we didn't have any kids!" (Kwok, 2001, pp. 115–116). The myth of these middle-class men's self-discovery through fathering is always a discovery of their better self, but never the dark side or perverse dimension of their personalities. The choice to become a good father is, in a way, always a pre-determined choice (that is to say, if you choose to be a father, you have to be good and to match the ideal image of a bourgeois liberal father). They are actually never free to overthrow the established law of such a patriarchal system and to choose not to play the bourgeois game of fathering. In other words, the "feminization" or naturalization of power is twofold in the sense that it applies both to the fathering and to the rediscovery of manhood among these middle-class men in Hong Kong. The search for the inner feminine side in these liberal men may reaffirm the power mechanism on both the subjected minors and those who exercise it. But the new feminine image of paternal power provides these men with an illusion of being liberated from the conservative role of a Chinese father while affirming as well as rejuvenating the patriarchal system in the face of the more severe challenges posed by late capitalist society.

## CONCEALING THE VOID OF SEXUAL DIFFERENCE

If the feminization of power in the liberal discourse could legitimize its exercise and make both the subjected group and the exerciser accept the imposition as if it were originating from their inner self, then the novel by Dong Qizhang (Dung Kai Cheung), *Dual Body* (*Shuangshen*), attempts to de-legitimize the discovery of one's inner self and to lay bare just such a process of a man's becoming a woman. Published in 1997, the historic year of Hong Kong's return to China, this fantasy story relates how a Hong Kong Chinese man wakes up one morning in Japan to find himself suddenly changed into a woman. What follows is his/her journey (from Japan to Hong Kong and back, and from the present to the past and back) to look for the real (sexual) identity originally belonging to him/her. Through such a journey in search of the self, the protagonist Lin Shanyuan (which literally means forest, mountain and origin or plain, all referring to nature) comes to understand more about the social positions of man and woman, becomes more emotionally attached to his/her rival younger sister, and is involved in several hetero-sexual/homosexual entanglements. The plot may remind readers of Franz Kafka's "Metamorphosis" or Virginia Woolf's *Orlando*, but its specific meaning could only be derived from its social context. At a first glance, becoming-female in Dong's novel is like a Deleuzian line of flight that does not aim at the liberation of women or men as a homogeneous collectivity but rather settles for a transformation and transgression of identity formation. The gist of any becoming, for Deleuze, is the loss of identity and becoming imperceptible in order to counteract the very notion of subjectivity. Becoming-woman is to de-stabilize the conventions of identity politics. This explains why the sexual metamorphosis in *Dual Body* was welcomed by neither feminists nor gay activists. Criticized for advocating a neutral gender that could transcend the oppositions of the two sexes (Yu, 1997), *Dual Body*, however, is not so Deleuzian in the sense of erasing the gender paradigm or tending towards imperceptibility. Actually it depends more on the essentialization of what man and woman are supposed to be. Although the novel makes use of numerous liquid images to suggest the fluidity of sexual identity, the drama of the story always hinges on the confusion and simple reversal of the conventional stereotypes of masculinity and femininity. For instance, readers are always presented with these queries while following the story line: What would happen if a man tried to make love to a woman who is actually a man? How does a man live with a body without a penis? How would a man feel when his female body is penetrated by the penis of another man? In what way could a man conform to female behaviour and finally accept the female identity? Physically turned into a woman and compromising more and more with his new femininity, Lin Shanyuan's inner self is still largely male, even though the memories of his past experience as a man (a boy, to be more precise) become blurred, if not vanishing entirely.

The interesting part of *Dual Body* is probably not its attempt to subvert the traditional hierarchy of rigid sexual roles. As a matter of fact, Dong always implicitly reinforces it. Neither does the story disguise itself as a work which celebrates the chaotic contemporary conditions of sexual roles and identities while surreptitiously bringing back the sexual stereotypes to restore the undisturbed balance. Perhaps what the novel endeavours to deal with is a rejection of the differentiation of sexual identities as a fixed and stable set of symbolic inclusions and exclusions. Sexual difference is treated in the story as a fundamental deadlock in human society. However, if this situation of deadlock is resolved or taken away, the symbolic universe may crumble. In other words, sexual difference does generate many conflicts in gender relations, but it is also the key element that constitutes meanings in the symbolic world. Sexual harmony will not arrive, as is expected by so many, if such a primary difference is eliminated. On the contrary, the disappearance of sexual difference may lead to the collapse of our world of meanings, thus unfolding the emptiness of our gender/subject formation. The semblance of changing into the opposite sex is only an excuse to cover up the traumatic lack of being or the pure void of negativity in the symbolic universe. In the preface to the novel, Dong refers to an old Chinese myth about an imaginary animal named *lei* (which literally means "category" in Chinese), whose body possesses both male and female sexual organs so that it can have sexual intercourse with itself. The story goes that people will no longer suffer feelings of jealousy if they eat this animal (Dong, 1997, p. i).

In his understanding of the ancient myth, Dong believes that the feeling of jealousy is triggered off by the impossibility of self-sufficiency and the unlimited desire for the other. I would rather say the intense feelings of envy, apprehension or bitterness towards the other are merely a screen to cover up the lack of being in oneself. But even when one becomes the other, as Dong reveals in the story, it still does not mean that one can become a full and complete being. The story tends to convey the phantasmatic message that there is always a kind of doubleness or bisexuality in our bodies and the subject can choose (consciously or unconsciously) to become either one. The entire process of becoming the other sex, however, is probably only a magic trick to distract our eyes from the void of the subject itself.

Dong appears to be interested in playing tricks in the gender performance game. In his earlier novella, *Androgyny* (*Anzhuozhenni*), he took up a female persona in the narration and successfully fooled the adjudicators of a fiction competition organized by a Taiwanese publisher. The story won a prize and its author was thought to be a woman. Apparently, Dong had no intention of covering up his male identity; this was due only to the misperception of the adjudicators. But what is revealing is that the so-called feminine writing or feminine-writing style is not inborn in the biological female but can be simulated by a man. The success of the gender simulation is based on some general assumptions about feminine writing or about femininity in literature. If the simulation is usually considered a challenge or a subversion of reality (that is to say, by telling people, in this case, how wrong the general perception of femininity is and then revealing its truth), then Dong's gender game as a performance or masking is actually a remaking of appearance that is used to fill out the void of reality itself. The following paragraph by Dong on fiction writing can help us understand more about how he makes use of simulation:

> Fiction has come to its full development. All possibilities of fiction appear to have been exhausted. Rebellious anti-fiction has also reached a dead-end. There can hardly be any real avant-garde form of fiction. Thus, whenever I start to write a story, a certain genre or a certain paradigm naturally bounces off my paper. The only choice left to me is to simulate something called fiction and to get a hold of its established rules and anti-rules. I try to write a novel, or to write my piece that does not look like a novel. It may not be a bad thing because simulation is not necessarily passive and submissive. Rather, it is a method for constituting new distances and new spaces. For me, simulation gives me an ambivalent

distance from the thing called fiction. It could be a faraway but also a very close relationship. (Dong, 1996, p. 7)

If we replace "fiction" with the word "gender," a new meaning may arise from the use of simulation in the gender performing game. Dong never refuses to play the game; neither does he ever try to play it in a witty manner in order to alter its rules. Rather, he follows the rules (and anti-rules) closely through the act of simulation, by means of which a gap or a distance from the thing simulated could be introduced, while rendering visible its inherent impossibility and failure. Harold Bloom's "anxiety of influence" gets on the nerves of a young writer like Dong. When all thoughts have been thought, simulation paradoxically becomes an alternative or a way out for the latecomer like Dong, because it serves as an appearance that conceals the fact that fiction writing is no longer possible nowadays. In the age of pluralism or at a time when anything goes, any revolution or transformation of gender is already rendered ineffective or invalid. Perhaps the strongest critique is no longer a direct confrontation with conventional gender concepts, and a full identification or a simulation could produce the greatest effects. The process of simulation could tell us that the original that is simulated actually does not exist. Becoming a woman or man is not a real identity, just a mask that covers up the void of subjectivity. Along the same line of thought, I find that the feminine transformation of a man in *Dual Body* is a fantasy that not only perpetuates the myth of gender fluidity (according to which one can choose and move from one sex to the other), but also functions as a symbolic fiction to save the appearance of full sexual identity from disintegration.

The final merging of Lin Shanyuan's body with that of his/her sister (the double body turning into double bodies) does not merely point to an ideal of unisex or sexual unity. It first and foremost reasserts the symbolic order of sexual difference. After all, it requires the essential concepts of the two different sexes to generate the ideal of neutral sex, unisex, androgyny or perfect sexual unity. The imaginary transgression of gender boundaries is in fact the very gesture that sustains the conventional symbolization of sexual difference and sexual identity. It is the simulation that saves the original. What it tries to cover up is not the truth under the surface but that there is no truth underneath. The myth *Dual Body* appears to uphold is the cliché that every man latently contains a woman, and by doing away with his masculine sexuality, the woman in him is allowed to emerge, and vice versa. But by writing the process of becoming a woman in a fantasy setting, Dong shows us that a person is devoid of any positive content no matter to which sex that person belongs. The traces of masculinity or femininity are all simulated, to fill out the ontological emptiness of subjectivity. After becoming a woman, the protagonist finds himself/herself excluded from the symbolic network. This leads us to recognize the fact that one always lacks the identifiable feature that would enable one to declare something as strictly belonging to oneself. Indeed every symbolic sexual identity one gains is ultimately nothing but a feature to fill out the void of subjectivity. During a critical transitional period in Hong Kong, the fact that Hong Kong people are becoming Chinese could probably be illuminated by the fantasy of becoming-woman in Dong's novel. It is not just a fantasy of regaining national entity to fill out the void of the post-colonial subject. In a world where the meaning of Chineseness keeps changing, the so-called national origin that Hong Kong people are now turning towards or emulating is also something simulated in order to cover up its non-existence.

The three different writings by men discussed above have all touched on the idea of feminization or becoming-female in their own ways. The process of becoming-female either in a literal or metaphorical sense in these texts is linked with contemplation of the masculine subject itself and the issue of Chinese identification. Hong Kong men appropriate the notion of femininity to reconstruct not only the male identity but also their national identity. But when the new meaning of masculinity or nationality is built around the idea of becoming-woman, it also suggests that there is no longer any positive consistency in a Chinese male subjectivity, which could only lie in the imaginary "woman" or in something that does not exist. It resonates with the (in)famous Lacanian statement, "There is no such thing as woman."

## NOTES

1. The Western media make a great deal of fuss over the cultural changes that have undermined traditional ideas about masculinity. The younger generation of men is particularly in trouble. For example, CBS's "60 Minutes" (October 31, 2002) reported that girls are graduating from high school and college and going into professions and businesses in record numbers, and now it is the boys who need help in school, where they are falling behind their female counterparts. The clinical psychologist William Pollack's 1998 bestseller *Real Boys* and the sequels have warned of the American crisis of boys, revealed their unique emotional, psychological

and physical needs and given parents practical advice about how to raise their boys in the development of traditional masculinity.

2. However, the rapid expansion of capitalism has changed modes of everyday life—including gender perception. The macho man based on Western models is no longer in vogue in China or across Asia. What has emerged instead is the feminized man whose image is spread widely by the popularity of male stars such as Lee Jun-ki, the male lead in the South Korean blockbuster *The King and the Clown* (dir. Lee Jun-Ik, 2005). Lee has a face prettier than that of any girl, and has sparked the new trend of the "feminine man" and become the archetype of *kotminam* (flower boy). But before Lee, South Korean actor Bae Yong-jun, with his TV soap opera series *Winter Sonata* riding the climax of the Korean Wave in Asia captured the hearts of many Japanese housewives with his feminine appearance and sensibility. The Taiwanese boy band F4 (Flower Four) that has swept across Asia got their start in the popular Taiwanese television series *Meteor Garden* (based on the Japanese *manga Boys over Flowers* [Hana yori dango]) and today exemplifies the metrosexual feminized boy image for the younger generation in contemporary Asia. But the Asia-wide craze for the "beautiful boy" image can always be traced back to the king of Japanese *dorama*, Kimura Takuya, whose TV series *Long Vacation and Love Generation* have transnationally circulated this feminized male type since the mid-1990s. Meanwhile, Shanghai Satellite Station's male-themed contest *My Hero*, that claims to seek out good men, features young men out-singing and out-dancing one another to the screams of teenage girl audiences. (The winners are selected by TV viewers who vote via mobile phone text messages.) Where the male contestants outshine their female counterparts in *Super Girl*, China's version of *American Idol*, is in the arena of beauty. Considered China's first generation of self-conscious metrosexuals, the finalists in *My Hero* are generally sweet and vulnerable, with good looks and feminine characteristics, and are the perfect objects of motherly or sisterly affection.

3. Kam Louie states that Chinese masculinity has been traditionally structured by two archetypes: *wen* which is associated with the Confucian gentleman-scholar, and *wu*, the martial masculinity symbolized by the Han dynasty military leader Guan Yu. The ideal balance of the two archetypal masculinities emphasizes that learning is a means to avoid descending to the sheer use of violence. Hence *wen* masculinity has always been prioritized in Chinese culture, though the two archetypes operate together (Louie, 2002). For more historical and ethnographic studies on the male gender in China from the eighteenth century to the present, see Brownell and Wasserstrom (2002).

4. However, some recent surveys show that the image of Hong Kong man, in the eyes of Hong Kong woman, is becoming less competitive than his Mainland counterpart. Hong Kong man is said to be "apparently shallow,

bad-mannered, selfish, macho and uncultured ... He doesn't read books, but cheap local magazines. He understands nothing about ideals. He thinks drinking red wine is 'high class,' and that earning a lot is his 'status marker' ... Who wants to marry a man whose interest is reading Japanese comic books?" (Lee, 2003). More career-minded Hong Kong women find Mainland men who are cultured and knowledgeable more attractive propositions.

5. For instance, Mark Gallagher points out that the Hong Kong action star Jackie Chan has revamped the Western action-hero persona by incorporating "into action-oriented narratives the burlesque body fundamental to comedy. His body's continuous, antic motion *feminized* through its implied vulnerability, calls into question conceptions of the ideal male body" (Gallagher, 1997, p. 24, my emphasis).

6. The advancement of consumer capitalism does, however, succeed in promoting the heterosexual male quest for "surface beauty"—the right hair, face, skin and clothes—that fuels an economy of beauty services and the fashion industry.

7. These local religious writings and campaigns are apparently influenced by the US men's movements, such as the Christian Promise Keepers and Robert Bly's mythopoetic men's movement in the early 1990s, which have been repeatedly mentioned in their publications.

8. Although men's liberation always gives rise to a conservative, anti-feminist men's rights movement, there are other men, who are usually liberal and middle-class, seeking to dismantle sexism and challenge traditional sex roles that distort both sexes. See, for instance, Stoltenberg (1989); Clatterbaugh (2000); Messner (2000).

## REFERENCES

Au, Raymond, and Philemon Choi (Cai Yuanyun) (1999). *Wo gai dui haizi shuo shenme: Ershiyi shiji hao baba zhenyan* [Proverbs for good daddies of the 21st century]. Hong Kong: Breakthrough Ltd.

Brownell, Susan, and Jeffrey N. Wasserstrom, eds. (2002). *Chinese Femininities, Chinese Masculinities: A Reader*. Berkeley: University of California Press.

Chan, Jachinson (2001). *Chinese American Masculinities: From Fu Manchu to Bruce Lee*. New York: Routledge.

Choi, Philemon (Cai Yuanyun) (2002). *Congwei yushang de fuqin* [Father in the making] (Rev. ed.). Hong Kong: Breakthrough Ltd.

Choi, Philemon (Cai Yuanyun), and Ou Xiangjiang (1998). *Nanren de mianju* [Men behind the masks]. Hong Kong: Breakthrough Ltd.

Clatterbaugh, Kenneth (2000). "Literature of the U.S. Men's Movements." *Signs: Journal of Women in Culture and Society*, Vol. 25, No. 3 (Spring), 883–894.

Danahy, Michael (1991). *The Feminization of the Novel*. Gainesville: University of Florida Press.

Deleuze, Gilles, and Félix Guattari (1988). *A Thousand Plateaus: Capitalism and Schizophrenia*. Trans. Brian Massumi. London: Athlone Press.

Dong Qizhang (Dung Kai Cheung) (1996). *Anzhuozhenni* [Androgyny]. Taipei: Lianhe wenxue.

Dong Qizhang (Dung Kai Cheung) (1997). *Shuangshen* [Dual body]. Taipei: Lianjing.

Douglas, Ann (1977). *The Feminization of American Culture* (1st ed.). London: Papermac.

Gallagher, Mark (1997). "Masculinity in Translation: Jackie Chan's Transcultural Star Text." *The Velvet Light Trap: A Critical Journal of Film and Television*, No. 39 (Spring), 23–41.

Gardiner, Judith Kegan, ed. (2002). *Masculinity Studies and Feminist Theory: New Directions*. New York: Columbia University Press.

Kwok, Lenny (Guo Danian/Kwok Tai Nin), ed. (2001). *Shi'er baba* [Twelve papas]. Hong Kong: Step Forward Multi Media Press.

Lacan, Jacques (1982). *Female Sexuality: Jacques Lacan and the Ecole Freudienne*. Eds. Juliet Mitchell and Jacqueline Rose. Trans. Jacqueline Rose. London: Macmillan.

Lacan, Jacques (1998). *On Feminine Sexuality: The Limits of Love and Knowledge*. Ed. Jacques-Alain Miller. Trans. Bruce Fink. New York: W. W. Norton.

Lee, Sherry (2003). "Spurned: Are Hong Kong Men Really Being Passed Over for Their Mainland Counterparts?" *South China Morning Post* (16 April), p. C5.

Louie, Kam (2002). *Theorising Chinese Masculinity: Society and Gender in China*. Cambridge: Cambridge University Press.

Lui Tai Lok (Lü Dale) (2001). "Jiu xiang congpang guankan haizimen xue qi danche" [Like watching from the sidelines as your children learn to ride a bike]. In Kwok Tai Nin, ed., *Shi'er baba* [Twelve papas], pp. 33–39. Hong Kong: Step Forward Multi Media Press.

Messner, Michael A. (2000). *Politics of Masculinities: Men in Movements*. Walnut Creek, CA: AltaMira Press.

Pollack, William (1998). *Real Boys: Rescuing Our Sons from the Myths of Boyhood*. New York: Random House.

Stoltenberg, John (1989). *Refusing to Be a Man: Essays on Sex and Justice*. Portland, OR: Breitenbush Books.

Turner, Matthew, and Irene Ngan, eds. (1995). *Hong Kong Sixties: Designing Identity*. Hong Kong: Hong Kong Arts Centre.

Yau, Lai To (Qiu Litao/Herman Yau Lai To) (2001). "Wo nü'er de mingzi bing bu jiao 'yishu'" [The name of my daughter is not "art"]. In Kwok Tai Nin, ed., *Shi'er baba* [Twelve papas], pp. 67–71. Hong Kong: Step Forward Multi Media Press.

Yu Ruomei (1997). "Yichang weixian de xingbie tiaoxi" [A dangerous sexual flirtation]. *Mingpao* (9 March), p. D11.

Zhong Xueping (2000). *Masculinity Besieged? Issues of Modernity and Male Subjectivity in Chinese Literature of the Late Twentieth Century.* Durham, NC: Duke University Press.

## GLOSSARY

*Anzhuozhenni*《安卓珍妮》

*Congwei yushang de fuqin*《從未遇上的父親》

Dong Qizhang (Dung Kai Cheung) 董啓章

lei 類

Lin Shanyuan 林山原

*Shi'er baba*《十二爸爸》

*Shuangshen*《雙身》

zhufu (*zhǔfū*) 主夫

zhufu (*zhǔfù*) 主婦

# Contributors

**Kuei-fen CHIU** 邱貴芬 (QIU Guifen) is Distinguished Professor and Director of both the Graduate Institute of Taiwan Literature and the Research Center for the Humanities and Social Sciences at National Chung Hsing University, Taiwan. She received her Ph.D. in Comparative Literature from University of Washington, Seattle. Before she joined National Chung Hsing University, she was Professor of Taiwan Literature in the Graduate Institute of Taiwan Literature at National Tsing Hua University. Since the early 1990s, she has been teaching and conducting research on postcolonial theories, feminist literary criticism, and Taiwan women's fiction. Her recent areas of research include documentary studies, historiography and popular culture. She has received many awards for her research on Taiwan literature.

**GUO Shumei** 郭淑梅 is an associate research fellow in the Institute of Literature at the Heilongjiang Academy of Social Sciences. She has published articles on female writings in Chinese journals.

**HE Songyu** 何嵩昱 is Associate Professor in the School of Chinese at Guizhou Normal University. He has published articles on modern Chinese women's literature.

**JIN Yanyu** 金燕玉 is a research fellow in the Institute of Literature at the Jiangsu Academy of Social Sciences. She has organized conferences and published numerous articles on Chinese women's writings.

**Jessica Tsui Yan LI** 李翠恩 received her Ph.D. in English from The Chinese University of Hong Kong in 2003 and another Ph.D. in Comparative Literature from the University of Toronto in 2007. She is currently a postdoctoral fellow in English at York University, Canada. She has published articles on feminist writings.

**LIN Shuming** 林樹明 is Chair Professor and Dean of the School of

Chinese at Guizhou Normal University. He received his Ph.D. in Chinese from Sichuan University in 2003. His publications include the book *Feminist Criticism in China* (in Chinese).

**Kwai-Cheung LO** 羅貴祥 (LUO Guixiang) is Professor in the Department of English Language and Literature at Hong Kong Baptist University. His research focuses on popular culture and literature in Hong Kong and his recent book is *Chinese Face/Off: The Transnational Popular Culture of Hong Kong* (2005).

**QIAO Yigang** 喬以剛 is Professor and Chairperson of the Chinese Department at Nankai University, Tianjin. She has published books and articles on female literature in China.

**SHENG Ying** 盛英 is Professor Emeritus, Department of Chinese, Nankai University, Tianjin, China. She is also a member of the Tianjin Writers' Association. She has published extensively on feminist writings in China. Her publications include *A History of Twentieth-Century Chinese Women's Literature* (in Chinese) (1995).

**Mei-hwa SUNG** 宋美華 (SONG Meihua) is currently Professor of English and Dean of the College of Foreign Languages and Literatures at Tamkang University, Taiwan. She received her Ph.D. in English from Brown University in 1983. Before she joined Tamkang University, she was Professor of English at National Taiwan University, where she had served as Chairperson of the Department of Foreign Languages and Literatures. She has a distinguished record of professional service, including the editorship of *Chung-wai Literary Monthly* and *Tamkang Review*, and has published numerous articles and books on English and comparative literature.

**Kwok-kan TAM** 譚國根 (TAN Guogen) is currently Chair Professor and Dean of the School of Arts and Social Sciences at the Open University of Hong Kong. He was Reader/Professor in English at The Chinese University of Hong Kong before he joined the Open University in 2007. He has held fellowships at the University of Illinois at Urbana-Champaign, the East-West Center and ASAIHL. Since 1995, he has been working on various projects on the politics and culture of globalization. He has published extensively on the topics of globalization, world Englishes, psychoanalysis, contemporary culture and comparative literature. His publications include the following books: *New Chinese Cinema* (co-authored, 1998), *Voice of Hong Kong: Drama 1997* (edited, 1998), *A Place of One's Own: Stories of Self in China, Taiwan, Hong Kong and Singapore* (co-edited, 1999), *The Politics of Subject Construction in Modern Chinese Literature* (1999), *Ibsen in China 1908–1997: A Critical-Annotated Bibliography on Criticism, Translation and Performance* (2001), *Soul of Chaos: Critical Perspectives on Gao Xingjian* (edited, 2001), *Shakespeare Global/Local: The Hong Kong Imaginary in Transcultural Production* (co-edited, 2002), *Sights of Contestation: Localism, Globalism and Cultural Production in Asia and the Pacific* (co-edited, 2002), *Anglophone Cultures in Southeast Asia* (co-edited, 2003), and *English and Globalization: Perspectives from Hong Kong and Mainland China* (co-edited, 2004).

**Lisa Lai-ming WONG** 黃麗明 (HUANG Liming) is Assistant Professor in the School of Humanities and Social Sciences at the Hong Kong University of Science and Technology. She was Assistant Professor in the Department of English at The Chinese University of Hong Kong before she joined the University of Science and Technology in 2006. Her research interests cover comparative poetics and literary theory. Her numerous publications on cross-cultural aspects of literary studies have appeared in *New Literary History*, *The Keats-Shelley Review*, *Connotations: A Journal for Critical Debate*, *Modern China*, *Journal of Modern Literature in Chinese* and *Tsing Hua Journal of Chinese Studies*. Her recent publication is the book *Rays of the Searching Sun: The Transcultural Poetics of Yang Mu* (2009).

**Suying YANG** 楊素英 (YANG Suying) is Associate Professor in the Department of English Language and Literature and has served as Director of the MA Programme in Language Studies at Hong Kong Baptist University. She has published numerous articles on linguistics, including "Globalization, Tribalization and Online Communication" which appeared in *English and Globalization: Perspectives from Hong Kong and Mainland China* (2004).

**Terry Siu-han YIP** 葉少嫻 (YE Shaoxian) is Professor of English Language and Literature at Hong Kong Baptist University. She received her Ph.D. in Comparative Literature from the University of Illinois at Urbana-Champaign. She has published extensively on Chinese-Western comparative literature, women's writings, literature and cultural change in China. Her publications can be found in academic books and journals published in Australia, Canada, Europe, the United States, Japan, China, Taiwan and Hong Kong. Her publications include *A Place of One's Own: Stories of Self in China, Taiwan, Hong Kong and Singapore* (co-edited, 1999), *Shakespeare Global/Local: The Hong Kong Imaginary in Transcultural Production* (co-edited, 2002), and *Sights of Contestation: Localism, Globalism and Cultural Production in Asia and the Pacific* (co-edited, 2002).

# Index